ROUTLEDGE LIBRARY EDITIONS:
POLITICAL THOUGHT AND
POLITICAL PHILOSOPHY

Volume 39

IN THE TWILIGHT OF REVOLUTION

IN THE TWILIGHT OF REVOLUTION
The Political Theory of Amilcar Cabral

JOCK MCCULLOCH

LONDON AND NEW YORK

First published in 1983 by Routledge & Kegan Paul plc

This edition first published in 2020
by Routledge
2 Park Square, Milton Park, Abingdon, Oxon OX14 4RN

and by Routledge
52 Vanderbilt Avenue, New York, NY 10017

Routledge is an imprint of the Taylor & Francis Group, an informa business

© 1983 Jock McCulloch

All rights reserved. No part of this book may be reprinted or reproduced or utilised in any form or by any electronic, mechanical, or other means, now known or hereafter invented, including photocopying and recording, or in any information storage or retrieval system, without permission in writing from the publishers.

Trademark notice: Product or corporate names may be trademarks or registered trademarks, and are used only for identification and explanation without intent to infringe.

British Library Cataloguing in Publication Data
A catalogue record for this book is available from the British Library

ISBN: 978-0-367-21961-1 (Set)
ISBN: 978-0-429-35434-2 (Set) (ebk)
ISBN: 978-0-367-24772-0 (Volume 39) (hbk)
ISBN: 978-0-367-24775-1 (Volume 39) (pbk)
ISBN: 978-0-429-28432-8 (Volume 39) (ebk)

Publisher's Note
The publisher has gone to great lengths to ensure the quality of this reprint but points out that some imperfections in the original copies may be apparent.

Disclaimer
The publisher has made every effort to trace copyright holders and would welcome correspondence from those they have been unable to trace.

IN THE TWILIGHT OF REVOLUTION
The Political Theory of Amilcar Cabral

Jock McCulloch

ROUTLEDGE & KEGAN PAUL
London, Boston, Melbourne and Henley

*First published in 1983
by Routledge & Kegan Paul plc
39 Store Street, London WC1E 7DD,
9 Park Street, Boston, Mass. 02108, USA,
296 Beaconsfield Parade, Middle Park,
Melbourne, 3206, Australia, and
Broadway House, Newtown Road,
Henley-on-Thames, Oxon RG9 1EN*

*Printed in Great Britain by
The Thetford Press Ltd, Thetford, Norfolk.*
© Jock McCulloch 1983
*No part of this book may be reproduced in
any form without permission from the
publisher, except for the quotation of brief
passages in criticism.*

Library of Congress Cataloging in Publication Data
McCulloch, Jock, 1945-

In the twilight of revolution.
Bibliography: p.
Includes index.
1. Cabral, Amilcar - Political and social views.
2. Guinea-Bissau - History - Revolution, 1963-1974.
3. Partido Africano da Independência da Guiné e Cabo Verde. I. Title.
DT613.76.C3M33 1983   322.4' 2' 0924   82-22969

ISBN 0-7100-9411-6 (U.S. : pbk.)

For Ann

With the help of ideas we are universal and dwell simultaneously in all places; the will puts us in a single place and settles us there.

                                                                Leonardo

CONTENTS

1 Introduction ... 1
   The historical context ... 1
   The theoretical context ... 3

2 The struggle for Guiné ... 11
   Introduction ... 11
   Specific conditions in Guiné and Cape Verde ... 12
   The Cape Verde Islands ... 16
   Political mobilisation ... 17
   Strategic aims of the struggle ... 20
   Military actions ... 22
   Portuguese tactics during the war ... 25
   The inevitability of victory: the domestic sphere ... 29
   The inevitability of victory: the international sphere ... 30
   Guiné since the war ... 32

3 The agronomic writings

4 The class analysis of African society ... 59
   The theoretical setting ... 59
   The class struggle in Guiné ... 62
   The peasant ... 67
   The social structure of the towns ... 69
   The Lumpenproletariat ... 73
   The petty bourgeoisie ... 75

5 Culture and personality ... 82

6 The state ... 92

7 The forces of production ... 100

8 Imperialism ... 110
   First- and Third-World theories of imperialism ... 110
   Cabral's theory of imperialism ... 115
   Towards a new theory of imperialism ... 125

9	Conclusion	129
	Notes	139
	Bibliography	145
	Index	155

1 INTRODUCTION

THE HISTORICAL CONTEXT

In most African states the first ten years of political independence brought to fruition none of the promised benefits of a freer and a more bountiful life. The decade closed with the death of the spirit of a once optimistic nationalism. Yet in 1970, almost ten years after the independence of West and East Africa, the colonies of Portugal, namely Angola, Mozambique and the insignificant territory of Guiné-Bissau, were still fighting for the right of national self-determination. The struggle in Guiné was begun in 1956 under the leadership of Amilcar Cabral in the same year that Patrice Lumumba began his rise to prominence in the Belgian Congo. It ended in 1974, almost thirteen years after the death of Frantz Fanon and the achievement of Algerian independence.

The revolution in Guiné is not in itself important because Guiné is not important. Unlike Angola, Guiné has no great mineral wealth. With a population of a little over 500,000, a severe climate, and an economy which at best could rely upon the export of groundnuts, timber and other primary produce, Guiné has never been attractive to European settlement or capital. The sole reason Portugal invested so much effort to retain the colony was out of fear that the loss of Guiné would jeopardise the military and political situations in the other colonies.

During the 1960s the Portugese made numerous attempts to have the Cape Verde Islands covered under the NATO umbrella as had been the case with the Azores. Portugal hoped to sell her African wars to the United States with the claim that the Cape Verde Islands would provide a vital communications link into the south Atlantic and that Guiné itself was strategically important in West Africa. The United States could, however, at the time detach both the Cape Verdes and Guiné from American strategic interests in the region. Once these moves had failed, Portugal was left to defend a territory of no strategic importance to anyone but herself. To western eyes the only fact of interest about Guiné proved to be that those in the independence struggle could achieve so much against a vastly superior force.

The success of the Vietnamese people in opposing and finally defeating the French and then the Americans was remarkable because of the disadvantages under which the Vietnamese fought in terms of weapons and technology. Both Indo-Chinese wars are testimony to the predominance of human will over the weight of purely material force. Yet even by this measure the achievement of the PAIGC in defeating the Portuguese is extraordinary. According to the UN census of 1969 the population of mainland Guiné was estimated at 530,000. In 1972 the total number of Portuguese troops in the country was in excess of 35,000. The ratio of foreign troops to indigenous inhabitants was far greater in Guiné than Vietnam and still the Portuguese lost.

The revolution in Guiné is fascinating because on a small scale it demonstrates the strengths and weaknesses of national liberation movements. It also illustrates in a most dramatic fashion the difficulties experienced by reactionary forces in attempting to contain such movements. The contrasts in Guiné are even more dramatic than in the case of Indo-China, for in Guiné the struggle was fought against an ancient colonial regime by a people who before the war had no national identity and no state. And yet, despite the smallness of scale of the revolution, the liberation of Guiné was instrumental in the destruction of the fascist regime in Portugal.

The revolution in Guiné is also fascinating because of its lateness. The war began at a time when France and Britain were dismantling their empires in West and East Africa and all three wars in Portugal's empire span the whole of the first decade of African independence. This lateness, and the strategic importance of Angola and Mozambique to the minority regimes of the south, identify these wars as the prelude to the final phase of Africa's liberation - the destruction of the minority regime in South Africa.

Guiné's road to independence was unique, because only in Guiné had Portugal been successful in engraving the image of her own lack of economic and cultural development. This lack of development was an important factor in the liberation struggle and this, as much as any other single influence, set the horizons for the type of war waged by the Partido Africano da Independência da Guiné e Cabo Verde (PAIGC). The very novelty of the situation made it necessary for the national movement to confront a number of theoretical questions about social structure, class alliance and international political forces which in aggregate came to represent a new interpretation of contemporary imperialism. It is certain that if the PAIGC's answers to these questions had been misconceived and, if the party had entered the struggle armed with the wrong theory, the war against the Portuguese would soon have been lost. A strategy such as that suggested in 'The Wretched of the Earth', relying upon peasant leadership and spontaneous eruptions in the cities, could not possibly have succeeded. Under such circumstances the nationalist movement would have been destroyed in a matter of months.

Amilcar Cabral was born in mainland Guiné in 1925. He received his secondary education in the Cape Verde Islands and later trained as an agronomist in Lisbon. Upon returning to Guiné, Cabral was employed by the Provincial Department of Forestry and Agriculture. As a result of his opposition to the colonial administration, Cabral was expelled from Guiné in 1955 but returned for a brief visit the following year during which time he was instrumental in founding the PAIGC. Over the next four years Cabral worked as an agronomist in Angola. He also made regular visits to Guiné and Portugal and published a number of important studies on agricultural practice.

Cabral was the leading intellectual force within the PAIGC and it was his analysis of the social structure of Guiné, based largely upon his understanding of Guinéan agriculture, which formed the basis for the success of the party in its fourteen-year-long struggle against the Portuguese. During 1959 the party suffered early reversals for, in attempting to organise strikes among the dock workers of Bissau, the movement made itself vulnerable to the savage repression the Portuguese immediately imposed. The reasons why the PAIGC finally arrived at the correct strategy can be found in part among Cabral's earliest writings, published while he was working for the Department of Forestry and, in particular, in that cluster of articles arising from the survey of agriculture he conducted for the Department in 1953. During his work as an agronomist Cabral had the opportunity to explore at first hand the relationship between Portuguese colonialism and the dominant features of Guinéan agriculture. This, in turn, led him to examine the relationship between social class, indigenous culture, and the political economy of colonial rule. In the period prior to the outbreak of armed struggle in 1963, Cabral had already arrived at a theoretical understanding of the principal elements defining social and economic activity in the country.

THE THEORETICAL CONTEXT

The speeches, essays and other writings of Amilcar Cabral represent an attempt to think of imperialism and the colonial relationship in a new way. Superficially, Cabral's writings don't present any new or particularly complex interpretation of colonialism. With the exception of a few rather brief essays, most of his work appears to be merely a description of a guerrilla war fought against the last of the great colonial powers. Yet the appearance in these essays of the terms 'mode of production' and 'productive forces' suggests that his understanding of imperialism was founded upon a new set of presuppositions. Cabral employed these terms before they became fashionable among the ranks of the avant garde and at a time when the concept of the mode of production was still largely a possession of Soviet Marxism. It is important to remember that during the 1960s Soviet visions of the Asiatic Mode of Production were achieving much the same effect as modernisation theory in the west. Both schools tended to reflect the difficulties in defining exactly what was happening in post-colonial Africa in terms of the working out of broader historical forces. The fact that most

of Cabral's important essays were written at this time only
emphasises the innovative quality of his work.
The classic theories of imperialism presented in the writings of
Hobson, Hilferding, Lenin and Luxemburg were addressed to
understanding changes internal to the European economic and
political orders. Lenin, who is the best-known and also the most
typical of the classic theorists, was concerned to expose the
causes of the Great War and to destroy the accepted myths
about the colonial empires. In none of the classic theorists is
there anything approaching a social psychology of imperialism
or a compelling analysis of imperialism as an ideology. This
proved to be a significant omission in the development of African
socialism, because of the importance of imperialist sentiment
and overt racism to that generation of colonial intellectuals educated in Europe after the war. It was these men and women who
were to lead the nationalist movements in Africa.

In the period beginning with the end of the Second World War
there was for the first time a perceived need within Marxist
scholarship for a new approach to the theory of imperialism. By
the early 1960s Marxist thinking had become inadequate, as
most Marxists clung ferociously to Lenin's 'Imperialism' as the
definitive text on capitalist expansion. When Cabral began his
intellectual career he was faced with these verities which dominated thinking on the left about colonial societies. But by chance
Cabral was placed in an advantageous position; his intellectual
life began at the end of the 1940s within the context of the
antique colonialism practised by the Portuguese in Guiné and
Cape Verde and stretched well into the post-colonial era or, as
Cabral preferred to call it, 'the age of rationalised imperialism.
In terms of the development of Cabral's own theory it was fortu-
nate that the war in Guiné was fought against the first of the
great colonial powers which, because of its economic and social
backwardness, was the last to decolonise. Portugal's backwardness taught Cabral two important lessons: it taught him that
economic and political control were not one and the same thing.
It also taught him that the absence of capitalist penetration could
be as debilitating as the pathologies arising from the impact of
foreign capital.

In 1960 at the opening of Africa's decade of independence,
modernisation theorists and most European Marxists could at
least agree on one thing: the lack of human achievement on the
African continent. This prejudice infected both Soviet and
Western Marxist thought throughout the 1950s and 1960s and
found expression in various guises such as schematic presen-
tations of categories of modes of production. In its most crude
form this allowed the integration of African societies into a
Marxist perspective as instances of the Asiatic Mode. Leaving
aside the numerous problems inherent in this concept, problems
such as the absence of hydraulic works, this tack reinforced
the prejudice that African societies were stagnant and that
Africa was a continent without a history. Unfortunately such

theorising only served to hold back the development of African socialism.

In contrast to these Eurocentric theories of imperialism, Third-World theorists have tended to flounder at the point where their analyses approach the question of class theory and class struggle. This has been particularly obvious in African political theory in the past decade. The chief problem appears to derive from the fact that it is necessary on the one hand to analyse primitive or communalist social formations (which are so very different from social strata in Europe) and to integrate this material into a sophisticated analysis of the internal dynamics of later capitalism. This area of difficulty has been compounded by the preoccupation of both First- and Third- World theorists with the question as to how Marx himself conceived of the transformation of primitive societies. All too often an account extrapolated from the pages of 'The German Ideology' describing the process of transformation would be matched against the pattern of capitalist developments which have taken place in Black Africa. This in turn would be identified as being typical of underdevelopment. These kinds of adaptations within the boundaries of Marxist and neo-Marxist theory serve to illustrate the problems which arise from the interlocking of First- and Third-World economies and raise numerous questions about the concepts of class and the mode of production, as well as throwing into question basic assumptions about revolutionary strategy.

As a result of these kinds of problems, Marxist and neo-Marxist theories of imperialism have tended to be conflated with theories of underdevelopment which are, in turn, particularly weak and unsubtle in their approach to class analysis. Consequently, the construction of theories about class conflict and theories of underdevelopment have become separated.

The evaluation of the status of pre-colonial societies is one major area in the approach to African history which has a direct bearing on the development of theories of imperialism. For too long the Marxist concept of the Asiatic mode of production absolved researchers from the responsibility of exploring the evolutionary trends present in African societies, in the period prior to effective colonial control. Consequently, little effort was made to discern either the differences between modes of production common to Africa and those common to European societies, or to distinguish between categories of social class, which are historically and functionally different in the two environments. In consequence the possibility of the existence of an endogenous reflex to change, bringing in its wake the development of more sophisticated economic and social formations, was ignored entirely. This neglect was reinforced by the attitude toward the African past adopted by the new nationalist elites. So much African political theory of the last twenty years owes its existence to the twin mythologies of negritude and the African personality. All too often any question directed to an evaluation of the pre-colonial past was resolved by reference to the myth that colonial rule had not altered in any significant way the foundations of African societies. Supposedly, colonialism had not affected that unique Black African ontology which would provide the basis for an African socialism. Consequently, for more than thirty years, the all-pervasive influence of negritude and the myth of the African personality preoccupied intellectuals with what were ultimately personal questions of meaning and identity. This influence was so deeply ingrained that until quite recently class theory was often clumsy and invariably ill-conceived.

The shallowness of African political theory is apparent even in the work of Frantz Fanon, who in other ways did so much to free political theory about Africa from the dead end into which the winds of change had driven it. But even in 'The Wretched of the Earth' the foundations of Fanon's class analysis are drawn from the ideology of the cultural renaissance movements which, in turn, have their ancestry in the writings of E.W. Blyden and Marcus Garvey. The work of Fanon, a West Indian, shows just how destructive this influence could be, for it contaminates almost all of his writings on the subjects of race, class and revolutionary strategy.

The need for a new approach to the theory of imperialism was brought about, above all else, by the political and economic degeneration which accompanied the first years of African independence. The growing repressiveness of most nationalist governments and their apparently inevitable decay into military regimes raised important questions about the relationship between political and economic autonomy. It also posed the equally important question as to the composition of the new ruling classes. Unfortunately the response to the need for an innovative theory was extremely slow in arriving.

The dimensions of an adequate theory of imperialism for Africa should refer to the issues of contemporary production, class formation, and national culture. Such a theory must also contain an account of Africa's historical evolution in the period prior to colonialism. Each of these questions, in turn, needs to be examined from the perspective of Africa's historical experience, rather than from the vantage point of the political and economic evolution of Western Europe. In the case of production and class theory it is necessary to accommodate an analysis of primary production with an account of class. During the later half of the 1960s the search for the origins of Africa's lack of development was revived through the application of underdevelopment theory and in the use of Latin American models, which traced the process of economic retardation to the dominance of European capital. Within socialist theorising about Africa in the period before the publication of 'The Wretched of the Earth', this meant little more than the search for a national middle class. Since Fanon it has often meant the search for a comprador bourgeoisie.

In underdevelopment theory higher levels of technology are associated exclusively with increasing economic and political repression. The abandonment of the belief in the liberative effects of technology, which is so central to the history of Marxist thought, has gone unquestioned. This has, in turn, led to a widening gap between Marxism and what is now sometimes termed neo-Marxism. In Marx, as in Hegel, there is no allowance for the occurrence of abortions in history. To Marx, as to Weber or Hegel, a model such as Fanon's superfluous national middle class, a class which achieves absolutely nothing, would appear quite absurd. Yet in underdevelopment theory in general and in Fanon's work in particular, the idea of pathological development is seen as normal. Underdevelopment theory treats capitalism itself as the special case.

In the works of African nationalists and in particular in the writings of such people as Sékou Touré, Lumumba, Mondlane, and Nkrumah there are a number of common elements which when taken together constitute an African theory of imperialism. Rather ironically these shared elements are most clearly codified in the writings of the West Indians, Aimé Césaire, and Frantz Fanon. Both Fanon and Césaire viewed imperialism and European civilisation as essentially barbaric. Imperialism, they believed, had a distorting effect upon colonial societies and a peculiarly corrupting influence upon the metropoles where it ran hand in hand with the rise of reactionary elements and, in particular, with the emergence of fascism. Although conceding that imperialism was an outgrowth of capitalism, Fanon and Césaire rejected completely the idea that there is a necessary connection between higher levels of technology and the quality of a civilisation. Fanon, in particular, has a tendency to see the relationship as inverse and to identify higher technology with cultural degeneration. Both Fanon and, to a lesser extent, Césaire emphasised two elements which place them at odds with Marxist belief; they rejected the primacy of class conflict within the metropoles as the determinant of contemporary history and they rejected the idea of a natural and effective solidarity between the metropolitan working classes and the nationalist movements. Fanon, in particular, was convinced that the European working class was reactionary. These two points, which are found in one guise or another in most African socialist literature, establish an irrevocable separation between such theory and Marxism.

From the vantage point of the 1980s the immediate response of African socialism to the challenge of the independence decade seems little more than an inverse reflection of the myths of Africa's social and cultural backwardness etherealised. The existence of rich traditions in sculpture, the visual arts, music and the dance were presumed to reinstate the African into the human family, if only at the cost of perpetuating the prejudice this posture was intended to destroy. Pablo Picasso's 'Les Demoiselles d'Avignon' is not really a convincing argument as to the strength of African civilisation. Certainly the traditional Marxist theory of imperialism was quite inadequate in analysing colonialism from within, but the intertwining of certain aspects of Lenin's essay with an unsubtle inversion of several of its central propositions only weighted down the development of an adequate interpretation of the colonial experience. It is now apparent that African socialism was little more successful in coping with the challenges of nationalism than were the governing elites which nationalism had brought to power.

In understanding the dilemma of the nationalist generation, it is useful to draw a parallel between the work of Cabral as one of Africa's leading revolutionary figures and the writings of Frantz Fanon, who was Africa's leading revolutionary theorist. The parallel between Fanon and Cabral is a fascinating one and it is encouraged by the fact that they were born within a year of each other. Both were members of a small middle class and both were educated in Europe in the period immediately after the end of the Second World War. Each was open to much the same range of intellectual influences with Fanon having a marked attachment to a kind of intellectualising that is so conspicuously absent from the writings of Cabral. Both were influenced by post-war Marxism and the cultural renaissance movements which preceded the nationalist decade. In their early twenties both men developed a passionate commitment to destroy the system of colonialism which dominated the worlds into which they were born.

The differences between Fanon and Cabral can be explained in part by their choice of vocations; Cabral became an agronomist and Fanon specialised in psychiatry. These vocations became the starting point from which each man set out to invent a new politics of colonialism. Fanon's intellectual curiosity about the colonial relationship invariably resolved itself into questions about personality and mental illness. The theory of the colonial personality is the major achievement of Fanon's most famous work. Yet Fanon occupied an insignificant position in the Algerian struggle for independence, and it is only in the West that his name is associated with the Algerian revolution. As a non-Muslim who spoke no Arabic, Fanon never really shook off the epithet of the 'Nigger Doctor from Blida' with which he was welcomed to North Africa.

In contrast to Fanon, Cabral was the founder of a political party. He was a successful and important political activist who is universally recognised as the founding father of the nation of Guiné. Like Fanon, his earliest published writings were written in his professional capacity, as an agronomist. Cabral's early studies of agriculture in Guiné were the first step he took in making a systematic analysis of the entire spectrum of productive and social relations within the country. The strength of much of Cabral's later work on class structure, in particular, can be traced to his knowledge of agricultural production. This point of difference between Fanon and Cabral is highly significant. Fanon always interpreted both oppression and the prospect of liberation purely in terms of psychological well-being. Cabral conceived of liberation as the freeing of the national productive forces which he believed would alter the entire gamut of social and political conditions within the country. This difference marks the point of separation between the two men and identifies them intellectually as belonging to two distinct generations.

In drawing a parallel between Fanon and Cabral, 'The Wretched of the Earth' appears as the final work in a lineage which has its roots in a past as distant in time and place as Aimé Césaire's 'Discourse on Colonialism'. If 'The Wretched of the Earth' is the baroque of African socialism, then Cabral's scattered speeches, essays and incidental writings represent a new beginning in African socialist theory.

There are a number of specific problems for the reader in approaching the political theory of Amilcar Cabral. He published no single major work and his analysis of colonialism and imperialism comes to us in the form of speeches and numerous articles scattered in English, French and Portuguese. The subjects of his writings range from technical studies of soil erosion to essays on culture and colonial rule. In each instance the form in which Cabral's work is presented was dictated by the purpose for which it was written. All of Cabral's writings, and this includes even the earliest of his published essays on agriculture commissioned by the Portuguese government, were written with the purpose of improving the life conditions of the people of Guiné and Cape Verde.

It is quite wrong to draw a distinction in Cabral's work between serious theoretical and less weighty practical writings. There are obvious differences between the talks Cabral gave to party activists during the period of the struggle and his speeches to international audiences in Cuba or before the United Nations. But these differences should not be taken as indicating the presence of various levels of seriousness within his written work. To divide these writings into a theory and practice order imposes a higher and lower degree of merit on the problems and arguments they contain. Such an approach always holds the assumption that only a specific social stratum is capable of understanding the complex social and economic factors which shape its existence. This in its most crude form refers to two types of political practice. In the context of a national liberation struggle, this distinction becomes a class distinction most ideally expressed between the petty bourgeoisie and the peasantry. Cabral's opposition to this distinction in practice and his opposition to this principle in theory, that is within his writings, is entirely in conformity with the ethos of revolutionary socialism.

A second range of problems arises in the interpretation of Cabral's work because his writings fall across three decades. These three decades are paradigmatic in the sense that they correspond to fundamental changes in both the theory and practice of politics in Africa. Cabral's work begins with his agronomic studies of the early 1950s. The imaginative horizon of these writings was set by the possibility of the modernisation of agricultural production. Politically, Cabral stops short at the proposition that the wealth created by Guinéan producers should stay in the country to the benefit of all Guinéans. The second period is that of the 1960s in which the beginning of radical social theory corresponds with the acceleration into political independence. Most of Cabral's political writings come from this period although, because of the nature of the archaic colonial power against which the PAIGC was fighting, his writings in this area are simultaneously late and premature. The 1960s is the decade of African nationalism. It is also the decade of modernisation theory to which there was no convincing response from the left until the work of André Gunder Frank. The early 1970s is the period of the failure of African independence and it belongs to the underdevelopment theorists. Yet invariably all the concerns of the underdevelopmentalists, that is, the root causes of poverty, political atrophy, and bureaucratic inflation, were the same as those problems occupying the attention of modernisation theorists during the previous decade. In a period of ten years neither Africa's liberation movements nor African socialist theory had made the advances which were hoped for at the beginning of the decade.

To African and Asian nationalists the history of theories of imperialism has always been in essence a history of Europe. In a more contemporary setting modernisation and underdevelopment theories contain a secret history of European enterprise at work. Having first adopted the disguise of benevolence, the enemies of this enterprise now wear the features of helpless compassion.

Amilcar Cabral is the leading political theorist of the second phase of the independence era. His collected writings, essays, and speeches prove that rather than being the last of the radical nationalists and falling in with the genealogy comprising Nkrumah, Fanon and Touré, Cabral is the first of the next generation. His essays, such as The Weapon of Theory and National Liberation and Culture, suggest a radically new analysis of the role of the colonial and post-colonial states, as well as exploring the mode of production common to West Africa. None of these terms appeared in the literature of African Socialism until ten years after Cabral wrote. Among other things Cabral anticipates the debate about the overdeveloped or autonomous state as well as its sequel. That is why the writings of Amilcar Cabral have a relevance far beyond the borders of the small West African state for which he gave his life.

2 THE STRUGGLE FOR GUINÉ

INTRODUCTION

The history of revolutions in our time, like the revolutionary theories accompanying them, has been played out against the decline of Europe's domination of the world. This decline has made it necessary to distinguish between the tactics and strategy appropriate to revolutionary movements within the First and Third Worlds. It has also meant that careful attention has had to be given to such factors as the social, cultural and historical peculiarities within individual environments. Since the end of the Second World War there have been numerous attempts by African and Asian nationalists to invent a new politics both in theory and in practice. Often the principles governing liberation struggles have been expressed in highly abstract terms, and they have tended, especially in the case of Africa, to drag revolutionary nationalism towards a preoccupation with questions of racial individuality and the genius of national culture.

Contemporary history has also witnessed a growing concern with questions of global strategy and the relative weight which should be accorded the nationalist revolutions in the colonial world. In terms of political success this issue has been resolved so decisively in favour of the colonial world that Third World theories of imperialism have all but broken away from plain Marxist and Soviet Marxist interpretations of revolutionary strategy. This has been further encouraged by a disenchantment with the modest achievements of revolutionary movements in the advanced countries. Frantz Fanon's dismissal of the colonial proletariat as a revolutionary class was motivated largely by his contempt for the failure of the French working class to support Algerian independence. It is in this context of the shift in the centre of gravity of the world revolutionary movement that Cabral's political theory lies.

Cabral's published writings on the revolution in Guiné were intended to do a number of things. They were intended to provide a history of the people's war against the Portuguese and to propagandise that struggle within the international community. These writings were also a stage on which Cabral could explore and analyse the process of the struggle in terms of the theoretical problems it posed. Cabral's history of the war in Guiné is the major source of documentation we have in understanding the revolution in the period to 1973. Because of the way in which they are phrased, the problems touching on political theory in

Cabral's writings come to us, as Althusser would have said, in a purely practical form.

In the pamphlet 'Our People are our Mountains'[1] Cabral comments that there are laws common to all national liberation struggles; for instance, it is not possible to attack the colonial power in his metropole with any real hope of military or political success. Similarly, on the military plane all national liberation struggles have employed the Maoist principle of forcing the enemy to disperse his forces, then attacking the enemy at the point of his greatest weakness. But, although it is useful to know and even to adapt the experience and theories of others to one's own ends, each struggle sets specific demands and requires its own theories. Cabral is quite adamant that it is impossible to create a theory of liberation without first participating in that struggle; under every circumstance it can be said that practice comes before theory.

In 1963, when the armed struggle in Guiné began, the leadership of the PAIGC was not familiar with the writings of the great theorists on revolutionary warfare. Cabral argues at one point that such knowledge which could be gained from reading Mao or Guevara would only be of secondary importance. The revolution in Guiné and the problems which the war against the Portuguese presented could only be solved in a way dictated by the peculiarities of the country, its history, and its people. Cabral does not presume to claim on the basis of the Guiné experience that theories of national liberation should in any sense be modified. In his view all such questions are subordinate to the laws which govern the evolution of each society, for it is these laws which must dictate the practice of revolutionary struggle and determine the possibilities for social transformation. Above all else, each liberation movement must operate in harmony with the specific stage reached by the society in which it occurs.

SPECIFIC CONDITIONS IN GUINÉ AND CAPE VERDE

The political and economic backwardness of Portugal was a major factor determining the character of colonial rule in each of her African territories. Nowhere was this more true than in Guiné-Bissau and the Cape Verde Islands.

At the beginning of the independence decade, when the rising tide of nationalism was sweeping the rest of Black Africa, the infant mortality rate in Guiné was in excess of 70 per cent. Until 1959 there was not one secondary school in a country with a population of over 500,000. There were few roads and virtually no industry. This lack of development was also reflected in the composition of the settler community. The few Europeans living in the colony tended to be poor and to live in closer proximity to the native population than was common in British and French West Africa. This poverty, although pushing the two communities closer together in a physical sense, meant that Portuguese colonials lacked the kind of cultural and intellectual sophistication which could have stimulated an interest in local African cultures. This cultural backwardness prevented African arts and society from exercising upon the Portuguese the kind of fascination which they held for both the British and French.

During the first decades of this century the artistic achievements of the peoples of Africa exerted a strong influence over the most imaginative and creative European artists. Cubists and Surrealists were inspired by the sculpture and carvings of Benin, Dogon and Makonde artists, for they recognised in their work a vitality and originality which European painting and sculpture lacked. Eventually the influence of African arts in Europe opened the way for a recognition of how African peoples conceived of their world and of how that world was consecrated in numerous complex mythologies. It was by this means that the African gradually acceded to a human status in the eyes of Europeans.

Despite its vast African empire, the Portuguese never came to understand the peoples it ruled. During the period of the liberation struggles this incomprehension proved disastrous, as Portugal found to its great expense that the African was not what he was assumed to be. In the jungles of Guiné, Angola and Mozambique the soldiers of Portugal discovered a different African, for in Portuguese Africa the myth of assimilation disguised a reality in which of all the great colonial powers Portugal had the least influence upon the peoples it claimed to have ruled justly for five hundred years.

In an article published in June 1960[2] Cabral set out to make known to the world the deplorable conditions existing in the Portuguese colonies. Writing under the pseudonym of Abel Djassi, Cabral provided an overview of life under Portuguese colonialism at a time when the western world was blissfully unaware of conditions in Mozambique, or São Tomé, or the Cape Verde Islands. The portrait which emerges could well have been written by E.D. Morel at the turn of the century, for it recounts a life of unremitting toil in which the African was used as an instrument for the most crude forms of capital accumulation. Social and political life in these colonies belonged to an earlier age.

In each of the colonies the national economy was dominated by monopolies which thrived under the protection of the Portuguese colonial administration. These monopolies extracted profits through various practices, including the use of contract labour and the payment of depressed wages. In all of the colonies taxation schemes were used to extract money and labour, thereby reducing the costs of administrating an already cheaply run empire. In Mozambique the iniquitous practice of contracting out labourers to work in the mines of South Africa was a major source of government revenue. This practice, like similar schemes of forced labour used in all of the other colonies, but especially in São Tomé, created conditions akin to slavery. In return for colonial status the peoples of Angola, Mozambique and Guiné received virtually nothing in the way of educational opportunity or health services. There is little justification for the claim made by Lisbon that the Portuguese presence helped advance the peoples of these colonies toward a better life.

During the final years of the empire, political repression of the most brutal kind was used to stifle dissent while foreign investors were encouraged to pour their capital into extractive mineral and agricultural enterprises. Implicit political support from among the major western powers allowed Portugal to maintain this system virtually intact at a time when the rest of the colonial world was changing so profoundly.

In fighting to hang on to her African colonies, Portugal had the advantage of being a fascist state. For Portugal there was no discomfort from the contradiction between state ideology and state practice which so troubled successive American presidents in Indo-China. The denial of basic political and civil liberties to the peoples of Guiné and Cape Verde was entirely consistent with the absence of these same freedoms among the peasants and working class of metropolital Portugal. Poverty and illiteracy was the fate of the majority of peoples living at both ends of this particular imperialist relationship. Life in Portugal and its colonies had somehow remained outside the mainstream of modern history.

The settlements in Guiné-Bissau and the Cape Verde Islands were among the very first permanent European footholds in West Africa. Even so, it was only after the Berlin Conference of 1885 that the Portuguese made a concerted effort to gain effective occupation of the mainland territory. This was achieved with the support of the British government, which acted in response to the threat posed by a French advance upon British territories from Senegal and Guinea. The present borders between Guiné, Senegal and the Republic of Guinea were effectively settled at the Luso-French Convention of 1886. However, Portugal's status as a colonial power did not mean that the Portuguese established the kind of sovereignty over Mozambique, Angola and Guiné which the British and French enjoyed in East and West Africa.

The Portuguese conquest of Guiné was resisted by all the major ethnic groups. This resistance included, particularly, fierce opposition from the Manjak, the Balanta, the Fula and the Mandingo. During the wars of pacification, which were to last for over half a century, the Portuguese exploited animosities between the tribes as a means of dividing and conquering the territory. According to official histories the war ended in 1917, although it was not until as late as 1936 that the peoples of the Bissagos archipelago were subdued. In fact, it was only during the early 1930s, at a time when Salazar's fascist state was in the process of construction, that effective control over the whole of the colony was finally established. This simultaneous rise of fascism in Portugal did much to shape the character of colonial rule.

Unlike Portugal's major African territories, Guiné had a very
small European population. There were no foreign-owned
plantations. This was principally due to the severe climate and
the lack of opportunities in agriculture and mining. Unlike
Angola and Mozambique, in which West German, British and
South African interests were so strong, in Guiné there was a
complete absence of foreign capital. The territories' economy was
dominated by a single monopoly, the Companhia União Fabril
(CUF), which controlled foreign trade. All exports were directed
to Portugal which also dominated the limited range of imports
drawn into the country. As elsewhere in her African empire
Portugal gained advantage through the export of her primary
goods such as cork, wine and fish, all of which have limited
appeal on a competitive world market.

In Angola and Mozambique restrictions were placed on the
development of local manufacturing industries so that locally
grown cotton was exported raw to Lisbon and manufactured
clothing was shipped back under monopoly conditions. All
attempts to establish local industries which offered competition
to metropolitan producers were proscribed. But the bulk of the
economic advantage gained by Portugal from her African wards
came through the servicing of foreign-owned monopolies investing
in Angola and Mozambique. The small and anaemic Portuguese
bourgeoisie simply lacked the facility, the capital, and the
initiative to exploit the mineral and agricultural wealth of Angola
and Mozambique. Invariably the Portuguese state merely acted
as an intermediary for foreign investors.

In comparison with the neighbouring colonies of Britain and
France, Guiné's economy remained largely unchanged until after
the Second World War. Samir Amin[3] has shown how the present
pattern of an export directed monoculture in Senegal and Ghana
was established well before the turn of the century. After 1860
the British had encouraged the growing of oil palm, while the
French promoted groundnut cultivation in both Senegal and the
Republic of Guinea. After 1945 massive investment pushed
further the monoculture that is now characteristic of the Francophone states of West Africa. In Guiné a similar pattern of reliance
upon a single export crop was also present so that by 1960
nearly three-quarters of the country's exports earnings came
from groundnuts. But in Guiné this pattern of cultivation for
export came much later and herein lies the explanation as to why
the wars were fought. If Portugal had possessed a higher level
of material development, then the wars in Angola and Guiné and
Mozambique would never have taken place. The principal reason
for Portugal's refusal to decolonise was the certainty that, in
doing so, she would lose every advantage which possession of a
colonial empire offered: a captive market for inferior manufactured goods, a cheap supply of raw materials, and the opportunity to act as an intermediary for international capital. Neither
Britain nor France had suffered greatly from the loss of their
colonial empires. The independence of Algeria had remarkably

little effect upon the French economy, but Lisbon rightfully feared that the loss of Angola would be a calamity.

Topographically, Guiné is quite unsuitable as the site for a successful guerrilla struggle. It is a small country, predominantly flat and divided into two major regions; the coastal areas consist of swamps, rivers, forests and ricelands; the interior is principally savannah traversed by a number of rivers. There are no mountains. This flat terrain set specific problems for guerrilla activity and it made the nationalist forces vulnerable to attack, particularly during the early stages of the war. There were simply no mountains to which the guerrillas could make a tactical retreat. In terms of comparison with other guerrilla struggles, the geography of Guiné was entirely unfavourable to a nationalist success.[4]

THE CAPE VERDE ISLANDS

The islands of Cape Verde lie nearly five hundred miles off the coast of West Africa, yet there are strong historical ties between the islands and Guiné which have bound together the nationalist movements in the two countries. In the period prior to 1879 the two colonies were administered as a single territory. The majority of Cape Verdeans have Guinéan roots and there has for several centuries been migration between the two territories.

As on the mainland there is a long history of resistance in the islands, which has seen revolts, mass migration to neighbouring colonies, and persistent refusal to pay taxes. But unlike mainland Guiné, the Cape Verdes have suffered from famines. In modern times these persistent famines have been so severe that during the period 1942-7 between 30,000 and 40,000 people died of starvation. A further 10,000 perished in the famine of 1958-9. The only vaguely constructive response by the Portuguese to these calamities involved a policy of forcibly expatriating thousands of Cape Verdeans, who were sent as contract labourers to the plantations of São Tomé and Angola.

High unemployment has always accompanied the recurring agricultural crises so that the peasants, who make up the vast majority of the islands' population, have lived under the constant threat of starvation. During the 1950s there was massive clandestine migration to Senegal by peasants seeking a decent life.

From the early days of settlement intermarriage between Cape Verdeans and Portuguese colonials had been common, so that by the beginning of this century the majority of the population was mestizo. This fact encouraged the granting of a number of privileges which the Cape Verdeans enjoyed over mainland Africans. Under Portuguese rule the Cape Verdeans were automatically granted the status of assimilados, which in theory, at least, accorded them equal status with Portuguese citizens. In Guiné this privilege could only be earned after meeting a number of severe educational and financial requirements. Cape Verdeans were allowed access to state education, whereas indigenes were restricted to mission schools, which offered an inferior education. In consequence of these advantages a large number of Cape Verdeans qualified to enter the civil service where they came to dominate the lower and middle rungs of the government administration. The pre-eminence of Cape Verdeans was to have long-term consequences for the nationalist movements and the success of the revolution in mainland Guiné.

POLITICAL MOBILISATION

In Guiné and Cape Verde in the period immediately after the end of the Second World War various attempts were made to establish trade unions as well as social and recreational clubs. Although anything but radical, these organisations had a nationalist flavour and they were soon disbanded by the colonial authorities. These pre-nationalist organisations did not attempt to appeal to the population outside of the urban centres, and none of them really sought to raise the issue of nationalism in any direct way. After these abortive attempts the PAI[5] was founded in 1956 as a clandestine political party. The initial strategy of the party was to concentrate all its efforts in the cities of Bissau and Bafata, but this soon proved disastrous. The massacre of dock workers at Pidjiguiti on 3 August 1959, in which 50 workers were killed and over 100 wounded, proved that open action against the government would be savagely put down.

The party gave up the attempt to organise the urban working class for a policy directed primarily towards the peasants. A clandestine organisation was retained in Bissau, but this was kept extremely small in order to survive constant police harassment. Over time a more elaborate urban party base was evolved so that by the mid-point of the war there was an extensive underground party present in Bafata, Bissau and Farim. From the first days of the struggle the prospect of armed action against the Portuguese troops in the cities was cherished as a distant goal. Such action, if in fact it proved necessary,[6] was always taken to represent the consumation of military and political victory.

The earliest demands for independence were issued by the PAIGC in December 1960.[7] The language used in the memorandum was firm but restrained, and the list of demands could as well have been presented in a more contemporary context by SWAPO or PALISARIO. In this memorandum the PAIGC called for the withdrawal of Portuguese troops and political police (PIDE) and demanded the carrying out of elections under UN supervision. The document also contains a number of detailed recommendations for the establishment of separate parliaments in Guiné and the Cape Verde Islands; however, the memorandum makes clear that any final decision for union between the territories must be arrived at through set procedures worked out by the respective parliaments. Significantly, the document contains no suggestion that the PAIGC should have any priority in an independent state.

The tenor of this early catalogue of demands is faithfully reflected in the PAIGC's official programme of the same year,[8] with the exception that the manifesto is more firm on the necessity for the 'conquest of power' by the peoples of Guiné and Cape Verde. There is nothing in either the memorandum or the party programmes at variance with the drift of the African nationalism which so dominated the decade when these important documents were written.

In conformity with so many nationalist movements born in the same era, the PAIGC was careful to distance itself from orthodox Marxist rhetoric. In an interview held in 1970[9] Cabral was asked the question as to whether or not the PAIGC was a Leninist-style party. He answered that, although in Guiné the concept of the political party, like that of European parties, grew from the workings of the class struggle, the outlook of the PAIGC was above all else grounded in the needs and experiences of the people of Guiné. Of necessity the structure and programme of the PAIGC followed the contours laid down by the reality of the struggle. Therefore, it was not a European-style party, nor was it a Leninist party, as that term is usually understood. Cabral went on to explain that, in the wider context of continental Africa, the class struggle has generated various types of political parties. Where they differ from the European experience is that these parties have the twofold role of overthrowing colonial rule and of building new nations. In terms of neither the historical circumstances under which they operate nor the social or cultural bases of their support could they be compared with the mode of political organisation which is dominant in Europe.

From the outset the PAIGC adopted the strictest principles in approaching the problem of political mobilisation. In assessing the potential of each social group a number of specific characteristics were taken into account. Firstly, a judgment was made of the extent to which each class was dependent upon the colonial authorities either for the enjoyment of benefits or for the class's very existence. Once this question had been decided, then assessments were made as to the potential of each class in the anti-colonial struggle and finally the class's revolutionary capacity for the period after independence had been won.[10] This careful and methodical approach was maintained throughout the war and it was instrumental in the success of the PAIGC.

After its early failure to mobilise successfully the minuscule working class, the PAIGC sought to discover the means by which to radicalise the peasants. The party militants soon learned that to be successful the weapon of ideology had to be linked directly to the reality of the peasants' daily life. To use a programme based on the slogan such as 'the land to those who work it' as the FLN had done in Algeria would have been futile in Guiné where land alienation had never occurred. Nor was it feasible to hope to mobilise these people through an appeal to the abstract principles of nationalism.

The initial period of mobilisation took over three years of constant work in which party cadres helped the peasants to come to an understanding of the external and often invisible conditions which ruled their lives. These conditions included the artificially low price paid for fruit, groundnuts and rice, the imposition of taxes for which the peasants saw no benefit, and their vulnerability to constant abuse by government officers and soldiers. Each of these fragments, which together constituted the face of colonialism in rural Guiné, was discussed in such a way as to link them in the peasant's mind into a meaningful whole. Through a slow and often difficult process of political education, the peasants came to understand that they were themselves the creators of the wealth which the Portuguese settlers and administrators enjoyed.[11] In theory and in practice the peasants of Guiné were never reduced to being the passive recipients of an explanation brought by strangers as to why their lives were so. Through the activity of creating their own knowledge, a life which hitherto had been essentially mysterious and determined by conditions beyond control became comprehensible. This process of mobilisation was designed to promote what Cabral in one essay refers to as 'the essential function of man - thought and political action'.[12] It was in these discussion groups that the defeat of Portuguese colonialism was begun.

Mobilisation involved the holding of hundreds of meetings and the distribution of thousands of pamphlets and documents. The process of political education brought a number of important changes. For example, rivalries arising from ethnic differences began to be erased, including the deeply felt hostility of native Guinéans toward the Cape Verdean minority which had always received favoured treatment under the Portuguese administration.

In the years of preparation between 1959 and the outbreak of the war in 1963 the party itself took form. Operating on the principle of democratic centralism and collective leadership, the party was carefully moulded into groups, sections and zones. The preparation for conflict also involved the storing of materials and the establishment of guerrilla bases so that, when the phase of armed struggle was finally launched, the nationalist forces were in fact better prepared for combat than the Portuguese. It is somewhat misleading to distinguish the period before 1963 as lying outside the realm of armed struggle. The work of the PAIGC at this time was carried on under fierce police repression, for the Portuguese did not wait for the first guerrilla attacks before declaring war against the civilian population. This repression increased considerably after the massacre in 1959 at the Bissau docks and continued throughout the war in which with every successive defeat PIDE and the army turned more brutally against both peasants and the urban population.

External factors were also important during these years of preparation. The PAIGC leadership was acutely aware of the

need to internationalise the struggle and this was done in a
number of ways, including the sending of delegations to the
United Nations. Assistance from the Republic of Guinea was
particularly useful, for it allowed the party to set up a political
base in Conakry including a school for militants.

The Congress of Cassaca, which was held on 13-17 February
1964, marked a turning point in the war.[13] During a seven-day
meeting of party representatives, when every aspect of the
party and the party's strategy were opened to criticism, a
number of important changes were made to the structure of the
party and the organisation of the armed forces. The country was
divided into a series of regions or zones in which strategic
bases were clustered. The party's political structure was modified and the autonomous guerrilla zones were abolished. In
addition to the local village guerrilla militias a regular army,
FARP, was created. In concert these changes allowed the advancement of the war from an initial stage of limited guerrilla action
to that of a mobile and properly co-ordinated armed conflict.
As an immediate result of this reorganisation the movement made
rapid progress both in the war itself and on the economic front
within the liberated zones. The Cassaca Congress was in every
sense a turning point for the party and for the peoples of
Guiné. It was as important within the development of the struggle
as were the general elections which were held during 1972 by
which the people of Guiné gained a judicial personality within
the international community.

STRATEGIC AIMS OF THE STRUGGLE

The strategic purpose of the PAIGC in resorting to arms was to
create the political conditions under which favourable negotiations for national independence could take place. The resort to
armed resistance in Guiné, as in all of Portuguese Africa, was
made necessary by the intransigence of the fascist government
in Lisbon. Above all else, the purpose of the guerrilla struggle
was political and from the beginning it was understood by the
party that victory on any one of the three African fronts would
mean the end of all the wars. Once the point of negotiation had
been reached in Guiné or Angola or Mozambique then negotiations
would, through the weight of public opinion in Portugal, force
negotiated settlements in the other territories. But, like the
MPLA in Angola and FRELIMO in Mozambique, from the outset
the PAIGC adopted the principle that the only point from which
negotiations could begin was from an accession to the right to
an unconditional independence.

The armed struggle was initiated from within Guiné and it was
from the outset directed from the country's centre. Using what
Cabral terms a 'centrifugal strategy', the guerrillas moved from
the middle towards the periphery as the struggle gathered
momentum. This strategy was a major innovation which had the

benefit of catching the Portuguese completely unaware. At the outbreak of the war in 1963 the Portuguese assumed that the PAIGC would launch an invasion of Guiné from Senegal. Therefore they placed troops on the border and erected a series of fortresses to stop infiltration. The assumption of an invasion was based on the experience in Angola and also more obliquely upon the principles of counter-insurgency theory which the US were to rely upon in Vietnam. In consequence the guerrillas made rapid gains, especially during the first months of the war.

When the strategy of sealing the border failed the Portuguese immediately turned their attention to the civilian population. They used napalm and white phosphorus and gun-boats and helicopters in a concerted campaign of terror. The Portuguese also used radio propaganda in an attempt to separate the civilian population from the guerrillas. At every step the strategy was a facsimile of American policy in Vietnam, except that the Portuguese lacked America's material capacity to wage war on a grand scale.

In terms of tactical principles the nationalists followed quite closely to established methods of guerrilla warfare, alternately concentrating then dispersing their forces to the disadvantage of a less mobile and less imaginative enemy. Cabral readily conceded that the party learned much from the experiences of the Chinese, Vietnamese and Cuban revolutions,[14] and that these methods met with immediate success.

During the initial phase the nationalists created autonomous guerrilla zones in which each group was linked directly to the party leadership. This phase lasted until the end of 1963 when the army units were created. In the development of the struggle the reorganisation of the guerrilla units, including the creation of an army and the integration of each of these forces into the peasant community, was allowed to develop in successive stages, organically 'like a human being'.[15] Each time a particular phase of the struggle was completed the next phase was carefully ushered in. This gave what Cabral termed 'a total harmony to our struggle'.[16] The small guerrilla groups which were the first active units were moulded and tightened until they constituted a regular army. This process was very gradual, yet, because of the movement's precocious military success, by as early as 1964 the majority of the former guerrilla units had been converted into regular forces.

At the beginning maximum autonomy had to be given to the guerrillas. This was made necessary by the problems of communication between these groups and the party leadership. Furthermore, because of the small population of Guiné, it was necessary to fight as economically as possible, especially in the early stages of the war. Autonomy enhanced security. The movement simply could not sustain heavy casualties and still survive. This policy was pursued in the knowledge that it entailed the calculated risk that individual guerrilla units would become uncontrollable. During the initial phase of the struggle the total integration of the guerrilla forces with the local population did encourage some guerrilla leaders to abuse their autonomy. Consequently, particular units became isolated and failed to co-ordinate their activities with the other units in their area. This problem was overcome at the Congress of Cassaca in 1964 at which existing units were reorganised and disciplinary action was taken against a number of guerrilla commanders.

The immediate objectives of the armed struggle included a programme of social and economic reconstruction in the liberated areas which, within three years of the commencement of armed struggle, included two-thirds of the countryside. In these regions there was no need for land reform as all land was owned communally, but there was need to improve yields. Cabral writes about the need for a 'technical revolution' in agriculture as the only basis for a prosperous Guiné. Considerable gains in production levels were achieved despite the concerted efforts by the colonial army to destroy staple crops.

During an interview in 1967[17] Cabral was asked if he thought the war would end with a battle such as that at Dien Bien Phu. He replied that the African wars would see a political solution and that in Guiné a European army would be defeated by political means. He went on to argue that such had in fact been the case both with the first Indo-Chinese war and in Algeria. The political aspect must always be dominant in a war of national liberation. In every instance success depends upon the rate of mobilisation of the people and not upon such technical factors as terrain or military capacity which in both Guiné and Cape Verde were unfavourable to the PAIGC.

Throughout the nationalist struggle in Guiné great care was taken to avoid the creation of a separate military apparatus. The army was always in theory and in its daily operations an instrument of the party. In an operational sense there was no rigid distinction between the two; all members of the army were also members of the party. As Cabral commented in an article published in 1969, 'Our fighters are defined as armed activists.'[18] The political bureau of the PAIGC directed the armed struggle as well as the economic and social administration of the liberated zones. Within the Political Bureau the War Council had immediate responsibility for the military actions. But the War Council was at each turn an instrument of the Political Bureau. Each front had its own command below which lay sectors and units. These had autonomy in day-to-day activities, but each major decision had first to pass through the hands of the party's general secretary; it was the secretary who presided over the Political Bureau and the War Council.

MILITARY ACTIONS

At the end of each year of the war Cabral wrote an annual report tracing the progress made by the nationalist movement.

These reports were written for a number of reasons including the need to propagandise the achievements of the PAIGC before a western audience. They were also intended to provide a history of the people of Guiné in the process of becoming a nation as well as to be a medium by which Cabral could resolve immediate problems confronting the party in terms of a broader theoretical perspective.

Because these are practical writings there is a tendency for Cabral to disavow any concern with questions of political or social theory. This is particularly evident in his responses to questions presented in the interviews which are appended to several of the annual statements. But this negative response to the issue of theory is always justified by Cabral's insisting on his fidelity to the principle directing the struggle; this principle was that the actual conditions and history of Guine must be the sole determinant of the kind of struggle waged by the PAIGC. Fortunately besides Cabral's occasional protests in favour of this prejudice such an antipathy to the problem of theory is not reflected anywhere else in his writings.

The year 1964[19] was important for the development of the armed struggle during which time two decisive events took place. In February the Portuguese launched the first of a number of major military operations and it was also the month in which the first party congress of the PAIGC took place.

The proximity of these events in time symbolises the interdependence of the political and military aspects of the struggle. The Island of Como was the first area liberated by the PAIGC during 1963 and therefore it was a prime target for Portuguese military action. The island had great strategic significance for control over the southern half of the country, and reconquest of the area would have represented a major political victory for the Portuguese. The battle of Como lasted for more than two months and it involved 3,000 Portuguese troops, including 2,000 hand-picked combat troops transferred from Angola for the offensive. In all, the Portuguese lost 658 men killed and a large number of wounded. The battle proved a resounding victory for PAIGC and it shattered Lisbon's hopes of achieving a quick military solution.

In the following year the PAIGC achieved important victories in the regions of Gabu and Boe as well as consolidating ground won in the liberated zones. Significant improvements in the cultivation of crops in the liberated zones were achieved and commerce in general was stimulated through the establishment of People's Shops. During 1964 the army managed to paralyse the activities of the two principle commercial companies operating in Guiné, the Société Commerciale d'Outre Mer in the south, and the CUF in the interior. In the region of Gabu the groundnut industry was brought to a virtual halt as the guerrillas established control over most trade routes in the interior.

At the social level there were a number of advances made including the construction of a small bush hospital, the training of sanitary workers, and the establishment of a boarding school at Conakry. There was also a massive literacy programme initiated in the liberated regions. Schools were set up and several thousand books distributed in an effort to overcome five centuries of colonial rule.

During the next four years the PAIGC established undisputed control over two-thirds of the country.[20] The Portuguese forces were confined to the urban centres and could not venture outside of the cities without fear of attack. In 1968 the nationalists launched numerous attacks including direct assaults against enemy fortified camps. There were also attacks made against supply boats which since early 1964 had become the principal means used by the Portuguese for moving supplies and men. Apart from ambushes and other such small-scale operations, the army carried out a number of commando raids against enemy barracks and even managed to attack an air base within ten kilometres from Bissau. Besides inflicting physical damage, these various forms of military activity had the effect of sapping the enemy's morale.

In the early months of 1968 the Portuguese began sending their wounded directly to hospitals in West Germany, where they could receive better medical treatment. This was also a convenient method of hiding the level of casualties, which had grown significantly over the preceding eighteen months, from the Portuguese public. The use of West German hospital facilities was an indication of the extent to which Portugal was losing ground in the war.

The actual losses suffered by the nationalist forces were no higher in 1968 than were the civilian casualties due to police and army violence before the outbreak of the war. This was so, despite the fact that the FARP were now operating on all three fronts. Clearly, the reorganisation of the armed forces and the arming of a large number of civilians had increased the nationalists' effectiveness against Portugal's troops. By 1968 the Cape Verde Islands were providing a valuable logistic base for the Portuguese military operations in Guiné and Angola. Yet, despite the importance of making ground in the islands, the PAIGC had not been able to advance from political to military action in Cape Verde. The Portuguese resolution to retain the islands was indicative of their strategic importance. South Africa operated an air base on the Island of Sal which was central to western interests in both Southern and Western Africa.

During 1969 the nationalist forces continued to make political and military progress.[21] The Portuguese had lost all capacity to move men and goods along the few highways linking the towns and the rivers which were now too dangerous to use with any confidence. Even within the controlled territory the Portuguese could not move without heavy armoured vehicles and without the certainty of losses. Thus the urban centres had become prisons for the soldiers, who even there were subject to harrassment and attack. By this time the Portuguese had given up all hope of re-establishing control over the liberated areas.

The isolation of the enemy in purely defensive positions meant that the previous reliance upon motorised and ground troops had been replaced by the use of aerial bombardments of the civilian population. For the liberation force to move beyond this phase of strategic stalemate, it was necessary to create an unbearable situation for the colonial troops. It was believed that this could be brought about by blocking off all supply routes on the rivers servicing the principal ports and urban centres. The complete isolation of the enemy-occupied centres was then the next step toward victory.

In April 1971 the nationalists launched an offensive which took advantage of the garrisoned position of the colonial forces.[22] Major successes were achieved on the Kinara and Catio fronts and also, for the first time, attacks were made directly against the cities of Bissau and Bafata. These attacks were mainly of psychological value as they spread uncertainty and insecurity among the enemy troops. This year was as a whole the best military period of the entire war, with one success following another.

This pattern of success extended into 1972 when four separate attacks were made against the capital and the airport.[23] Further attacks against the towns including Bula were carried out in 1972 and early 1973, and were part of a general increase in the tempo of the war planned by Cabral. This line of approach in increasing military activity was dictated by the militancy of the Portuguese who, according to Cabral 'understand only one language - the number of corpses'.[24]

The increased military activity of the colonial forces relying now upon aerial bombardment was understood by the PAIGC as being entirely normal for a liberation struggle. In September 1972 there was the first clash between the Portuguese and peasants in Cape Verde, which indicated a deterioration of conditions in both Praia and throughout Santiago. But, above all else, the major achievement in the struggle during 1972 lay in the holding of general elections and the creation of the first people's National Assembly in Guiné. With universal suffrage and a secret ballot, response in excess of 80 per cent was achieved in most liberated areas.

Tragically, Cabral did not live to see the National Assembly constituted in March 1973, and his history of the struggle ends suddenly with his murder on 20 January of that same year.

PORTUGUESE TACTICS DURING THE WAR

In their suppression of nationalism in Guiné and Cape Verde, the Portuguese imitated the tactics and strategy used by the United States in their anti-nationalist war in Indo-China. Initially, the Portuguese employed outright repression of the native population, combined with political work aimed at setting the indigenous population against itself. With the outbreak of guerrilla conflict in 1963, the level of repression was stepped up so that by the closing stages of the struggle the Portuguese had effectively declared war against the entire population of Guiné. As the colonial administration gradually lost control, it replaced with violence all other means of social control. The principal factor preventing the saturation bombing of the civilian communities was a paucity of weapons. In all other respects the ethics and strategy used by the Portuguese military was identical to the American intervention in Vietnam, and it was equally unsuccessful.

The opening phase of the struggle took place at Pidjiguiti on 3 August 1959 when Portuguese soldiers and civilians fired on striking dock-workers. This incident was followed by a wave of repression by the PIDE, which effectively excluded all possibility of political concessions. Cabral notes that this was accompanied by an export drive on rice, which created severe food shortages in the countryside and the towns, thereby helping to stifle political dissent. In the Cape Verde Islands there were severe famines during 1958 and 1959 which the Portuguese did nothing to alleviate. Perhaps as many as 10,000 people died during these years of drought, which followed similar famines stretching throughout the previous decade. The only positive response by the colonial authorities was forcibly to contract out Cape Verde labourers to other colonies, principally São Tomé. These famines and the forced expatriation of workers took place in the same year that the Gold Coast achieved political independence from Great Britain. As the tide of decolonisation gained momentum in the other states of Black Africa, the level of political and economic repression in the Portuguese colonies increased. In Guiné and the islands the erosion of political authority, which had always been extremely fragile, soon gave way to naked force. It is probable that the inept response to the recurring famines in the islands was as much a result of Portugal's desire to keep the population servile as simple indifference.

In 1965 as the result of successive losses in Guiné, Angola and Mozambique, the Portuguese government decided its best chance to remain in Africa lay in internationalising the war. Lisbon set out to achieve this end by attracting foreign investors, principally British and American firms, to invest heavily in developing the mineral and agricultural resources of Angola and Mozambique and even, if possible, of Guiné itself. Laws governing foreign investment were changed so that foreign firms could hold the majority share in any venture. There were also to be no restrictions on the repatriation of capital or profits. British, American and South African concerns were quick to take up such generous terms.

Diamonds and petroleum attracted investors in Angola, while concessions were granted to Esso to explore for petroleum in Guiné. There were also additional rights granted for the exploration for bauxite. In addition to extractive rights, the

Portuguese government set up vast hydro-electric schemes at Cabora Bassa in Mozambique and in Cunene in Angola. Both of these schemes were intended to be the focus for major European settlements, promoting mineral and agricultural enterprises. The Cabora Bassa project was so dominated by South African capital that even today all electrical output from the facility is lined directly to the Republic. The people of Mozambique receive no direct benefit whatsoever from the scheme.

This programme of attracting foreign investors to the African territories was in a sense a rationalisation of a trend which had been evident for a long time in Portuguese Africa. Portugal simply lacked the capital to exploit the extensive resources of Angola and Mozambique. The wars in the three territories were being fought by Portuguese soldiers with weapons provided under the NATO treaty on behalf of the white settler communities, in the three countries but, more importantly, these soldiers were fighting to preserve US, British and South African economic and strategic interests in the region. By 1968 Portugal had over 160,000 troops fighting in Africa in a war which was costing in excess of $US400 million per year. In the jargon of the present US administration, these Portuguese troops were in effect surrogates fighting for America and South Africa.

But, despite these manoeuvres, the political and military situations in all three colonies continued to deteriorate. Cabral reports that during 1967 the Portuguese concentrated upon bombing the liberated regions, especially in the south and east. The apparent aim of these excursions was to drive the people in these areas from the land and into the cities where the colonial government still held authority.

In the article Ten Years After Pidjiguiti[25] Cabral gives a detailed account of the activities of the Portuguese army during the whole of 1968. In May of that year there had been a change of military governor, with General Schultz being replaced by General Spinola. This change indicated the importance the Portuguese government attached to the war in Guiné, for Spinola had been the architect of important gains made in Angola.

Under Spinola there was an apparent change of outlook although, as Cabral comments, in essence the policy remained the same. In a programme of what Cabral terms 'false gentility' a number of political reforms were made with particular attention being paid to the urban population. There were various concessions granted such as the construction of new schools, health centres and chapels and the distribution of scholarships for study in Lisbon. This was accompanied by an extensive programme of propaganda, extolling the virtues of the overseas territories 'where all men are equal before God and before the law'. In its appeals for peace the government promised the construction of a better Guiné. An uncharacteristic liberal rhetoric had suddenly replaced the old paternalism.

In April, after a visit lasting only a few hours, the head of the Portuguese government, Marcello Caetano, called for a reconciliation with the PAIGC in which the people of Guiné would work for a better world under the Portuguese flag. And yet, even while the prospect of peaceful change was being voiced, the spectre of a neo-colonial Guiné was accompanied by programmes of aerial bombardments of peasant villages and the burning of crops, presumably intended to reduce the peasants to starvation. Cabral defined this mixture of propaganda and military operations as a policy of 'smiles and blood'.

Portugal continued to lose ground so that by July of 1971 the situation had become desperate. In a report covering the first eight months of that year[26] Cabral emphasised the growing strife within the metropolitan society between Caetano and the Portuguese people, whose sons were being forced into exile in France or Spain, or else were condemned to fight in the jungles of Africa. Caetano maintained the policies of Salazar and he stifled any possibility of reform. Yet, with each successive year the burden of the wars in Africa was growing as was the consciousness of the Portuguese peasantry and working class that they were approaching economic ruin. The inhibiting effect of over half a century of fascist government and the imperialist and racist mentality of the ruling class acted to prevent Portugal from withdrawing from what was clearly an unwinnable situation.

In 1972 the Portuguese arrived at the final strategy for remaining in Africa. This strategy represented a last desperate lunge against the tide of nationalist successes in all three territories. The Portuguese sought to introduce a large number of European settlers into Mozambique, in the zones of Cuanza and Zambezia, and also into Angola. In all there were to be over one million new emigrants brought into southern Africa in the hope of cementing a hold on the colonies through the sheer weight of numbers. A long-term strategy of Portugal had always been to maintain European immigration at a sufficiently high level to guarantee white numerical superiority over the literate black population. This new immigration programme was geared specifically to halt the nationalist movements by strengthening the settler communities, and thereby enhancing Portugal's claim to sovereignty within the international community. The plan, however, was begun too late and the promise of a million new white farmers in southern Africa was never realised.

This final gesture, like the entire history of Portugal's African wars, was a failure. The strategy of crude, almost reflexive violence, that saw the slaughter of dock-workers at Bissau in 1959 and the massacres at Meuda in Mozambique in 1960 and Luanda in March 1961, made armed struggle unavoidable. In every instance where political concessions were made they were accompanied by an increased military effort against that part of the population which lay outside of government control. In Guiné that sector of the population was in a majority by as early as 1964.

THE INEVITABILITY OF VICTORY: THE DOMESTIC SPHERE

Within the period of armed struggle there were two developments, which were fundamental to the success of the revolution. The first was the need to centralise the daily activities of the guerrilla forces so that they were co-ordinated and synchronised according to an overall strategy. Yet countervailing this was an equally important need to retain authority within individual units so that some initiative could be maintained at the local level.

The problem of the relationship between the army and the party, which was resolved at Cassaca in 1964, was really an expression of a far wider problem, which is perennial to national liberation movements and new nationalist governments alike, that is the problem of how to reconcile the often contradictory needs of the desire for responsiveness to popular demands and the need for efficacy in decision-making. The PAIGC managed to resolve this problem both at a military level, which is evident in the great success against colonial troops and, politically, within the liberated zones in the construction of a new society.

A second range of difficulties arose from the existing patriarchal and tribal institutions. The peasants accepted the authority of local leaders and chiefs and therefore were reluctant to accept the authority of PAIGC cadres. After the armed struggle had begun, this encouraged a tendency towards authoritarianism at the local level, and some local chiefs came to exercise considerable power once the authority of colonial officials had been destroyed.

At every separate stage of the struggle the party needed to show sensitivity to the cultural individuality of each tribe. Initially, the PAIGC avoided placing a party member from the same tribal group in charge of a particular tribe for fear of encouraging localism. It was also necessary for party cadres to be sensitive to the importance of magical and local religious practices. In this way peasants were not alienated through the violation of beliefs which to outsiders may have appeared to be irrational, but which were to the tribe sacrosanct.

This sensitivity shown towards local practices is indicative of the subtlety of approach used by the PAIGC. In Cabral's history of the war it is obvious that no attempt was ever made to force the people of Guiné to change either their beliefs or behaviour merely because change would have been useful to the party. Change only came about because the peasants had finally decided that such change was necessary. This preference for an organic pattern of change is the reason why the internal development of the struggle cannot adequately be conveyed through an account of political or military achievements. As each set of needs or contradictions was resolved by the community, the struggle would be moved onto a new plane from which point it would advance again as these new conditions were in turn superseded. In essence the anti-colonial war was from the first not so much a military struggle as a process in which a new

30   *The struggle for Guiné*

society and a new state were being invented. That is why the
Portuguese were fated to lose.

THE INEVITABILITY OF VICTORY: THE INTERNATIONAL
SPHERE

From the outset the PAIGC used every means available to propagandise its claims for national independence on the international stage. Even prior to the outbreak of armed struggle, the party appealed directly to the UN General Assembly against the intransigence of the Portuguese, for national elections under UN supervision. During the war the PAIGC received some direct support through the OAU; it also benefited substantially from aid granted by Tanzania, Algeria, the UAR, Congo (Brazzaville), Cuba, China and the other members of the socialist bloc. Besides material aid, the PAIGC placed great importance on moral and political support within international organisations such as the UN. The Portuguese, on the other hand, received military aid from the United States through the agency of NATO. Portugal also received major financial and military support directly from South Africa which of all states had the most to lose with the emergence of nationalist governments in Angola and Mozambique. Besides the US and South Africa, Portugal found no difficulty in purchasing arms from France and Belgium and West Germany. The West Germans also provided hospital facilities for wounded Portuguese troops and technical instructors for aircraft and other armaments supplied to Lisbon.

On 2 February 1970 Cabral appeared before a US Senate House Committee on Foreign Affairs, investigating America's responsibilities in the African wars.[27] Cabral's appearance was memorable for his disarming candour. Cabral explained to the committee how the various arms supplied under the NATO agreements were being used in contravention of UN resolutions handed down in favour of the nationalist movements. To a question about outside (that is, Soviet or Chinese) sponsorship of the PAIGC Cabral replied that, unlike the Americans in their revolution, the people of Guiné had no need of a Lafayette. They could fight their own war for themselves, so long as the Portuguese were not granted the advantage of virtually unlimited supplies of American arms.

Senator Derwinski asked Cabral to what extent his movement's arms were supplied by Cuba and the Soviet Union. Cabral replied quite simply that unfortunately the extent was not great enough. Cabral also made no attempt to hide his party's support for the cause of the NLF in South Vietnam. It is worth remembering that this interview took place in 1970 at a time when, under President Nixon, the US had stepped up the war in Indo-China in order to extract a 'peace with honour'.

The linking of the struggle in Cape Verde to the war in Guiné only increased the determination of the Portuguese to retain a foothold in West Africa. Cape Verde was used persistently by Lisbon as a bargaining point with Washington in order to gain US support. The Portuguese government tried at every opportunity to have the Cape Verdes covered within the ambit of the NATO treaty, as was the case with the Azores. Although this was not successful, there is little doubt that this tactic worked to lessen American sensitivity to criticism that NATO weapons were being used illegally against nationalist movements on all three fronts.

In June 1970 an international conference was held in Rome attended by delegates from 74 countries, brought together to discuss Portugal's African wars. The conference was valuable in politically isolating Portugal and in giving the liberation movements the opportunity for an international audience. The conference closed with a Papal audience being granted to representatives from the liberation movements, including the PAIGC. This event alone had enormous impact upon Portuguese Catholics. The Declaration from the Rome Conference stressed the importance of NATO aid in allowing Portugal to continue the wars, and the fact that Portugal was also receiving covert support in the form of arms sales from France, Britain and West Germany. The declaration also linked the wars in Mozambique and Angola with South Africa's strategic interests in Namibia and Rhodesia, much to the embarrassment of the American government. The Conference represented a major political victory for FRELIMO, PAIGC and the MPLA.

Besides such victories on the international stage, there is a wide variety of reasons for the success of the PAIGC in its political and military struggle against the Portuguese. In his statement before the US Foreign Affairs Committee, Cabral cited three sets of conditions upon which he believed success would depend. Success would depend first and foremost upon the determination of the people of Guiné and Cape Verde to 'throw off the colonial yoke'. Above all else, victory in a national liberation struggle is the result of human forces and only secondly of material resources. The other factors Cabral cites are the moral, political and legal attitudes and conduct of the Portuguese government and the attitude of other nations within the international community, particularly in the forum of the United Nations. Cabral concludes that over time the various complex contradictions between each of these three spheres within Portugal, Guiné and the international scene at large would decide when and how the war would be won.

The nationalist forces in all three Portuguese territories shared the advantage of fighting on the side of history. They each possessed the political and moral capacity to expose and exploit the profound weaknesses of the Portuguese position. But they did so, and this was particularly so in the case of Guiné, in the absence of the material advantages of plentiful weapons or a favourable terrain or a large population. These obstacles make the achievements of the nationalists in Guiné all the more remarkable.

GUINÉ SINCE THE WAR

In September 1974 Guiné-Bissau became the first of the former African territories to be recognised as an independent state by Lisbon. Independence came eighteen years after the foundation of the PAIGC and after more than eleven years of armed struggle. It had been necessary for the African wars to destroy the fascist regime in Lisbon before it was possible for Portugal to concede her African wards the right to self-government. Of all the nationalist parties in Portuguese Africa, the PAIGC was the best-organised and the most successful in military and political terms. Yet since 1974 there has been a dramatic contrast between the success achieved during the war and the post-war problems the new government has experienced in operating and administering even basic institutions.

At independence, Guiné inherited a tiny secondary sector which had been severely run down as a result of the war. For seven years there had been virtually no investment. The local market for all goods was small and there was a uniform lack of skills, especially in the urban areas. Nearly the entire wage-labouring population was concentrated in the capital. Roads and all forms of communication were poor. The PAIGC also inherited a large trade deficit, the management of which was only cushioned by an influx of foreign aid. In fact, the inflow of foreign aid has been so great that Guiné enjoys the dubious distinction of being the largest recipient of aid, per head of population, of any African country.

Cape Verde gained independence the year after Guiné and with the mainland it was ruled by the PAICG operating as a bi-national organisation. However, the dream of unification remains remote. There is hardly any trade between the two states and very little room exists for the development of reciprocity between their individual economies. Both Cape Verde and Guiné have retained strong trading links with Portugal and both have pursued a vigorous policy of non-alignment, which has proven useful in attracting aid from both Eastern European and Western blocs. Since independence, the People's Stores have been retained as the dominant institutions for the supply and distribution of goods and they control over 60 per cent of all internal trade, as well as exercising a monopoly over the sale of imported goods. In 1976 the government of Guiné acquired a majority share in all local Portuguese firms, thereby ending the domination of the economy by a few foreign-owned monopolies.

The main problem facing the new nation at independence lay in the production of food. Before the war rice output had stood at over 120,000 tons per annum and there was even a small export surplus. By 1974 annual production had fallen to less than 30,000 tons. During the first three years after independence production of both rice and groundnuts increased substantially. Groundnut production in particular was quick to recover as the introduction of a world market price parity scheme increased the producers' return for this crop by over 300 per cent in the space of just three years. This recovery, however, was brought to an end with the droughts which began in 1977. Since then outputs have fallen drastically so that, like most African nations, the new government of Guiné is faced with the problem of feeding a population which cannot feed itself. The droughts also brought to an abrupt halt the first attempts at crop diversification in sugar, fruits, cotton and tobacco. The possibility of Guiné's farmers producing a wide variety of crops had originally been proposed by Amilcar Cabral in the early 1950s.

At independence the government of Luis Cabral, Amilcar's half-brother, began a pattern of investment in what can only be termed prestige projects. A motorway was to be built from the airport to the capital in order, no doubt, to speed the passage of foreign dignitaries to their hotels. A vehicle assembly plant has also failed to produce the export earnings for which it was built, and a more modest fruit-processing factory has run into problems of mismanagement and a lack of produce resulting from the drought.

During the last two years of Luis Cabral's rule there were complaints of corruption in the Peoples' Stores and allegations of political killings and widespread repression of all opposition. This, combined with the falling rice production, undermined support for the government, so that the coup which took place in November 1980 came as no surprise.

The Cape Verde Islands have fared little better than the mainland. Since 1968 the islanders have lived with constant droughts which have devastated agriculture. Output of maize, the staple crop, has been reduced to one-third of local needs and unemployment has soared among the islands' predominantly peasant population. At independence the iniquitous practice of share cropping was ended, but a decade of drought has meant that the situation of the islanders has not improved. Under the Portuguese the usual response to drought was road-building projects which, of course, were useless in alleviating in the long term the conditions which the droughts always bring to the islands. In contrast, the PAIGC has responded with a series of reafforestation programmes and public works constructions, concentrating upon water and soil conservation.

The outlook for Cape Verde is extremely grim. The islands have virtually nothing of value to export and, since independence, foreign aid has been the only thing standing between the people and famine. However, as in mainland Guiné, government mismanagement and lack of imagination have not helped. A new parliament house is presently under construction which, when completed, will cost over $US 17 million. Although the project is being funded entirely by foreign aid, it is hardly an appropriate enterprise for a country such as Cape Verde to undertake.

The coup in November 1980 saw the overthrow of Luis Cabral and the accession to power of a new government, relying entirely upon the army as its base of power. There was virtually no rice available in the capital in the month prior to the coup, which has since been dubbed 'the rice coup'. The initial explanations given for the coup made much of the obvious and long-standing antagonism between Cape Verdeans and native Guinéans, antagonisms which the Portuguese had exploited so skilfully. Luis Cabral himself is of Cape Verdean origin and, although this was an element in his overthrow, there were more important factors. In early November a new constitution was introduced which effectively centralised power into Cabral's hands by making the head of government also the head of state. This move, like so much government practice during the preceding four years, ran directly against Amilcar Cabral's principle of democratic centralism on which the party and the state had been founded. The centralisation of power and overt repression, including the murder and jailing of political opponents, had replaced the participatory democracy which Amilcar Cabral had hoped to see as the guiding value of an independent Guiné. Independence had spelt the atrophy of the PAIGC and the swelling of the state bureaucracy. In the economic climate created by the droughts this proved fatal.

The intrusion of foreign aid was also a factor in the overthrow of Luis Cabral. This aid encouraged graft and inefficiency at a time when the institutions of the new nation were quite fragile. The state, which existed during the liberation war, was not in any sense as complex in its operation or its functions as the state which has emerged since independence. The drought further increased the odds against successful transition by frustrating expectations and increasing reliance upon foreign benefactors. The possibility of important oil discoveries in the area south of the Bissagos Islands, ownership of which is at present disputed by the Republic of Guinea, may provide a way out for the new government. But oil discoveries could well place as great a strain on the bureaucracy as the influx of foreign aid on which the country is at present living. In the Cape Verde Islands the impact of the 'rice coup' led to the formation of a new ruling party. On 20 January 1981 on the eighth anniversary of the murder of Amilcar Cabral, the PAIGC was disbanded and replaced by the PAIVC (African Party for the Independence of Cape Verde). Despite protestations that this change in no sense alters the relationship between the islands and Guiné, the formation of a new ruling party was a direct response to the anti-Cape Verdean sentiments which the coup aroused in Bissau. As a result the prospects for unification are now somewhat remote.

The November coup indicates that the revolution in Guiné has, at least for the time being, gone sour. So many of the contradictions and potential weaknesses in the revolutionary movement identified in Cabral's writings have grown fat on foreign aid and political nepotism. It is difficult to imagine a less propitious environment than Guiné in which to stage a social revolution. The country has so little natural wealth and so great a need for basic infra-structure. And yet, if an assessment were made in retrospect of the chances of an anti-colonial movement being successful in this same environment, the outlook would have been equally pessimistic. In 1956 as now Guiné had virtually no working class, no industry, no mountains for a guerrilla force in which to hide and only a handful of western educated intellectuals. Despite these handicaps, the PAIGC was probably the most successful of all the nationalist liberation movements of the decade.

At the time when the United States was pursuing her war in Vietnam she was also suffering through her surrogate, the Portuguese colonial army, a series of defeats of far greater strategic significance in Mozambique and Angola. In an important respect the failure of the Portuguese to achieve a victory in Guiné was the key to all three wars. That is why a small country without resources and, until 1956, a country without a history of its own is so important. The rice coup does not change that nor should the coup be taken to signify the death of the revolution in Guiné. It merely gives more reason to admire the achievements of a small nation, which gained its independence against impossible odds, and it makes it all the more important to understand how that victory was achieved, for therein may lie a lesson for the rest of Africa.

3 THE AGRONOMIC WRITINGS

After five years of study in Lisbon, where he graduated as an agronomist specialising in the agriculture of colonial societies, Cabral returned to Guiné in 1951 to work for the Provincial Department of Forestry and Agricultural Services. During the next four years, prior to his expulsion from the country for political activities, Cabral worked as a research officer with the Department studying the problems of agricultural production and soil erosion. His earliest writings are found in a number of studies of agriculture published during his years with the Department.

In November 1953 Cabral was placed in charge of a team appointed to undertake a census of all agricultural production in Guiné.[1] This census was to be the first of its kind in Portuguese Africa. The work had originally been commissioned at a meeting of the Food and Agricultural Organisation in London in 1948 but because of various delays research was not begun for almost five years. It is certain that no such census would ever have taken place if the Portuguese government had not been subject to pressure from within the international community. However, once the decision to commission the work had been made it was seen by Lisbon as a useful tool for the promotion of an export economy for the colony.

At the meeting of the FAO in London in 1947 the government of Portugal agreed to carry out an agricultural census in all of its overseas territories. This work was to commence within eighteen months following strict guidelines laid down by the FAO. After numerous delays, some of which were due to specific problems confronting such a task in Guiné, in August 1953 Cabral was appointed to lead the research team. After the completion of two test runs in the district of Begine the work was finally commenced on 22 September 1953.

According to the prescriptions of the FAO the census was to document a number of specific characteristics of local agriculture; this included estimates of the total areas under cultivation, the number and characteristics of the agricultural population, the numbers of livestock and the level of production of each separate crop. The collection of this data required the use of work and sampling methods which were sensitive to the specific conditions under study. In Guiné it proved necessary to modify many of the research tools used in the collection of data as well as to adjust sampling procedures in line with the peculiarities of the country.[2] Fortunately a full population census of Guiné had been completed in 1951 so that the research team was free to concentrate upon investigation of agricultural production.

Initially it had been hoped to include cattle-raising activity within the census. But as was the case with the production of oil palm, coconuts and wax, it proved impossible to obtain reliable figures from indigenous farmers. As cattle were an important element in local production, this omission in the survey was significant. Difficulty in obtaining accurate information was also felt in the documentation of tree crops. In both cases farmers were afraid that if they gave accurate details of their output they would face increased taxation on their crops. The average annual tax burden for farmers in Guiné was set at nearly 25 per cent of annual income, which placed a severe strain on producers and encouraged farmers where possible to understate their output.

The problems in collecting data on cattle and tree crops meant that in these areas the survey could not present anything other than an estimate of production levels. Cabral also warned that because of difficulties in collecting accurate returns on the dominant crops the figures cited should only be treated as approximations.

For the purposes of the census the area of Guiné was divided into territorial units using the grid of Portuguese administration. In each of the administrative sectors the population was divided according to the number of homogeneous units, that is according to the number of tribal units. Even so only the economic activity of the major tribes was studied. This in turn was defined as those tribes which made a substantial contribution to the agriculture of the region. Although the survey was intended to cover as many villages as possible the research team did not presume to achieve an exhaustive study of the activity of each specific tribe.

In Guiné in the 1950s the land was cultivated in small plots worked by family units. There were no plantations and no land shortage. Because of this pattern of ownership the samples reflected the dominance of family agricultural exploitation. The survey also reflected the fact that in Guiné the choice of individual crops and the choice of cropping combinations varied from people to people. Each particular tribe tended to have one crop which dominated its agriculture. Before the gathering of information by field officers was begun Cabral personally visited each local council in the areas to be studied in order to explain to the local people the purpose and the methods of the census.

The preparatory field work indicated that it would be necessary to study between 1,200 and 1,500 individual farm holdings each of which represented a family unit. This estimate went far beyond the projections of the original FAO Commission of 1949 but because of the peculiarities of Guiné it was discovered that any lesser figure would be inadequate in calculating the levels of production with any accuracy. Although it was necessary to ignore the data on oil palm production and forestry and the potential for growth in these two industries, Cabral was satisfied that the information contained in the final census presented an accurate account of the most important features of indigenous agriculture. From this data it was possible to draw accurate conclusions about the potential of local production in all the principal crops.

In all, the collection of data took five months of field work, covering a total of 2,248 individual holdings and 350 villages in 41 administrative districts. Each census agent surveyed only a small number of individual holdings per day in order to ensure that returns were both detailed and accurate. The final results of the census were not published until more than three years after the field work had been completed.

The census showed that, although there are more than twenty-five tribal groupings in Guiné, four ethnic communities, the Fula, Balanta, Mandinga and Manjac, dominated agriculture in the country. The Fula and the Balante alone shared almost two-thirds of total production. These two groups also happened to be numerically the major tribes and they were evenly dispersed throughout the country, unlike the smaller tribes which tended to predominate in particular districts. In the case of each of the ethnic groupings the essential purpose of cultivation was for the production of subsistence food crops and cash crops accounted for only a little over 21 per cent of the total area under cultivation.

In terms of crop choice there was found to be a clear division between rice growing, which supplied the basic food staple particularly among the Balanta, and groundnuts (mancarra), which was the export crop. As with the production of foodstuffs the survey showed that the Fula, Balanta and Mandingas dominated the global production of cash crops. Within this grouping the Fula were found to be the most committed to production for export and they therefore also tended to dominate production of millet, which was the principal crop grown in consociation with groundnuts. The Fula dominated the cultivation of groundnuts both in terms of area under cultivation and output, while the Balante were found to predominate in the production of plain rice.

When global production figures of the major crops were compared floodplain rice appeared as the major crop, with around 90,000 tons being produced per annum. This was followed by groundnuts and cereals with output at 63,000 and 50,000 tons respectively. Of the wide variety of crops grown in Guiné it was discovered that the main crops, groundnuts, rice and cereals, gave the highest yields per acre and in each case these yields were quite encouraging given the conditions under which they were grown and harvested.

The survey indicated clearly that the farmer in Guiné was faced with a choice between groundnuts and rice. Both of these crops gave a good yield per unit of area cultivated, with groundnuts being only slightly superior in this respect. Cabral argues in favour of rice as the best crop because for the cultivator it brings a higher immediate return. Although there appeared to be two principal reasons for this judgment, Cabral cites only one of these in the survey. A major drawback with groundnuts is the effect this crop has upon the diet of the farmer and his family. Millet is the food crop grown in consociation with arichide. Where groundnuts are grown cereals tend to replace rice as the staple element in the farmers' diet. But according to Cabral millet is only a poor substitute for rice; its food value is low and it is a food more suited to cattle than for human consumption. Therefore before any consideration of the price paid for the cash crop relative to surplus rice the groundnut cultivator was worse off than the rice grower because he had to rely upon a poorer food staple. The second reason for Cabral's favouring rice is not found anywhere in the survey nor in Cabral's other agronomic works but appears in his political writings. Under Portuguese rule indigenous farmers were paid an artificially depressed price for their cash crops. In the case of groundnuts this figure was set far below current world market prices so that Guinéan producers were receiving only a fraction of the return on their crops which was available to farmers in Senegal and the Republic of Guinea. Clearly the major beneficiaries of the groundnut industry in Guiné were the large Portuguese monopolies, especially CUF which dominated all export trade.

The perennial crops could not strictly be counted as part of agriculture since there were very few orchards and the collection of bananas, papaya, feigeoa and mangoes came principally from casual trees. In Guiné the richest tree crops, kola nuts, gave only a small global yield and production was dominated by two or three of the numerically insignificant tribes.

The census also contains estimates of the areas burnt-off and the areas left fallow by each of the major tribes. According to the data the Fula and the Mandinga were the leading practitioners of both these traditional methods although all tribes were found to use burning-off as a means for claiming land for cultivation. In the case of the Fula and the Mandinga the incidence of burning-off and fallowing was found to be closely related to the cultivation of groundnuts. But in order to understand what this means in the broad terms of Guinéan agriculture Cabral suggests that it is necessary to compare the form of land usage associated with groundnuts with the use made of nursery facilities in rice and cereal cultivation. The Balanta, a tribe specialising in rice growing, was found to be the most concerned with seed reproduction and the control of crops, while the Fula and the Mandinga, both of which grew cereals in consociation with groundnuts, made the least provision for future production. Therefore the preference for groundnuts or rice may indicate different attitudes toward the land. Groundnuts tend to be associated with the perennial and cyclical modes of agriculture that are typical of peasant farming.

Despite specialisation in the choice of crops, Cabral found that all the peoples of Guiné were capable of cultivating all of the principal crops grown in the country. Therefore agricultural vocation only reflected traditional patterns of land usage. Given the proper technical and economic guidance any of the tribes could achieve the diversification of crops which Cabral deems essential to a prosperous economy.

The most important questions the researchers identified as having arisen from the census concerned the possibility, given the current social and technical conditions, of increasing the average size of holdings. The survey did discover some significant variations in the size of holdings with the Islamicised tribes in general working large plots. But Cabral concluded that even though the total true area cultivated represented less than 15 per cent of the land surface (and less than half of the arable land then in use), in the light of current technology it would not be possible to increase average holdings. Only a combined advance in the technical means used in agriculture and an improvement in the farmers' living conditions would make the extension of land under cultivation productive. Given existing circumstances any expansion of this area would most likely result in a decrease in the level of production. In the case of groundnuts the researchers concluded that the yields per acre should be increased before any attempt to expand the area under cultivation. Furthermore, rather than move towards an agriculture based on groundnuts, a far better policy would favour secondary crops such as manioc, sweet potato, sugar and oil palm. Each of these is superior to cereal crops in nutritional value and all have potential for commercial exploitation. Similarly a rational exploitation of fruit crops such as bananas and citrus fruits could also be valuable both to individual producers and to the national economy.

The census indicated that there was need for increased yields and production of primary and secondary crops. The raising of levels of output of the most profitable crops, notably rice and other foodstuffs, would be the best way to bring about an improvement in the living conditions of farmers and their families. This in itself is cited as a precondition for any wider programme aimed at bringing about a structural improvement in agriculture. The existing pattern of cultivation in which certain tribes favoured particular crops would also be an important factor in the prospects for success of any such programme. Fortunately the three major tribes, the Fula, the Balanta and the Mandinga all showed the capacity to cultivate all of the suitable crops and therefore agricultural vocation merely reflected the traditional land usage conditioned in turn by climatic and socio-economic factors. The levels of rice production among the Fula and the Mandinga could quite easily be increased by improvements in the method of cultivation and by diligent practice.

In summary the recommendations contained in the survey emphasised the importance of crop diversification. By implication rather than by direct comment the census concluded that an economy based upon groundnuts would not benefit the farmer and that the future prosperity of Guiné must rest with the development of rice and secondary foodcrops. Yet in the light of Cabral's previously published studies of soil erosion and the groundnut industry the conclusions presented in the census are rather tentative. This is hardly surprising given the official nature of the report.

Cabral had attempted to prepare the ground for the conclusions of the census by the publication in 1954 of two articles based upon the preliminary results of the field work. These articles, On the Contribution[3] and Brief Notes on the Objectives and Methods of the Survey[4] differ from the final work in the severity of the criticisms made of colonial agricultural policy. In Brief Notes Cabral argues that there must be only one aim of the census; the census must help to improve the lot of the indigenous farmer, and it must not merely extend the existing pattern of exploitation of the soil.

The intention of the Portuguese government was of course to create a lucrative export agriculture, the success of which would be measured in terms of corporate profits rather than by benefits accruing to the producer. Cabral argues very strongly that the census should seek to discover the reason why some areas in Guiné were rich while others were poor, both questions relating to the political and economic foundations of agriculture. In the end the value of the census would depend upon how it was used, whether it was to be an instrument to improve the lot of the indigenous farmers or to extend colonial control by increasing the area devoted to export farming. Unfortunately, this strong criticism of export agriculture is all but absent from the final document.

The second article, On the Contribution, published in October 1954, that is some eight months after the completion of the field work, contains the rudiments of a political economy of Guiné. As in the preceding article, the tenor of Cabral's argument is in marked contrast to the final work. In On the Contribution Cabral analyses the agriculture practised by the various tribal groupings. Each of these peoples is distinguished according to language, religion, diet and traditional patterns governing the division of labour. In turn this diversity influences the material and cultural aspects associated with agricultural production. Cabral comments that in aggregate this means that each of the ethnic groups is quite individual, both in terms 'of their economic infra-structure and their social superstructure'. Yet despite these important and obvious variations, each of the peoples of Guiné lives within an identical socio-political situation; that situation is defined by the nature of colonial rule.

All of the peoples of Guiné also live within a reality based upon a traditional fund of knowledge of the land and the ways in which it should be cultivated. To understand that reality is to understand the basis of the Guiné economy. Cabral argues that the importance of agriculture is such that it is essential for rural production to reach in social terms the same level of importance which it has in purely material terms. The only possibility for the country to progress is for government to take the rationalisation of agriculture as its first priority.

The purpose of the article On the Contribution was to define the relative importance to agriculture of each of the principal tribes. This was done by comparing the areas under cultivation with the total production levels for each tribe. This method appeared to indicate a significant variation between the numerical importance of several of the tribes and their place within the scale of production. Obviously agricultural production in Guiné is influenced by such factors as the level of technology and the productivity of labour. Of the major tribes the Fula, Balanta, Mandinga and Manjanco were found to be the major contributors, dominating nearly 90 per cent of total agricultural output. A secondary contribution was made by the Mancanha, Papel, Beafada and Felupe peoples while the remaining twenty tribes, principally because of their numerical size, were found to have only a tiny share in production. Cabral concluded that this classification of tribes proves that agricultural practice, in terms of the choice of crops (which in turn influences the whole of a people's material existence) transcends ethnic and cultural diversity. Besides this general community of interests linking various tribes together the agriculture of all the peoples of Guiné is defined by the background against which it is carried out; that background is one of shared poverty.

Despite Cabral's claim that there are important variations for several tribes between their relative importance in the national population and in their contribution to the total area under cultivation the figures do in fact indicate a close correlation. Such a correlation between population size and the area cultivated is of course to be expected, given the uniformly low level of technology which existed in Guiné. Cabral's reason for emphasising the small degree of variation he could identify, notable in the case of the Mandinga, Mancanha and Felupe, was to draw a distinction between ethnic boundaries and the more important boundaries established by agricultural activity. The tribal boundaries are therefore not as important as the divisions established by the specialisation of crops. Therefore the economy of Guiné should be seen as an agricultural economy in which various crops are grown with varying degrees of efficiency. The fact that these crops are produced by different ethnic groups is of little importance.

Cabral had hoped that the Census would be a tool for the development of local agriculture and he accepted only one measure of the success of such a programme; success would be achieved to the extent to which the lives of peasant cultivators were improved or worsened by changes in the type of crops grown and the technical and economic conditions under which cultivation was to take place. This principle is more obvious in the Brief Notes and On the Contribution than in the Census itself, which was finally published only after Cabral's expulsion from the country. Yet even as it stands it is possible to discern in the Census a fairly strong disapproval of the path in which agriculture was being pushed. In the Census there is ample evidence that, given the severe limitations on the labour capacity of family units working small plots and the rudimentary character of the technology being used, that the choice of crops was absolutely vital to the welfare of every ethnic group.

In Brief Notes Cabral mentions the importance of studying labour methods used for each of the crops, although there is no reference to this in either the Census or in On the Contribution. Presumably this would be one of the factors accounting for those variations between tribal population and levels of production of which Cabral makes so much. It is puzzling that in none of the articles arising directly from the research for the Census does Cabral attempt to answer the important question he poses in Brief Notes; why is it that some of the peoples of Guiné are poor while others are rich? The answer to that question can be found in two places; most immediately it is suggested in a cluster of writings Cabral published on export cultivation and its impact on the soil. Secondly, it is found in Cabral's political analysis of the social structure of Guiné which he wrote ten years after the Census was completed.

Cabral supplemented the Census with the publication of a number of individual studies on soil erosion and the consequences of the practice of burning-off and fallowing. In effect these studies constitute a critique of groundnuts by accounting the costs associated with intensive cultivation for export. These articles are On the Cultivation of Groundnuts and Millet in 'Portuguese' Guiné (September 1954),[5] Burning Off and Fallow in the Cultivation of Groundnuts and Millet (September 1954),[6] and Burning and Fallow in the Circle of Fulacunda in 1954.[7] The first two studies were originally presented as papers at the Conférence Arachide-Mils at Banbey in Senegal in September 1954 but were not published until four years later, that is some two years after the foundation of the PAIGC. Collectively these writings give a compelling portrait of a country on the threshold of a shift from a system of cultivation for subsistence to cultivation for export. In the early 1950s these two modes of cultivation existed side by side.

In Burning and Fallow Cabral set out to evaluate colonial agricultural practice by establishing a comparison between the colonial and indigenous forms of land usage. The influence of the colonial presence in Guiné, as in much of West Africa, was felt most acutely in changes in the traditional choice of crops. The resulting pattern of indigenous agriculture can be measured in a number of ways. Cabral chose to examine the effect of crop change upon the soil, the immediate and long-term benefits to the cultivator and the methods associated with cultivation of the new crops compared with traditional produce. Cabral's choice of Fulacunda as the area for this brief study is itself significant for at the beginning of the 1950s this region was the subject of a concerted effort by the Agricultural Board to extend the acreage of groundnuts. Fulacunda was also a region in which each of the major ethnic groups was fairly evenly represented and in which all of the principal crops were grown. This was in contrast to regions such as Gabu and Bafata both of which were centres of the groundnut industry. In Gabu the cultivation of groundnuts for export was so advanced that there had even been some attempt made to introduce agricultural machinery.

In Guiné agriculture had a highly individualist structure with subsistence cultivation being carried out on small plots of land by family groups. With the shift to colonial cultivation for export this basic structure was completely altered as were the techniques associated with an intensive agricultural regime. In those areas in which it became dominant the cultivation of mancarra (groundnuts) for export completely changed the traditional social and economic structures. Farming for export had what Cabral defined as 'the character of industrial production'. Traditional patterns of burning off and fallowing were soon abandoned as new land was rapidly burnt off to increase the acreage of cultivation. In every case where the economic structure of the native agricultural system clashed with the technical requirements of production for export the traditional methods were discarded.

In the area of Fulacunda Cabral found numerous forms of cultivation which varied from rice growing to the harvesting of spontaneous fruit crops. With the spread of groundnuts this area was given over to export cropping as immigration, particularly into the area of Buba, took place. Although groundnuts had in fact been grown in the area for many years nomadic farming for subsistence had hitherto always predominated. The traditional agricultural process involving groundnuts had followed a very strict pattern in which there were a number of successive steps. In this pattern there was initially the burning off to free the land for cultivation, then the rotation of cereal crops, followed by groundnuts and finally the land was returned to fallow. This method had for generations been used by the peoples of Fulacunda, and in particular by the Brame who were the oldest cultivators of groundnuts in Guiné. But this method had never been used within the context of intensive cultivation.

In 1953 the colonial administration decided to create what Cabral termed 'a new agro-economic structure'. In Fulacunda as a whole, nearly 10 per cent of individual family holdings were broken up to make way for the new programme. A change was also felt immediately in the ratio of burnt-off land to land in fallow. With colonial cultivation the ratio was in fact negative, as new land was quickly burnt off in order to extend the area available for mancarra. This acceleration of the normal cycle was further increased by the inflow of a number of immigrants who had been attracted to the district by imagined material gains to be had in the intensive pattern of cultivation. However, the long-term effects for the land were to be anything but beneficial.

In his research Cabral discovered that in all traditional native agriculture there was an even balance between the area cultivated and the areas burnt off and left fallow. This balance, which had been arrived at by the experience of generations, was essential for the protection and preservation of the fragile soil and therefore to guarantee the long-term survival of a productive agriculture. Unfortunately with the changeover to groundnuts the attitude of the farmer was now determined by external socioeconomic factors which set no upper limits on production in contrast to subsistence cultivation in which strict limits were determined by need. Under traditional methods, for instance, burning off only took place as the need for land arose and no more land was burnt off than was required immediately by the community. The growing of groundnuts for export set a new rhythm for production that led directly to a lowering of the fertility of the soil. The reduction of the period of fallowing and the increased use of burning off would eventually destroy the fertility of the land. Therefore in the long term the ecology associated with groundnuts would place the native farmer in a precarious economic position. It is in this sense that Cabral concluded that the rhythm of this type of export agriculture was inherently destructive. Perhaps it would only be possible to improve the life of the agricultural workers by the maintenance of traditional land usage; perhaps in Guiné it would prove necessary to return to the native system of farming before any progress could be made.

This warning on the dangers posed by groundnuts to soil fertility and texture is further developed in the articles Burning-Off and Fallow in the Cultivation of Groundnuts and Millet and On the Cultivation of Groundnuts and Millet in 'Portuguese' Guiné, both of which were first published in 1958. The line of argument Cabral developed in each of these articles followed on directly from the earlier studies.

In traditional and colonial methods of agriculture, burning off is used in order to render land suitable for cultivation. However, this practice encourages a degeneration of the soil which can only be countered by the use of fallowing. The technical and economic realities under which agriculture in Guiné was practised made these two methods indispensable. Cabral noted that with the development of an export agriculture there was a sudden increase in the areas burnt and a steady decline in the fallow period. Consequently the degeneration of the soil which was already characteristic of indigenous cultivation was greatly accelerated. In a country such as Guiné the relationship between the areas burnt off and the areas fallowed is an index to the dynamism of agriculture. It is also an index to the likely extent of erosion. In the district of Fulacunda the highest ratio of burning off to fallow was found to occur among those groups such as the Fula, Beafada and Mancanha, who practised colonial cultivation, while the lowest was among those such as the Balanta and Papel who grew subsistence crops. This comparison indicated that where groundnuts were the principal crop there was a complete disregard for the survival of the soil.

In all traditional methods of cultivation the farmer employs an intimate knowledge and understanding of the character of the soil in his daily work. Fallow is the means by which he guarantees that the soil will remain fertile. This is reinforced by the practice of growing a wide variety of crops which included manioc, sorghum and haricots. The cultivation of groundnuts would decrease the future possibilities for agriculture by leeching the soil of essential minerals and by encouraging erosion. In Fulacunda wherever the colonial aspect of cultivation was dominant the period of fallowing was shortened, fires occurred more often on the same piece of land and new areas were constantly being opened up to increase output.

The question of soil erosion is a continuing theme in all of Cabral's agronomic writings. His first published article, In Defence of the Land[8], was in fact a study of the severe erosion in Cape Verde where large areas of agricultural land had been devastated. In these islands the rate of erosion was such that within the space of a single generation entire tracts of once-fertile land had been made barren. A comparison of rainfall statistics over the same period proved that this degeneration was not due to any perceptible change in rainfall pattern. The effects of drought which had plagued the islands for centuries were in fact due to the lack of groundwater caused by the soil's incapacity to retain moisture. The first step in combating this cycle of erosion and drought is of course research into its causes, which in the case of Cape Verde would have required considerable expenditure of funds by the Portuguese government. Naturally no such work was ever commissioned and the island peoples continued to suffer from the famines which were the inevitable companion to drought. Cabral's tentative conclusions were that soil erosion was due largely to ignorance of the limits to cultivation imposed by the climate and vegetation of the islands and that without some fundamental change to agricultural practice erosion and drought would continue.

In Understanding the Problem of Soil Erosion in Guiné[9] Cabral examined in greater detail the threat posed by an inappropriate use of the land. He made reference in turn to such factors as soil type, climate, topography and land use, all of which when combined condition the health and fertility of the soil. In Guiné, as in every country, the use made of the soil by man requires its transformation. In all tropical areas such as Guiné, where unfortunately the problem had practically been ignored, high rainfall is conducive to erosion. In the case of Guiné this was exacerbated by the fact that non-industrial cultures are particularly vulnerable to erosion because of the lack of knowledge of what to do once erosion has begun. This does not imply that such cultures are any less sensitive to the characteristics of the soil they work.

Erosion is not confined to any one mode of exploitation of the soil. It is simply a disease of the soil promoted by human use and the extent of damage done to the soil will vary according to the use made of it. Therefore the aim of all methods of cultivation should be to maintain and carry out a balanced programme of exploitation. This can be achieved either by studying the agents of erosion in order to control them or by improving the soil in order to protect it. A technical solution to the problem of erosion can be implemented by mechanical means, such as drainage and the building of dykes, or by biological methods. A biological approach requires the control of erosion by selective use of plants and the rotation of crops. The use of mechanical means is invariably expensive in construction and of course requires continuous maintenance.

In On the Cultivation of Groundnuts and Millet in 'Portuguese' Guiné Cabral continues his account of the effects of a monocultural economy by examining in detail the role played by the Agricultural Board in the spread of groundnuts. Already by 1954, with the exception of the Balanta and Papel tribes whose principal crop was rice, groundnut was established as the basis of most indigenous agriculture. For all tribes much the same method of cultivation was used, with groundnuts and millet being grown within a rotating cycle. Cultivation of groundnut was always followed by a period of between two and five years of fallow.

The activities of the Agricultural Service in regard to groundnuts had been limited in the main to the distribution of improved seed varieties. The Service, however, had also encouraged experiments with light machinery in the region of Gabu. Cabral noted that the intention of the Agricultural Service was to establish a programme of technical assistance to the indigenous cultivators in order to improve production. Hopefully great strides could be made in improving both yields and the quality of future crops. Cabral admitted, albeit reluctantly, that given indigenous techniques and the limitations inherent in the agroclimatic characteristics of the country, that conditions in Guiné were favourable to the cultivation of groundnuts and millet.

Cabral believed that the development of a groundnut industry was entirely dependent upon the action of the Agricultural Service. This in turn was likely to be determined by research into techniques, soil types and improved seed varieties. But this does not imply that Cabral favoured the development of a groundnut industry or economy for Guiné. At the end of his article he comments that 'the empire of groundnuts' is not necessarily the fate of Guiné; neither is it a lucrative crop for the indigenous cultivator. In Guiné wherever millet occupies an important place in the farmer's diet the farmer is poor. Cabral concludes with the comment that 'The progress of agriculture in Guiné necessitated the displacement of the groundnut/millet consociation with other crops that are more lucrative and more beneficial and the economic value of which is more positive.'[10]

Cabral was aware from the early 1950s that further cultivation of groundnuts would damage the society and economy of Guiné in a number of ways. Most immediately he believed that groundnuts would offer the indigenous cultivator a poor return for his labour. This return would fluctuate according to prices set on a world market over which the cultivator had no control. His return would be both low and erratic. Secondly, the increased cultivation of groundnuts for export would bring a reduction in the practice of fallowing and encourage the constant opening up of new land by burning. In the district of Fulacunda these practices had already brought about a depletion in the fertility of the soil and the appearance of the first evidence of erosion. The fragile soils in Guiné simply could not support intensive forms of cultivation, and yet intensive exploitation was a necessary aspect of an export economy. Groundnut cultivation meant a switching over from traditional food crops and the substitution of millet for rice and other nutritional foods in the staple diet. An economy which relied on groundnuts would soon create a poorly fed society which in the end would be unable to feed itself.

If production for export were to be increased it would be necessary to mechanise agriculture. This would encourage the growth of two distinct sectors within the economy; there would be a small group of large mechanised estates owned by Europeans growing only groundnuts while a majority of indigenous farmers would continue to cultivate small plots of land. Although in the short term, because of an abundance of arable land, this would not necessitate land alienation, in time the quest for fertile soil would create a pool of landless farmers. In terms of the social structure the establishment of estates would strengthen the power of traditional chiefs, especially among the Fula, and it would encourage the growth of a larger European settler community. All of this promised a bleak future for the people of Guiné. A monocultural economy geared to the export of a product giving only a poor return to the producer and bringing in its wake an irreversible decline in the living conditions of the indigenous cultivator.

In the period between 1953, the year of the census, and 1960 the production of groundnuts for export increased from 64,000 tons to over 100,000 tons. In 1960 nearly 60 per cent of foreign trade revenue was obtained from this one crop. Naturally this increased production was achieved at the expense of the traditional subsistence economy. During the colonial period all foreign trade in Guiné was controlled by the Companhia União Fabril (CUF) which managed to exercise a monopoly over most economic activity. In 1960 the manufacturing sector consisted of less than ten small factories husking rice, processing groundnuts and producing paper pulp. With the departure of the Portuguese in 1974 the major industrial plant was a beer factory in Bafata established to supply the Portuguese troops. This pattern of minimal development was perfectly consistent with the history of the Portuguese efforts to create a groundnut economy. The Portuguese in fact used a wide range of taxes to encourage groundnut cultivation. In 1954 the average European settler paid a total of 18 escudos per annum in taxation as against the indigenes' 218 escudos. The peasants were further exploited through the marketing system in which Portuguese and Lebanese middle men collected groundnuts at a low price for re-selling to the CUF.

In Senegal a groundnut economy had been established by the French after 1860, while the British in West Africa concentrated upon the cultivation of oil palm and cocoa.[11] In the period between the end of the Second World War and independence there was a large investment of funds throughout Francophone Africa aimed at stimulating an export economy, although most of these funds were finally absorbed in administrative costs rather than in improving productivity. During the nineteenth century groundnuts had been introduced into Senegal without any substantial fall in local food production, because there was abundant arable land. However, in the post-war period there developed a direct substitution in land use between groundnuts and local foodstuffs so that a commercialisation of agriculture resulted in a declining food production. In Senegal the history of the groundnut industry shows that increased production has always meant the breaking of traditional practices of fallowing. This has led to a degeneration of the soil and widespread erosion.

In evaluating the success of the groundnut industry in Senegal, Samir Amin estimates that in real money terms in the period since 1938 there had been a constant falling return to the producer for his crop.[12] Amin also discovered that in the period since 1960 producers have tended to withdraw from the market in order to concentrate upon the production of food crops. Although this substitution meant a fall in money incomes, the farmers benefited directly by an improvement in their diet. Amin's final judgment on groundnuts in Senegal is that the benefits, when measured in terms of the immediate living conditions of the cultivator, would have been far greater if the funds devoted to the spreading of groundnuts had been invested in rice, tree crops, oil palm and a variety of fruits. This judgment is made quite apart from the question of the long-term national development of Senegal, which of course had been intended to be financed by groundnut production. On this second question Amin is even more adamant that groundnuts had been disastrous.

In 1954 Cabral published two articles which offer a very different perspective on agronomy to that found in the studies of burning off and fallowing. These articles, when read in conjunction with Understanding the Problem of Soil Erosion in Guiné, suggest a more theoretical interpretation of cultivation as a labour activity in the context of the particular conditions present in tropical Africa.

The first of these articles is entitled On Land Utilisation in Black Africa,[13] which was first published in April 1954. In Black Africa the physical aspects of land utilisation are well known; the high humidity, the high rainfall and the constantly high temperatures impose particular limits on agriculture. Because of these factors there is a peculiar drainage pattern, with the soil being vulnerable to leeching of minerals and the threat of erosion. In Guiné, as in all tropical environments, the soil is low in organic matter and nitrogen. However, the existence of large forests which contain spontaneous sources of food has to some extent discouraged agriculture. The combination of these factors provide the parameters within which agriculture must take place.

Cabral explains that in Black Africa as elsewhere the mode of land usage represents the evolution of human society. In the process of history man ceases to be a gatherer of food and becomes himself a producer of food. All history is the confrontation of man with nature, although very often the centrality of land usage in this relationship is forgotten. In Africa there are numerous forms of agricultural production; in Zimbabwe production is very much individual; among the Yoruba all agricultural work is performed by men, while among the Balanta of Guiné most work is done by women. In all instances there is some form of family co-operation in the production of food. The land is the source of individual and collective life.

Cabral is careful to develop the idea that the practice of agriculture is set by both a physical and by a social horizon. But in the case of West Africa the physical factors are insignificant when compared with the social and economic influence of colonialism, for in order to satisfy the exigencies of a new social condition the African had abandoned his traditional knowledge of the land. Everywhere this has meant the breaking-up of communities and the destruction in fertility of the soil.

Cabral argued that economic factors, namely the promise of material advantage, were the cause of European settlement in Africa. During the latter half of the last century the Europeans moved from the business of selling commodities among the African to the exploitation of the land itself. His object had been to utilise the itinerant system in producing goods for export. He modified the purpose of production, without modifying the actual system of cultivation. This in turn created new needs. Over time a system of private property in land emerged, with land being held either by European settlers or by assimilados.

Despite the pull of structural obstacles to any change in the *raison d'être* of agriculture, the itinerant system now acquired new characteristics. Land was taken from forests and the period of cultivation recklessly increased. It became common for the soil to be cultivated until it dried out. Very often agricultural techniques drawn from European practice would be applied without allowance being made for the environmental differences between the two continents. Consequently the land and the men who worked it were pauperised. These men acquired without their consent a new social condition and a new set of needs.

European settlers often introduced new plants and new techniques and sometimes local industries processing raw materials were established. Within this extended process colonialism first established, then accentuated, at each separate step, the contradictions within local agriculture between the initial purpose of production for need and the aim of production for an infinite surplus. Cabral's solution to this contradiction was to align agricultural practice according to the same principles which ruled traditional cultivation; that land is best used where the benefits accrue to the society as a whole. The wealth of Black Africa must be applied to Africa itself and not repatriated for the benefit of others. To achieve this Cabral argued that it is necessary to establish an agrarian structure which excludes destructive exploitation of the land and thereby prevents the exploitation of man by man. A careful selection and application of everything useful in the traditional and European methods of cultivation would establish a proper working relationship between the cultivator and the land. Under these conditions a gradual evolution in agriculture could make possible the development of other branches of production and with this guarantee the progress of Africa. As early as 1954 Cabral was convinced that a capitalist system, albeit at a discount under the tutelage of Portuguese colonialism, was destructive of natural resources and antithetical to basic human needs. At every single point, whether judged in terms of the needs of the soil, the needs of the producers or the needs of consumers, colonial methods and principles of cultivation were destructive. The rapacity which motivates the quest for high profits would in the space of one or two decades destroy the foundation from which those profits were dragged.

The same range of problems attendant with colonial agriculture were explored in On The Mechanisation of Agriculture in Guiné.[14] In this article, as in Understanding the Problem of Soil Erosion, Cabral examined the delicate ecological balance between the specific instruments used in the production of crops and the subsequent relations among producers. The introduction of machines in the cultivation of groundnuts in Guiné would have repercussions upon the entire economic and social environment. Cabral explores this problem through an historical survey of land usage.

The history of agriculture can be segmented into various phases according to the method of traction used; for instance, with advances in man's mastery over nature animal traction replaces simple hand methods of tilling the soil. This in turn is superseded with the introduction of heavy machinery. In Guiné these three particular phases of agricultural production co-exist and there are important differences between the regions where one form dominates over another. Therefore in order to improve agricultural production it is necessary to study and perhaps to modify the existing methods of cultivation.

The transformation and increasing complexity of the means by which man confronts nature and thereby produces the means for his subsistence brings about a transformation of man himself.

Therefore the question of mechanising agriculture is a political question which requires the satisfaction of a number of specific pre-conditions; there must first be a thorough understanding of the character of the soil and the terrain; there must be the development of technical skills for the operation and dissemination of machinery and finally there must exist an economic, social and political climate conducive to mechanisation.

In any context the introduction of heavy machinery creates a wide range of changes in the whole of agricultural practice. It will firstly require a great increase in the area under cultivation which in turn means deforestation; it will also require a far more intensive method of cultivation which in turn opens up the threat of erosion. More importantly mechanisation will increase production both per acre and in global terms but will reduce the number of workers involved. The introduction of machines will create a need for technicians and thereby establish a distinction between specialised and manual labour. The technician will demand a high wage and a higher standard of living than the manual worker, and his labour will be seen as having greater value because it produces more. Through their social and cultural effects upon the character of labour, machines transform man by transforming labour activity.

When judging the effectiveness and cost of mechanisation it is necessary to take account of that whole range of inputs which mechanisation brings in its wake; the need for fertilisers, the need to clear larger and larger tracts of land, the cost of training a new stratum of technicians, the costs of fuels and lubricants, and the displacement of the traditional rural work force. When judged against this range of costs perhaps the higher yields promised with mechanisation will appear less attractive.

Mechanisation by definition transforms the productive forces and no matter how limited that transformation is it will produce an effect on the entire structure of the economy. In every instance there is a reciprocal relationship between the levels of technology, and the economic structures in a given environment. With any form of mechanisation this is felt most acutely in the area of labour supply and demand. In all of rural Africa there is a basic lack of people to work the land. Mechanisation would not solve this problem because it would create a demand for specialised labour which was also scarce. Cabral commented that in the case of Guiné there was no lack of hands to work the land but farmers were reluctant to work for others as wage labourers. This preference would not be changed by the introduction of machinery.

In Guiné there are two kinds of agriculture: there is the indigenous cultivation in which the land belongs to the community and there is non-indigenous agriculture in which the land belongs to commercial interests. In the latter production is for export and there is an abundance of capital, while in the indigenous form the farmer has little or no access to funds. In 1959, when Cabral wrote, these two forms of agriculture were largely identical in terms of the methods of production. They were distinguished by socio-economic factors and not by technology. Mechanisation would radically alter this situation. The position of the indigenous farmer was conditioned by the fact that all economic activity within Guiné was integrated, to some degree or other, into the Portuguese national economy. Some of the commercial products, such as some palm oil, were consumed locally, but the bulk was exported as raw material. Because of this pattern of integration it was quite possible for the indigenous farmer to mechanise his plot and yet receive no additional benefit. The conditions in the marketplace, then as now, were entirely dependent upon factors over which the farmer had absolutely no control.

In On the Mechanisation of Agriculture in Guiné Cabral concluded that the only way in which mechanisation could be geared to the benefit of the indigenous farmer was for such change to be carried out under strict state control. Mechanisation would change the conditions of life for all indigenes; it would create a new type of rural worker, and it would transform the social environment of every worker. The machine is purported to serve man; but the machine transforms him. The key question in any programme of mechanisation is the fate of the thousands of rural workers who would be displaced.

The most important elements in the essay, On the Mechanisation of Agriculture in Guiné, are carried by implication rather than discussed outright. These elements, if phrased in a Marxist terminology, concern the way in which Cabral envisaged the relationship between a change in the forces of production and the shifts and transformations this would bring about in the relations among producers. Obviously the introduction of tractors would influence the choice of crops, encouraging an acceleration in the spread of groundnuts in preference to rice and secondary foodstuffs. Under existing social and economic conditions in the colony this would ensure that the bulk of cultivation was for export. The use of machinery would under most conditions depress the demand for labour and encourage rural unemployment by replacing capital-intensive for labour-intensive methods. The high cost of machinery could in the long term affect the concentration of land into the hands of a few thereby creating a landless sub-proletariat. This line of argument is repressed within the text and it is difficult to judge the degree to which Cabral would have been willing to accept the conclusions his analysis finally implied. Most probably in 1954 he would have balked at the implications of a class critique of colonial agriculture suggested in his account of mechanisation.

In this article there is some indication that Cabral viewed technology as inherently revolutionary and that the conditions of its usage were secondary to its necessary effects upon ownership and the social distribution of the product. He proposed that mechanisation be controlled under the guidance of a state monopoly, but his enthusiasm as to the likely effectiveness of this as a safeguard against the negative features of mechanisation lacks conviction. In fact in On The Mechanisation of Agriculture Cabral gives the impression that machinery has an immutable influence upon human society, an influence which lies somewhere beyond the reach of human purpose. However this line of argument is at odds with the predominant drift in all of the other agronomic writings in which he emphasised the variety of levels of causality between agricultural production and social formation. In general these factors are deemed to be as various as are the elemental forces conditioning agricultural productivity itself.

In all of Cabral's agronomic writings there is strong emphasis upon the importance of establishing and maintaining a harmony in the relations of man with man and man with nature. In this vision of the ecology of human labour, strength is seen as being achieved through balance rather than through force. It is in this sense that Cabral argued in Understanding the Problem of Soil Erosion and On the Mechanisation . . . that traditional methods of cultivation are superior to those of colonial agriculture for export. Within the traditional community the farmer produces in such a way and in such quantities that the long-term survival of the soil and of the community is guaranteed. Colonial practice sets no upper limits to production. This is why Cabral was so critical both of the plans for mechanisation and of the groundnut industry as a whole. In an economy like that of Guiné, the alteration of a single element within the productive process would change the conditions of work, the structure of labour and the division of the product. Although it is tempting to interpret Cabral's attack upon mechanisation as being sympathetic within the ethos of those cultural renaissance movements, such as negritude, which were so popular during the 1950s and the early 1960s, his attitude had no affinity whatsoever with their anti-modernist philosophy. This temptation arises also because of another and quite unusual element in Cabral's work which was to re-appear at various points of his political writings and which gives those writings their distinctive flavour. This is Cabral's professed belief that in human history change is initiated and directed by alterations to the level of technology. In Marxist terms Cabral implies that the dialectics of social transformation lie within the forces of production and not within the struggle between classes. This thesis is stated quite clearly in On the Mechanisation of Agriculture in Guiné where Cabral divides human history into various phases according to the dominant methods of traction, whether manual, animal or mechanical. Human invention and the conquest over nature that invention allows transforms man and society with the force of a natural law. That at least is the implication of Cabral's attack upon mechanisation.

Cabral's agronomic papers carry within them an anthropology reminiscent of Marx's Economic and Philosophical Manuscripts. In this anthropology the achievements of human history are seen to be measured against the continuing conflict against nature as the subject of labour. In the article Understanding the Problem of Soil Erosion in Guiné Cabral attempted a resume of human history in terms of man's conquest of the soil, for when man became conscious of the soil and of the means by which to cultivate it the historical process began. The possibility of subsistence from the soil allowed men to co-operate and to form societies. At that point the soil itself assumed importance not only in crude economic terms but also in a political sense. With the change from the use of human hands to machinery in production the historical process itself changed.

Despite man's growing confidence in the face of natural forces, there arose a secondary conflict between man and nature. A most obvious instance of this is found in the phenomenon of soil erosion. Cabral observed that human history is full of examples of the fall of great civilisations and empires brought about by a lack of understanding of the soil. In the case of the decline of Egyptian, Hebrew and Roman civilisations the influence of soil erosion was important. The warning to colonial agriculture in Africa is perfectly clear.

Cabral's view of human history suggested at this point of his agronomic writing is essentially tragic. Cabral envisaged history as a process in which man, in his quest for control over nature, slowly destroys himself. The crucial step in this progressive destruction occurs under the capitalist mode of production when man ceased to seek subsistence from the soil and began to seek to maximise production so as to enrich himself economically. He took more than he needed and in so doing he abused nature and the soil. He destroyed the forests and he exploited the land in an extremely disorganised way. The extent to which individual men are responsible for this casual destruction is mediated by the economic structure of the society in which they live; farmers do not deliberately set out to destroy the source of their livelihood. They are merely the tools through which societies operate. Within this history capitalist agriculture appears as but one of a number of modes by which the earth and its produce are expropriated.

Cabral's agronomic writings are unusual in a number of senses. It is unusual for a post-war nationalist to bother with the rural sector in developing a revolutionary practice. In fact it is unusua for the writings of any nationalist to present an analysis welding together an understanding of the material basis of a society with the way in which that society was being transformed under the impact of colonialism. Cabral begins his politics of colonialism from the opposite point to every other nationalist from Lumumba to Nkrumah to Touré, all of whom took the condition and situation of their own class, the petty bourgeoisie or nationalist middle class, for the horizon of their political imagination. In effect, because the agronomic writings contain an economic history of Guiné they hold the promise of a sophisticated class analysis of a colonial society undergoing the experience of social transformation.

56 *The agronomic writings*

Cabral's studies of the groundnut industry are important for a number of reasons. All of these writings were published in the period 1949 to 1956, that is some twelve years before Samir Amin's studies of export agriculture in West Africa. Chronologically these agronomic papers are pre-nationalist, yet conceptually they rightfully belong to the post-nationalist period. In these studies Cabral exposed the process by which a traditional productive process was being replaced by an essentially destructive cash crop regime even while the agricultural workers maintained control of the land and of the instruments for its exploitation. Cabral's agronomic writings chronicle the displacement of subsistence agriculture by a capitalist mode of production. In fact there is little in Samir Amin's study of groundnuts in Senegal that is not already present in Cabral's research completed more than a decade earlier. For example Amin argues that in Senegal the increase in groundnut production had been accompanied by the need to import food into what had originally been a self-sustaining economy. Cabral's research gave prior warning that with the spread of groundnuts this would be the fate of Guiné.

Cabral's work differs from Amin's in the important sense that he examines the groundnut industry from the vantage point of production whereas Amin concentrates upon the process of distribution. Amin's main concern is with the influence of price on the international market and the way in which price functioned to the advantage of European economic interests. Amin wishes to trace the mechanisms of a global system of expropriation of the national surplus, in the cases of Ghana, Senegal and the Ivory Coast, and to discover the ways in which a transfer of wealth is achieved. The effect of this relationship upon the class formation within the exploited sector is, despite Amin's protestations to the contrary, of secondary importance within his analysis.

Although Cabral's work is founded upon an analysis of production as distinct from the distribution of the surplus, there is little material in his agronomic writings on the subject of the methods of production. The essay on mechanisation indicates that a change in the level of technology would in turn revolutionise the methods of production and the existing relations among producers. One must assume in reading Cabral's writings on class that in Guiné the instruments of production were uniform across the various tribal groupings, and that there was no significant variation in the levels of technology or in the ownership of the instruments of production which affected the levels of productivity. This is in fact borne out in the Census, where there is no evidence of any significant variations among the various tribes or between the various major crops in terms of output. Most of the variations can be explained by the influence of differing population concentrations.

The discussion of technology opens up the question of tribal divisions and the importance of these divisions within Guinéan

agriculture. This question is important since tribes are used as
the basic unit for analysis in all of Cabral's agronomic works.
Tribes represent the basic division of the units of production.
The distinction between rice growing and groundnuts falls along
tribal lines, so that the Balanta and the Manjaco grow rice while
the Fula and the Beafada are the principal growers of groundnuts. Cabral explains this specialisation as being largely
unimportant in that all the peoples of Guiné have the ability to
cultivate the entire range of crops which can be grown in the
country. In traditional practice particular tribes grow particular
crops because they live in a region in which those crops have
been established. The Portuguese efforts in promoting groundnuts had been most effective among the Fula and Beafada, while
the Balanta had shown resistance to changing their traditional
pattern of cultivation. During the long years of the national
liberation struggle this division between groundnuts and rice was
to correspond to the division between the tribes most and least
sympathetic to the PAIGC. The hostility of the Fula can be
explained in part by the favoured position of the Fula chiefs
under the Portuguese administration. The Fula's willingness to
adopt groundnuts helped to reinforce this favouritism. Cabral's
reluctance to give weight to the importance of tribal boundaries,
which were reinforced by the groundnut and rice division, was
to be reflected in his later political essays and speeches in
which he played down tribal distinctions in favour of the predominance of class as the principal source of cleavage in Guinéan
society. This creates a weakness in both the agronomic and the
political writings by underestimating the role of tribal divisions
in favour of nascent class distinctions which simply do not
provide sufficient means for demarcating groundnut cultivators
from rice growers.

The contemporary significance of Cabral's agronomic writings
lies in their portrayal of the process by which an undeveloped
economy was being transformed into a condition of underdevelopment. When read twenty years after they were first published, the agronomic essays give the impression that Cabral is
a writer who belongs to the post-independence era, when in
fact these studies were written more than a decade before the
debate about underdevelopment became popular.

Revolutionary theorists of the Third World and African Socialists in particular pay little if any attention to the role of material
production when building theories about revolutionary change.
The kind of massively detailed and intricate study of political
economy found in Lenin's 'The Development of Capitalism in
Russia' is, with the exception of Cabral's agronomic writings, a
solitary work. This refusal of the radical left to examine relations
between producers and the means of production and to explore
the economic horizons of a given society in detail is the result of
two particular trends. In the capitalist world critical theory has
been engaged in a near-compulsive preoccupation with such
factors as ideology and the state apparatus in order to explain

the conservatism of the working classes in Western Europe and North America. Recent events in Poland will no doubt spawn a whole new literature created to identify the inhibiting factors in the West which have dampened proletarian radicalism over the past thirty-five years. In the Third World the thrust of socialist theory has been blunted by the appeal of radical nationalism. In its wake has grown a preoccupation with relations between the various sectors of international capitalism which are given precedence over and above internal class relationships. In consequence class analysis has disappeared into the higher reaches of international relations.

The agronomic writings prove that Cabral was acutely aware of the fate which awaited Guiné if groundnuts were established as the staple crop. A degeneration in the ethics of agriculture and the destruction of the soil, both of which Cabral had witnessed first-hand in Cape Verde, were unavoidable if Portugal succeeded in establishing a groundnut economy. Yet, despite this wealth of evidence foreshadowing the threat of underdevelopment, the concept of underdevelopment does not appear in Cabral's subsequent political writings. More correctly, Cabral chooses to treat what is popularly known as underdevelopment as yet another instance of the capitalist mode of production in which there are specific sets of relations of production and a specific level of technical mastery over nature. By contrast in all theories of underdevelopment and especially in African variations of the theory, nesting as they do in the shadow cast by Frantz Fanon, underdevelopment and by implication capitalism itself are treated as extraordinary and even pathological.

It is *because* of the experience contained in the agronomic research that the concept of underdevelopment is absent from Cabral's later writings. Cabral saw nothing extraordinary or pathological in the spectre of a groundnut economy in Guiné. It was simply the line of development which best suited Portuguese interests and least satisfied the needs of local producers. This is the reason why the failure of the Portuguese to initiate any economic development before the early 1950s appeared to Cabral to be as damaging as were the efforts of the French and British in neighbouring colonies to create underdeveloped economies.

Since independence the PAIGC has done much to establish the kind of export economy which Cabral protested against in 1954. By 1978 the level of groundnut exports had reached record levels, while the production of rice had actually fallen. This can in part be explained by the severe drought conditions which have persisted throughout the latter half of the 1970s and also by the relatively buoyant international market for groundnuts. However, even given these factors, the question of priorities still remains puzzling. It would be ironic if the PAIGC managed to achieve what the Portuguese could not - an agricultural economy relying upon a single crop with tourism supplementing foreign exchange earnings.

4 THE CLASS ANALYSIS OF AFRICAN SOCIETY

THE THEORETICAL SETTING

The underdevelopment of a class theory for Africa arose in part out of the failure of African history to produce an authentic independence. This failure found a perverse celebration in the literature of African socialism with its rhetoric extolling the virtues of an independent and free African man forged against a background of worsening life conditions and an ever-receding future. It also found expression in an even more seductive guise under the banner of underdevelopment theory, with its bright new formulas set to replace the bankrupt ideas of political modernisation which for twenty years were so popular. Armed with the best of intentions, the underdevelopmentalists deflated the prospect of a resurgent Africa by denying the possibility of constructive change. The mechanistic models of Latin American underdevelopment, the cultural determinism of Ivan Illich, and the Marxism of Jalée and Amin banded together to create a new pessimism as underdevelopment came to be seen as Africa's fate. A close examination of the vicissitudes of class theory in the African setting shows that all too often the battle for a radical sociology brought the replacement of one set of myths by another.

During the first two decades after independence there was no general agreement, even on the left, as to the applicability of class analysis to the new states of Africa. Throughout the 1960s and early 1970s western observers were evenly divided between a liberal school which favoured the use of various branches of elite theory and a school, both Marxist and non-Marxist which preferred class analysis.[1] This dispute was compounded by the fervour of African nationalists in promoting the myth that African societies were classless.

There were a number of obstacles which have hindered the development of class analysis in the African setting. Among the most important reasons for the continued unpopularity of class theory has been the minuscule size of the middle classes in relation to the peasantry. This factor has in turn been compounded by the source of wealth enjoyed by the new ruling classes. Most members of the nationalist elites are salary earners. It is not ownership of the means of production but, rather, position within the instrumentalities of the state that has been the chief source of wealth. The members of these elites are rarely homogeneous either in terms of interests or background and they exhibit a high level of competition for promotion and advancement. In this contest for pre-eminence, control of the state apparatus is the principal means of accumulating wealth.

The difficulties confronting class analysis have not been confined to the urban setting. The relative absence of land alienation in West and Central Africa has meant that the African peasant has generally not been separated from ownership of the land. This, added to the fact that rural populations are numerically dominant, makes it tempting to characterise these new states as being composed of rural masses and urban elites rather than of competing social classes. Invariably, this view of African societies has been accompanied by an assumption that the rural populations are homogeneous and that there are no discernible divisions between upper, middle, and lower peasantries.

Two other factors which have contributed to the difficulty of inventing a theory of class conflict in the African setting concern traditionalism (for the want of a better term) and the influence of the economic and political relationship between the metropoles and the former colonies. Even though ethnic bonds may not completely obviate class ties, these ethnic ties are often cited as obstructing the development of objective patterns of political values and thereby excluding the use of class categories in the understanding of African societies. Supposedly, because of the influence of these ties, the pull of city life is simply too weak to disengage either the urban proletariat or the new bourgeoisie from attachment to traditional loyalties.

Most class analysts do admit having difficulty with the fact of ethnicity, especially where tribal affiliation cuts across class boundaries, thereby blocking what would otherwise be clearly defined lines of interest. Consequently, it is common for ethnicity to be seen as hindering the crystallisation of classes and the expression of coherent class interests. This in turn has encouraged a belief in the immaturity of African societies shared by both modernisation theory and Marxist class analysis.

While factors such as ethnicity, communal landownership, and the absence of an industrial base all throw doubt upon the existence of particular social classes, the fact of the 'external estate' puts into question the status of the indigenous social system as a whole. In general, the supporters of neo-colonial theory, in particular the 'classic theorists' such as Nkrumah and Fanon, argue that the metropolitan bourgeoisie must be seen as the ruling class, even though it is physically absent from the national territory.

This type of argument opens up a number of problems concerning the degree of autonomy exercised by the indigenous ruling classes and the degree of change brought by independence. This in effect tends to metamorphose class theory into a theory of imperialism. Such a change is important since none of the Third-World theorists of imperialism presents anything like a theory of class struggle such as was adjacent to Lenin's 'Imperialism' or even the liberal ideology contained in Hobson's essay of 1902.

The class analysis of African society 61

The rhetoric of African nationalism has been influential in justifying the rejection of class analysis. With few exceptions the nationalist generation espoused the myth of a classless Africa in reference both to the historical past and to the period of the anti-colonial struggle. Such diverse individuals as Nyerere, Nkrumah, Senghor, Mondlane, Lumumba, Touré, and Mboya were all at one time or another enthusiastic supporters of the idea of Africa as the classless continent. Those social cleavages that did exist were seen to be a consequence of the colonial experience. Supposedly, once the colonial powers retreated, African societies would return to normal and these embryonic class divisions would disappear. Leaving aside the practical drift of Tanzanian socialism, this myth sustains the sentiment of the Arusha Declaration.[2] Of course the idea of classlessness was simply a rhetorical device which was useful at a particular time, but it became so much a part of political discourse that the idea of classlessness erupted even in those rare attempts at serious political analysis. So it is that in 'The Wretched of the Earth' that Fanon of all people should cling to the myth that class conflict is peculiar to European civilisation and those societies temporarily under its domination.

There were a number of elements which encouraged the nationalist generation's romance with the idea of a classless Africa and, while the mixture of these elements varies from individual to individual, they are common to the literature of radical and reformist nationalism. In nearly every instance the communal ownership of land is taken as proof of the absence of antagonistic social classes. For radicals such as Fanon, Machel, and Mondlane the non-separation of the African worker from ownership of the instruments of production was proof that African societies were not bedevilled by class frictions and therefore could quite rapidly achieve a transformation to socialism.

The second element in the nationalist rhetoric, originated from within the literature of negritude which was such an important stimulus in the awakening of African nationalism in the period after 1945. The nationalist generation found comforting anger in the poetry of Aimé Césaire and Léon Damas and by the beginning of the decolonisation era the negritude movement could claim for itself an important place in the struggle for national sovereignty. So much of the aesthetics of negritude such as the belief in the existence of basic personality traits peculiar to the negroid people were absorbed into the mainstream of African socialism. The traits associated with the African personality were essentially a residual category drawn in contrast to those negative qualities such as individualism and avarice identified with occidental man. This belief in the African's sensitivity toward his fellow man and his preference for human purpose over the accumulation of things was, under the influence of African socialism, transformed into an explanation for the absence of class divisions in the past. More important still, because African societies did not contain antagonistic classes, there would be no need for Africa to suffer a period of class struggle in achieving socialism.

African socialists created a number of problems for themselves through this kind of mythologising on class and the African personality. These problems were made all the worse by the nationalist generation's wish to appear radical. Marxism appealed to members of this generation to the extent to which it outraged the sensibilities of British and French governments. In consequence an outward appearance of radicalism, which was characteristic of African socialism, further postponed any serious consideration of questions of class conflict. It also had the effect of reinforcing a prejudice which was so common among nineteenth-century European historians. Since one of the most basic tenets of Marxism is that all history is the history of class struggle, it followed that the classlessness of pre-colonial Africa was proof that Africa is a continent without a history. A complete absence of an awareness of such problems as this is indicative of the shallowness of socialist theory in the African setting. More importantly, it is consistent with the interests which those doctrines extolling the communalist ethos of the African mind and African society were to serve.

In the light of the intellectual climate which existed in Europe and Africa during the independence era it is hardly surprising that it was not until the middle of the 1970s that the first successful works on class analysis in the African setting began to appear. In this context the writings of Amilcar Cabral represent an important attempt to apply a theory of class conflict to post-war Africa. Cabral employs class theory, both at a basic level in describing a specific social formation and at a more abstract macro-historical level in analysing the mechanics of imperialism, and in tracing its impact upon African states. Apart from the latter writings of Frantz Fanon, no one has made a more adventurous attempt than Cabral to explore the influence of colonialism through the creation of classes.

THE CLASS STRUGGLE IN GUINÉ

Cabral's analysis of the social structure in Guiné rests upon the principle that any such analysis is useless unless it is directed to the purposes of an actual struggle. Consequently his account of class is, at least formally, confined to an exposition of the characteristics of Guinéan society. Any relevance that this analysis may have to a general theory of class struggle in Africa is, by Cabral's own admission, merely incidental. By contrast, in 'The Wretched of the Earth' Fanon had begun from the exact opposite point of reference. In his account of class struggle, Fanon's concern was with the invention of a general theory describing the broad dynamics of nationalist movements against colonial rule. The FLN's war against the French was peripheral to Fanon's central purpose. For this reason alone Cabral's analysis is the more subtle. Ironically, Cabral's work is also far more relevant to the task of forging a general theory of class conflict in Africa.

In the essay A Brief Analysis of the Social Structure in Guiné[3] Cabral begins by setting out the three variables which were employed by the PAIGC in determining the revolutionary capacity of each social faction. These three variables are in fact a key to Cabral's analysis of Guinéan society. Firstly, the party defined the position of each group in terms of its degree of dependence upon the colonial regime. This of course varied considerably across the range of the numerous rural communities. Similarly there were important variations present within the urban milieu. The second factor taken into account was the attitude of each group towards the national liberation struggle; for immediate purposes it was important to determine the degree of sympathy or antagonism which was felt toward the nationalist movement. The final element in constructing this class profile was the determination of the likely behaviour of each faction during the post-independence period. In aggregate, these elements enabled the PAIGC to distinguish between a class's immediate response to the nationalist cause and the likely attitude of that class towards revolutionary change in the period after national independence. This kind of distinction is implied in much of the literature of African socialism, but rarely is it presented in a systematic fashion. In Cabral's writings a recognition of the interplay of these three variables allowed him to distinguish between various levels of contradiction, which could then be analysed in terms of the alignment of the principal classes.

In A Brief Analysis Cabral defines class principally, but not exclusively, in terms of a group's position within the dominant pattern of ownership of productive wealth. But in employing this method Cabral soon encountered a number of problems in defining and then identifying individual social classes. Most of these problems could be traced in origin to the diffuse character of the capitalist mode of production in Guiné. For example, the peasants who engaged in groundnut cultivation also grew foodstuffs for subsistence and for the purposes of limited exchange. These peasants maintained effective ownership of their land as the means of production and they also retained ownership and control over the instruments used in their daily work. In combination these factors made it difficult to establish the points at which the boundaries of the subsistence and colonial economies occurred. Cabral omits to refer directly to this problem of definition, and yet its influence is felt throughout his account of class analysis in Guiné and, most especially, in his rather protracted discussion of what to label the working class in Guiné.

The second major element comprising Cabral's definition of class is that of culture. This element is important, particularly in Cabral's account of the peasantry and the petty bourgeoisie. In the case of both of these classes Cabral argues that the nature of cultural attachment is central to understanding political behaviour and outlook. Cabral discovered that the material and social advantages enjoyed by members of the indigenous petty bourgeoisie were countervailed by the psychological discomfort of being forced to live in the shadow of two cultures both of which had become a vague source of anxiety. This was to have an important influence upon the responsiveness of various strata within the petty bourgeoisie to the appeal of the national liberation movement. In the case of the peasantry, living in ethnic communities without any form of state organisation, the PAIGC soon concluded that a positive attachment to traditional culture was a stimulus for opposition to colonial rule.

In discussing the role of culture in setting the ideological horizons to class identity, Cabral emphasises the differences between the experiences of the peasant and petty bourgeoisie. Cabral then goes on to argue that in Guiné there was no evidence of a natural antagonism between the peasants and the petty bourgeoisie and that in Guiné (as elsewhere in sub-Saharan Africa) there is no primary or even secondary contradiction between urban and rural populations.[4] During the colonial period the town and the country dwellers are allies, because both peasant and proletariat share a mutual experience of servility. Furthermore, in colonial Africa all urban dwellers have family and personal connections in the countryside which dampen any possible hostility. In short, in Cabral's work there is no obvious nostalgia for pre-capitalist communalism and no suggestion of that antagonism to urban life which is unfortunately typical of African socialism.

Cabral has remarkably little to say about the theoretical foundation on which his class analysis of Guiné is based and it is not possible to glean much further understanding from a reading of his analysis as a whole. The brief references to ownership and the role of culture as the corner stones of Cabral's approach tell us very little about the final form his analysis will take. In fact the sophistication of his final work is inexplicable given his dismissive attitude toward questions of theory. And yet the remarkable success of the PAIGC in its struggle against the Portuguese army proves that Cabral's analysis of the social structure in Guiné was accurate.

In various speeches and articles published after 1956 Cabral discusses the relationship between colonial rule and the emergence of classes in Africa. At times his reflections turn in the direction of a meta-theory of class conflict and historical materialism. This material is far more suggestive than is that relating to the problems confronting class analysis in the contemporary setting. In the important essay, The Weapon of Theory, Cabral argues that throughout all human history the existence of classes is the result of a complex interaction between material production and the distribution of wealth predominant within each human community.[5] In certain cases that wealth may be usurped by another nation as occurred with the colonial conquest of Africa. Classes are created and develop as the result of friction between the level of the productive forces and the dominant pattern of ownership of the means of production. Once a certain level in the accumulation of a material surplus is achieved in primitive communalist societies, then a qualitative jump occurs and classes appear.[6] Factors external to the socio-economic whole can influence the development of the internal class structure. In the modern world this is particularly obvious in the role played by transport and communications. Within certain situations external factors can slow down the formation of classes or even cause a regression in the social formation as a whole. The history of colonialism is the history of just such a retardation which has given the societies of Africa their individual characters. However, once the play of this external influence ceases, the social formation reassumes its independent form. Under normal circumstances the evolution of a class society sets its own particular rhythm.

Cabral argues that, because of the impact of colonialism upon Guinéan society, it was necessary for the PAIGC to frame the question of national liberation according to the specific conditions in the country. No general theory drawn from the experience of other people such as the Vietnamese, Chinese, or Cubans could be suited to a country where, prior to the colonial presence, no state existed and in which the middle class was so small and so weak. Cabral concedes that it is useful to be aware of the theories used in similar struggles in other countries but that such theories could not tell the people of Guiné how their society works nor how to create their own revolution. In the context of Guiné Cabral explains that the task of the national liberation movement was to instil a working-class consciousness in a society in which there was no working class. This is the formula Cabral employs to define the project of making a socialist revolution in a backward country.[7]

Cabral knew from his years with the Agricultural Board that Guiné was divided into more than twenty tribal groupings of which four main factions comprised nearly three-quarters of the total population. Besides these basic tribal divisions there was a further distinction between Islamicised and Animist groups. Before the outbreak of the war almost 70 per cent of the population was Animist. The tribes belonging to this group had no form of state organisation, and with the exception of the Manjaco they had no traditional chiefs. Prior to the Portuguese occupation there was no concept of private property and no monetary system among a majority of the people. In contrast, the Islamicised groups comprised around 30 per cent of the population, with the Fula and the Mandinga being the most typical of those tribes having chieftainships. In analysing the structure of rural Guiné, Cabral identified the numerically and economically important Fula and Balanta tribes as representative of these two social extremes.

Among the Fula there are clearly established social divisions and Cabral identifies three specific tiers or strata. Firstly, there are the chiefs who with the notables and religious figures retain considerable privileges in the ownership of land and in the exercise of rights over the labour of peasants. On the second tier are the artisans and itinerant traders, the Dyulas, who are the bearers of an embryonic industrial development among the Fulas. The artisans play an extremely important role in socio-economic life, while the Dyulas have the potential to accumulate money. The artisans are dependent for their survival on the chiefs who are the only group able to afford their products. In the early days of the liberation movement the mobility of the Dyulas was important in helping to propagandise the movement. The peasants form the lowest strata of Fula society and, although they have effective possession of their own land, they have no rights and are exploited by the chiefs for whom they are obliged to work for part of each year.

In contrast to the Fula, to whom Cabral refers at various points as having a semi-feudal structure, the society of the Balanta conforms closely to the ideal of primitive communalism. Among the Balanta there is no social stratification and there are no rankings according to wealth or privilege. In each village there is a council of elders who arbitrate upon day-to-day decisions. Property, that is land, belongs to the village, with each family receiving the land necessary for its subsistence. The instruments of production are owned privately by the family which is the basic productive unit. Among the Balanta there are no clergy and the only grounds for social distinctions arise from age sets. In most of the Animist groups, but notably so among the Balanta, individuals both male and female are the owners of what they produce.[8]

Between the polarities represented by the Balanta and Fula lie numerous tribal groupings which in one way or another conform to either extreme. Cabral is inclined to play down the importance of the tribal division in preference to the dominance of class factors. In Determined to Resist[9] Cabral claims that when the Portuguese arrived in Guiné the tribal system was already in a state of decline. This decline was due to the play of a number of historical factors, including changes brought about by the endogenous development of the economy. Supposedly, this was the case in most of Black Africa and Cabral's designation of the social structure of the Fula as semi-feudal was intended to emphasise that point. The influence of colonialism merely accelerated the disintegration of the tribal units; it did not initiate the process. In Guiné the Portuguese sought to use the tribal structures for their own purposes. This tactic contributed to the decline of those structures while maintaining the illusion that tribal identity was still dominant.

As an economic system the tribal institutions did not engender respect among the PAIGC because, in effect, they had already been replaced by the emergence of a class system in which all peasants were united by a shared situation within the process of production. The PAIGC, however, did pay respect to the influence of the tribal structures in terms of language, religion,

The class analysis of African society 67

and culture. Despite the continued role of the family, the village, and the tribe as the primary units of production, Cabral is quite emphatic that the tribe as such was relatively unimportant during the liberation struggle.

Support for the PAIGC, which varied between the various ethnic groups as well as between classes, was by Cabral's own admission strongest among the Balanta and Mandinga and weakest among the Fula. The resistance of the Fula to the appeal of the PAIGC was particularly important despite Cabral's protestations that tribal identity was very much secondary to that of class.

THE PEASANT

As in the rest of tropical Africa the peasant class in Guiné formed the majority of the population. Cabral admitted having difficulty in defining the peasantry because the Guinéan peasants shared few of the characteristics displayed by the peasant classes in the Chinese or Algerian revolutions. In Guiné there were no large agricultural estates such as those found in Angola, and there was little or no land alienation. The Census of 1954 showed that the area of arable land under cultivation was less than half of the total area available. In Algeria, as in Vietnam and China, indebtedness to landlords and land hunger among the peasantry had been extremely important to the success of the national liberation movements. In Guiné the land remained in the hands of the village communities and the peasant was exploited through the depressed price paid for agricultural produce which was always set heavily in favour of the Portuguese and Lebanese traders.[10] Consequently, it was not easy for the PAIGC to explain to the peasant how he was being exploited. The question of the need to destroy Portuguese colonialism was essentially abstract for a rural population which had little or no contact with European officials. And yet Cabral believed that, because of its numerical dominance, the peasant class had to be the principal force in the anti-colonial struggle.

Among the Fula the peasants were a severely depressed group. They were exploited by their own chiefs who were closely allied to the Portuguese administration. Above all other groups the Fula peasants had the greatest objective interest in opposing the Portuguese and yet they clung stubbornly to the reassurance offered by their traditional chiefs. By contrast, the Animist tribes and most especially the Balanta, who had a history of opposition to colonial rule and had maintained their traditions intact, were the most receptive to the national liberation struggle.

This distinction between the Islamicised groups, best represented by the Fula, and the Animists, typified by the Balanta, led Cabral to draw a distinction between a class as a revolutionary force and a class as a physical force. Being the physically dominant group in the society, the peasantry was the creator of the material wealth of the country. It was also, under conditions of Portuguese colonialism, the most exploited class. And yet Cabral soon discovered that neither of these factors in themselves was sufficient to produce spontaneous support for the nationalist movement. The Fula peasants actively opposed the anti-colonialist struggle, even though that cause promised them relief from the oppressive conditions of their lives. Neither the presence of an objective interest in the destruction of the existing social order nor the experience of direct and barbarous exploitation could create a national liberation consciousness. Cabral concluded that, because of the limited conditions of its existence, the narrowness of its social experience and the archaic mental horizons of its life, the peasantry could not initiate revolutionary change. In his formal pronouncements on the peasantry Cabral views it as a class which is carried on the shoulders of other classes. It can lend its weight to a revolutionary movement only under the ideological leadership and guidance of another class. Cabral discovered that in Guiné the peasantry was not a revolutionary class.

This rather pessimistic interpretation of the Guinéan experience presented in In a Brief Analysis is countered in Cabral's other writings, especially his essays and speeches on the subject of national culture, which suggest a very different interpretation of peasant life. In Identity and Dignity, written six years after A Brief Analysis, Cabral emphasises the importance of peasant culture as a stimulus to revolutionary movements and he argues that support of the liberation movement was more dependent upon the kind of cultural affiliation of the peasant than upon any other single factor. The Fula whose chiefs had come under the influence of the Portuguese administration were the least sympathetic to the PAIGC of all the tribes. In his notes on national culture, Cabral explains that this acquiescence to colonial rule was authorised above all else by the erosion of the pull exerted by traditional culture. In those instances where colonial contact had been most pervasive, the internal economic and social organisation of the community, its traditional institutions, had been undermined. The office of chief now functioned as an adjunct to institutions and purposes located outside of the village. Consequently, the traditional institutions lost their vitality, and the relationship between culture, as the celebration of the communities' success in the daily struggle to satisfy human need, became less and less affirmative. At the conclusion of this process would lie institutions which had no appeal and a productive life that offered none other than material rewards. Ten years earlier Frantz Fanon had observed the results of the same process of detribalisation in the breaking down of traditional society in Algeria. There the destruction of all ties binding the individual to an affirmative collective life had set the pattern for a ghost-like existence. Within Fanon's theory of the colonial personality it is this which makes the African peasantry so volatile and so predisposed to self-destructive behaviour. By contrast, Cabral stops a considerable distance short of such a conclusion.

Within Cabral's theory as a whole there are two levels of
explanation suggested for the inability of the peasantry to act
as a revolutionary class. In some instances, as among the Fula
of Guiné, the erosion of national culture and the detachment
of that culture from the ongoing activity of tribal and national
life are cited as the reason for the peasant's inability and lack
of desire to change the world in which they live. This approximates, if vaguely, to Fanon's theory of the colonial personality.
This factor is implicit within Cabral's theory and it only becomes
visible if Cabral's comments on the role of culture are matched
with his account of the social structure in Guiné. Even so, without this element, Cabral's support of the latent revolutionary
capacity of the peasant class would be meaningless. Conversely,
Cabral also believed that the narrowness and brutality of village
life, which ties the individual so much to blind necessity,
strangles any initiative for change. The influence of those
features which Engels thought characteristic of peasant life,[11]
such as the demography of a productive process, which isolates
producers from each other, the variations in the degree of
exploitation and the habits of submissiveness, are all implied in
Cabral's rejection of the peasant as a revolutionary class. The
peasant is so immersed in daily toil that he cannot understand
or even envisage a life in any way different from his own. Therefore Cabral's dismissal of the peasantry as a revolutionary class
is due, paradoxically, to factors which may be identified as
synonymous with the colonial experience and with factors which
are endemic to peasant life. Cabral makes little effort to sort
out these two elements, thereby leaving his account of the
peasantry rather ambiguous. Needless to say this picture becomes
even more muddled when one examines Cabral's writings on culture and his view of political education.

THE SOCIAL STRUCTURE OF THE TOWNS

Although Portuguese colonialism was unusual in that it brought
less dramatic change to Guiné than was characteristic of British
and French colonies, it did create the necessary social and
economic conditions for the emergence of new social strata. In
Guiné the social structure in the towns showed considerable
diversity, with the most obvious division being that between
the minuscule European community and the black African population. In 1960 there were less than 3,000 Europeans in the colony,
all of whom occupied relatively privileged positions. This community tended to retain the pattern of social stratification characteristic of metropolitan Portugal. At the top lay a small stratum of
senior officials and managers of major enterprises; below this
came a group of middle-ranking officials, small traders, and
those engaged in commerce and the liberal professions. The lowest
stratum consisted of skilled workers whose conditions of life were
far superior to those enjoyed by any of the indigenous population

The African population in the towns consisted of four major strata; at the apex were a very small number of Africans, invariably of Cape Verdean descent, who were either high- or middle-ranking state officials or engaged in the liberal professions. Cabral himself was a member of this elite which numbered less than twenty. Below this lay a lower middle class of petty officials working in the lower rungs of public administration and business. Cabral emphasised that this middle stratum of the petty bourgeoisie held contracts and therefore were guaranteed permanent employment. Next came the wage-earners. The lowest social stratum consisted of déclassé elements. The déclassés were the new arrivals to the cities who comprised the young as well as the genuine social dregs such as prostitutes and beggars.

At the beginning of the revolution in Guiné the number of wage-earners congregated in the principal towns of Bafata, Bissau, Bissora and Bolama totalled less than 20,000. Cabral points out that, because of their position within the overall structure of the national economy, these workers did not warrant the title of proletariat or working class. The social and economic conditions attendant upon Portuguese colonialism meant that these workers could be compared only in the most vague way with a proletariat in a European setting. Among the wage-earners, as Cabral prefers to term such workers, were various groups of which the dock-workers of Bissau and the people employed on the cargo boats proved the most important to the PAIGC. Other factions of this class included domestic servants, those employed in small retail stores, and those working in the service industries such as porters.[12] Wage-earners in the service and processing industries worked without a contract and therefore were liable to be dismissed at any time without notice. These men and women lived under conditions of perpetual uncertainty.

The political participation of craftsmen and manual workers was very important during the earliest days of the nationalist movement in Guiné and it was the manual workers who formed the basis of support of MING at its foundation in 1956.[13] Even so, as with the peasant class, the wage-earners were not easily mobilised and many clung steadfastly to the small advantages they enjoyed under Portuguese rule. This particular faction suffered from what Cabral terms a petty bourgeois mentality.

By contrast, the small number of European workers in the colony had a very clearly defined political outlook and they were fiercely opposed to the nationalist movement. In the main these workers were skilled and they feared, quite rightly, that any liberalisation would be at their expense. Unlike the members of the expatriate petty bourgeoisie, these Europeans maintained their opposition to the liberation struggle throughout.

Initially, the PAIGC directed all its efforts at political mobilisation towards the dock-workers of the capital, Bissau. The first political opposition to the colonial government took the form

of demands for higher wages and better conditions. These
workers proved to be highly conscious of their economic position
and they were able to organise strike action with little outside
direction. This early success gave the party what it saw as its
'little proletariat'. However, because of their strategic position
within the economy and the smallness of their numbers, they
were extremely vulnerable to police repression and the early
strikes were brutally suppressed. The massacre of striking
dock-workers at Pidjiguiti in 1959 proved a turning point for
the liberation movement. From that moment onwards no direct
action was taken in the cities and the PAIGC concentrated upon
building a guerrilla base in the countryside among the peasantry.

In writing of the character and composition of the working class
in the successive contexts of colonial and neo-colonial rule,
Cabral favours the proletariat as a revolutionary class. However,
this judgment is tempered by the relative dependence of the
working class on petty-bourgeois leadership in the colonial
situation and the inability of the working class and the petty
bourgeoisie to distinguish between substantive and formal
national independence.[14] By itself the working class cannot lead
the colonial or post-colonial revolutions. Cabral argues that the
neo-colonial period is characterised by a sudden expansion in
the size of various classes and the increased differentiation of
the social structure as a whole. Independence brings about the
growth of an urban and rural working class and it is from this
class that there comes the possibility of the completion of the
task of national liberation. In the neo-colonial situation the
working class has the capacity to fight the national ruling class
and through it the imperialist bourgeoisie. The task of the
working class in the post-independence period is to capture
state power. It is this which really distinguishes the two phases
of the national liberation struggle.

In his account of the neo-colonial phase in particular, Cabral's
judgment of the necessity of the leading role of the proletariat
appears traditionally Marxist. Yet the working class or wage-
earning class in Guiné does not in any conventional sense constitute a proletariat, either in terms of its social context, its
origins, or its political character. Cabral himself admits this by
refusing to use the term proletariat or working class when
referring to those employed in service and domestic industries
in Guiné. Cabral, however, does this without any presentiment
of underdevelopment theory. There is no suggestion in his
writing that there could be no working class in Guiné because
Africa stands at the wrong end of the imperialist relationship,
which by its very nature warps the social structures of the
periphery. Cabral's intention is merely to emphasise the immediate differences between Guiné's social structure and the social
landscape found in other, namely European settings.

In 'Return to the Source' Cabral's designation of the proletariat
as a revolutionary class is tempered by various references he
makes to the need for working-class elements to open themselves

to the influence of peasant culture. In his important essay National Liberation and Culture Cabral explains how contact with the peasants changed the mentality of urban working-class elements working as cadres for the PAIGC. Through the experience of living with the peasants, 'They [the working class] discover at the grass roots the richness of their cultural values (philosophical, political, artistic, social and moral), acquire a clearer understanding of the economic realities of the country, of the problems, sufferings and hopes of the popular masses.'[15] They also discovered the spiritual and intellectual capacity of the peasant to comprehend and to transform his own limited world. Through this contact the political consciousness of the working-class and petty-bourgeois elements was enriched and they abandoned the kind of reflexive prejudices they had previously held about the idiocy of rural life. It was in this sense that the national liberation struggle in Guiné proved that the peasant class was anything but a passive receiver of an alien and superior culture transmitted by party leadership drawn exclusively from the urban milieu. Paradoxically, within this same essay, Cabral argues that the struggle against colonialism can only be erected upon the shoulders of the working class, that is, on the basis of the culture of the wage labourers.[16] This paradox is expressive of Cabral's ambivalence toward both the petty bourgeoise and the peasant class.

In practice this culture will be somewhat diffused, because of the presence of petty bourgois strains within the nationalist movement which it fosters. Even so, the prospects for the success of the national liberation movement rest largely upon the correct identification of the working class within the national culture. Thus, within Cabral's writings on class and his essays and speeches on the subject of culture and identity, the same perception of revolutionary consciousness as being by definition proletarian consciousness is found. And yet the working class was not to be the revolutionary class in Guiné.

In exploring the dynamics of the class structure of Guiné, Cabral explains with apparent regret why he found it necessary to dismiss the working class as the principal revolutionary force. It could play the part of the dominant class neither in terms of a physical force nor in the sense of being the predominant source of leadership for the movement. This leadership would have to come from another stratum. Cabral gives as the reason for this the simple fact of size. In Guiné the working class was too small and it did not represent an important fraction of the total working population. Size alone would disqualify it as the locus of the revolution for, in Guiné as elsewhere in Africa, the working class was essentially ancillary to the peasantry as the major producer of wealth. Guiné was simply not a commercial colony and there was no industry to create a working class nor even, as in Frantz Fanon's Algeria, a large urban sub-proletariat. Within Cabral's theory, revolutionary leadership can only come about through the alliance of various strata within which the working class can play a revolutionary role. This is a subtle but important distinction from the claim that the working class is the revolutionary class, which Cabral at times appears to favour.

Cabral's concern with the revolutionary capacity of the working class was the result not so much of a desire on his part to be orthodox but rather from his anxiety. The sad history of nationalist struggles in Africa throughout the 1960s had shown the weakness of movements which were based upon petty-bourgeois leadership. These movements had all ended in disappointment and frustration. Cabral thought that he had discovered the reason for this failure in the absence, within these movements, of the leading hand of working-class elements. This helps to explain how it came about that the working class, its political consciousness, and culture occupy the place of a myth in Cabral's theory, which contains the wish for the arrival of a world not yet formed and perhaps not even possible in some Black African states.

THE LUMPENPROLETARIAT

In Guiné there was one important urban group for which Cabral could find no ready name. They were neither a Lumpenproletariat in the sense that they were not the residue formed with the creation of a proletariat, nor were they elements discarded from the proletariat itself. In Guiné the members of this urban class were typically not failed or dispossessed peasants who were such a significant group in Algeria where land alienation was widespread. In origin this class derived from two sources: firstly, under the impact of Portuguese colonialism, there was a trend for peasants to move to the cities in a voluntary exodus in search of work or the other benefits which urban life appeared to promise. Because of the lack of opportunities for work, part of this exodus formed a pool of permanently unemployed.[17] This process of class formation is very close to that described by Engels in 'The Peasant Wars in Germany' in which he identifies as pariah strata of déclassés which come into existence whenever a town is created. As the feudal ties binding this group to the countryside are loosened these elements are coalesced into a pre-proletariat. Of course the assumption in Engels's study is that the growth of such a class is synonymous with the emergence of a proletariat which, in Guiné, was not the case. As Cabral explains in A Brief Analysis, there can be no Lumpenproletariat when in fact there is no proletariat.[18] When writing of this group Cabral always employs the term déclassé, thereby emphasising the indeterminate position of its members.

A second stratum of the urban unemployed originated from peasants fleeing the effects of the war in the countryside. As the liberation struggle progressed throughout the 1960s this stratum swelled. The use of napalm and aerial bombing was an encouragement for peasants to seek safety in the cities of Bafata and Bissau. Cabral makes no distinction between these particular déclassés in terms of their political potential or the degree to which they had been integrated into city life. But Cabral does distinguish between two political factions within the déclassés' group. The first are the genuine déclassés which is comprised of beggars, prostitutes, and the permanently unemployed. In terms of social composition, this group corresponds most closely to Marx's characterisation of the Lumpenproletariat. This group had been heavily infiltrated by the secret police.[19] The second faction consisted mainly of young people who were connected in one way or another with the petty bourgeoisie and the working class. The members of this group had recently arrived from the countryside and retained strong ties with families and friends in the rural sector. Because of their experience of city life, they had come to compare the living standards of their own families with that enjoyed by the Portuguese settler community. In this they shared a common experience with the members of the indigenous petty bourgeoisie. These youths were a great source of support for the PAIGC in whom they saw the chance to end the injustices of the colonial system which in the urban setting were only too obvious.

Cabral's account of the déclassés indicates that in a metaphoric sense the radical stratum of the déclassés took the place of a class of intellectuals. In Guiné of course there was no such class, but rather a very small number of members of the petty bourgeoisie who had some tertiary education. Because of their indeterminate social status and their limited opportunities, the radical déclassés felt themselves to be dispossessed and unattached to the society in any positive way. Often they were literate in the sense that they spoke Portuguese. These characteristics combined to produce the capacity for a critical interpretation of the meaning of the colonial relationship in terms of everyday experience such as work opportunities, social development, and exploitative labour practices. As Cabral comments elsewhere, in colonial Guiné an intellectual is a person with a primary education. Among the déclassés the PAIGC found its own intellectuals.

It is inexplicable that there are no references to the Lumpenproletariat or déclassés in any of Cabral's later writings. This is especially significant when one remembers that the later writings contain most of Cabral's judgments on the subject of political consciousness, cultural ties, and neo-colonialism. Yet in his earlier writings and in particular in his account of the neo-colonial period, Cabral argues that under such circumstances economic development encourages the growth of a Lumpenproletariat. Cabral's silence about the déclassés appears to be the result of a basic difficulty he experienced in conceptualising the place of this class in his social theory. In his brief study on the revolution in Guiné, Gerald Chaliand[20] describes this group as a temporary proletariat with a middle-class mentality, which played an important role in the struggle by supplying middle-level cadres for the party. Their basic characteristics according to

Chaliand are their rootlessness and their blind hostility towards authority. Chaliand's extraordinary mixture of terminologies is symptomatic of an uncertainty which is also present in Cabral's own work. But in Cabral's case this hesitance exposes the great strength of Cabral's approach to social analysis.

Cabral is able to distinguish between various factions within the déclassés group, although this group appears to form a single stratum. Certainly there is no cleavage within its ranks, according to the broader productive process, and Cabral is not easily able to divide this group into factions on the basis of obvious social characteristics or values. Cabral's social analysis never works in a mechanistic way or on a single plane and he never presumes to deduce the boundaries of a class solely on the grounds of its immediate political ambitions and behaviour. Neither does he presume to deduce political behaviour by reference to the productive process alone. That is why Cabral was able to recognise the potential of the déclassés, even though in Guiné this group would appear to be entirely unpromising as a source of support for the national liberation movement.

In Fanon's 'The Wretched of the Earth' the Lumpenproletariat is defined as a uniform class composed of landless labourers eking out a dismal existence as criminals and prostitutes in the urban slums. Fanon refuses to distinguish between expatriate workers and those types Marx knew as 'social scum'. Having done this, Fanon then proceeds to apply his concept of the Lumpenproletariat to the whole of Black Africa. Fanon's intention was to prove how inappropriate Marxist categories of social class were in the colonial situation. The subsequent record of so-called Lumpenproletariat elements in Algeria and Zaire have been in direct contradiction to Fanon's thesis.

The comparison between Fanon and Cabral serves to emphasise the greater subtlety of Cabral's analysis of social process and political behaviour. Even so, this comparison does not explain why Cabral should have been able to identify distinctions within the ranks of the déclassés which Fanon failed to perceive in the case of Algeria.

THE PETTY BOURGEOISIE

The major problem facing socialism in Africa has not been due to the atypical nature of the social structures colonial rule left in its wake but, rather, to the complete absence of particular classes. In Guiné, as elsewhere, this was most obvious in the absence of a clearly defined capitalist strata, conscious of its own interests, capable of forming a political party to represent those interests and capable therefore of dominating the state and the state apparatus. In Guiné there was no class which remotely resembled this type of national middle class. Even in those colonial settings where the rudiments of a national bourgeoisie did come into existence, indigenous middle classes in

Africa have, in general, because of their numerical and economic weakness, been unable to establish an independent position in regard to international capital.

At various sites in post-colonial Africa an independent stratum of indigenous capitalists has emerged in the sectors of trade, transport, and agriculture. This is in addition to the more obvious and affluent bureaucratic capitalist stratum which has dominated the attention of writers such as Hamza Alavi, Colin Leys, and Issa Shivji. While it is certainly true that in the progressive states the potential for growth of the capitalist stratum (outside of the state sector) is weakened by the continued expansion of state economic activity, this class does exist and it does represent one of the most important changes to be brought by national independence. The origins of this new national middle class are to be found in the petty bourgeoisie of colonial Africa.

In the radical histories of the colonial period the most commonly referred to social category is that of the petty bourgeoisie. This term is used to cover a wide range of social factions all of which are taken to share a number of essential characteristics: they are an urban class literate in the colonial language, they are relatively prosperous, and often they are active in the trading sector. Sometimes the petty bourgeoisie is defined as being congregated within the lower ranks of the state apparatus. Although prominent in the nationalist movements, this petty bourgeoisie is usually politically reactionary. Above all else, the petty bourgeoisie are seen as the natural inheritors of political power, however incompetently they may have wielded that power.

In Marxist literature the term petty bourgeoisie has always been used to denote a stratum associated exclusively with small-scale production and small-scale ownership. It is, in essence, a class representing a transitional phase in the development of capitalist production and it declines in size with the maturation of the capitalist mode of production. Because of its economic and social character, the petty bourgeoisie cannot sustain its own intellectual position or ideology and therefore it tends to oscillate between the ideologies of the working class and the bourgeoisie. It was in this sense that Marx designated these elements as constituting a petty bourgeoisie and not, as has so often been supposed, because the petty bourgeoisie were engaged in small business.[21]

In aggregate Marxist characterisations of the petty bourgeoisie emphasise its limitations for independent political action. Under special circumstances the petty bourgeoisie may serve as a governing class or it may even over time transform itself into an authentic bourgeoisie. But the petty bourgeoisie can never of its own accord and on the basis of its own class ideology constitute an independent ruling class. In any context the petty-bourgeois class is vulnerable because of its economic situation and its largely porous ideology. But in the African context the petty bourgeoisie is doubly disadvantaged.

The class analysis of African society 77

The rise of a petty-bourgeois stratum in Guiné, as elsewhere in tropical Africa, was tied closely to the expansion of the instruments of colonial administration. Cabral himself was a member of this class, as were most of the founders of the nationalist movements in British and Francophone Africa. The petty bourgeoisie, like every other group, fashions an inventory of concepts with which to order its social experience. But, in contrast to the peasantry whose lives are so dominated by social habit and obligation, the colonial petty bourgeoisie is exposed to a wide range of influences. The members of the indigenous middle class are caught between an urban existence and a lingering affiliation to a rural life which they have left forever. They enjoy relative economic benefits but these benefits are considerably lower than those accruing to European workers with the same level of skills. Most distinctively the indigenous middle class is the only group which can aspire to participate in the cultural life and consume the cultural products of the colonising community and it is this which marks its social experience as unique.

Among the indigenous classes the petty bourgeoisie is the class most infused with what Gramsci called 'external values'. Cabral explains that in the colonial situation these values are all too often accepted by the individual as merely personal experience and only rarely are they understood as being the product of a collective existence. Like its European counterpart, the colonial petty bourgeoisie accepts the bourgeois myth of individualism in which the path to improvement is assumed to rest solely in the force of personal effort. But, unlike the European middle classes, the colonial petty bourgeoisie is subjected to the contrast between traditional African and European cultures. This contrast is often presented in such a way that the choice of cultural styles becomes traumatic. In 'Black Skin White Masks', Fanon described just how debilitating that choice could be. Cabral emphasises that the differences between the petty bourgeoisie and the mass of the people are in essence, a division between cultural contact and change on the one hand and fidelity to traditional culture on the other. The petty bourgeoisie stands in a position somewhere between the masses and the European colonials. It is in every sense a marginal class.

In Guiné, Cabral identified two distinct factions within the petty bourgeoisie. The first consisted of higher- and middle-ranking officials employed in the state apparatus and those few indigenous members of the liberal professions; the second level was composed of petty officials and those individuals working in commerce with a contract guaranteeing permanent employment. Among this second faction there were also a number of small farmers engaged in production of groundnuts on a larger scale than the peasantry. Cabral does not distinguish politically between these two factions and there is no suggestion that the division between the higher and lower strata within the petty bourgeoisie corresponds to greater or lesser degrees of conservatism. In the case of Guiné there was one important ethnic feature common to the petty bourgeoisie elements working in the public sector. The Portuguese had recruited Cape Verdeans to fill the few vacancies in the civil service open to indigenes and they had also shown preference for assimilados in these same jobs. This favouritism created a ground-swell of antagonism toward Cape Verdeans which was to have long-term consequences for the success of the revolution. At the time of Cabral's assassination this division had become a source of hostility within the ranks of the PAIGC, and it was cited by the Portuguese and the South Africans as the reason for his death.

During the struggle against the Portuguese the petty bourgeoisie divided itself into three clearly defined strata. Part of the petty bourgeoisie was heavily committed to the Portuguese presence and threw its full weight behind the colonial system. Those who took the road against the PAIGC were, for the most part, members of the liberal professions or else higher officials within the civil service. A second group which, like the first, was numerically a minority was committed to the national liberation struggle. The majority of the petty bourgeoisie was, however, undecided and continued to vacillate between an outright nationalist stance and conformism to the colonial presence. Although there was a degree of correspondence between the radical and conservative streams and the principal divisions between the higher and lower strata of the petty bourgeoisie, Cabral found no clear necessary relationship between economic position and conformism.

The earliest protests against the colonial presence in Guiné originated from amongst the ranks of the petty bourgeoisie, and it was these elements which predominated in the leadership of the MING, the forerunner of the PAIGC. Cabral argues that even from this early date the dilemma facing the petty bourgeoisie was a matter of choosing between allying itself with the forces opposing national liberation or else throwing its weight behind the workers and peasants, thereby relinquishing its vocation as a petty bourgeoisie. This latter choice was of course the harder for members of the new middle classes because it entailed giving up the small advantages which accompanied its support of the colonial state.

Cabral identifies three specific factors determining the capacity of the petty bourgeoisie as a revolutionary class. The possibility of the petty bourgeoisie following a revolutionary path depends upon the nature and size of the party, the character of the struggle (in particular whether or not the struggle is violent), and the nature of the colonial state. Cabral is aware that the role of the petty bourgeoisie in European history has been that of an auxiliary class which is drawn along by the flow of events without ever being capable of placing its own stamp upon those events. It may ally itself with the leading movement of a particular historical epoch but it has never constituted itself into an independent force. Even so, Cabral still believes that in nationalist Africa it is always the petty bourgeoisie which leads, if only by default.

In the post-independence period when the immediate goal of national independence has been achieved, the petty bourgeoisie will undergo drastic change. This is true irrespective of whether that independence is genuine or nominal. The history of African nationalism shows that most often imperialism has managed to retain effective control over the nominally independent states lying within its orbit. When this happens the petty bourgeoisie will transform itself into a pseudo-bourgeoisie. The vehicle for this elevation will usually lie within the instrumentalities of the state. Cabral views such a development as inherently progressive, since it will strengthen the economic activity of local elements, stimulate private agriculture, and encourage the growth of small but important urban and rural proletariats. Cabral is emphatic that this pseudo-bourgeoisie should not be confused with a national middle class. It is not and cannot be a national bourgeoisie because the conditions for its existence rest solidly upon its compliance with and support of imperialism.[22] But this dependence does not mean that the rise of the pseudo-bourgeoisie can be dismissed as being of little importance. Nor should it be viewed with pessimism.

The phase during which such a class emerges is absolutely vital for, above all else, it signifies the sharpening of class contradictions.[23] The only stratum which is capable of a critical awareness of the machinery of imperialist domination is the petty bourgeoisie. Paradoxically, it is also the petty bourgeoisie which is the sole class capable of directing the operation of the neo-colonial state. Therefore, Cabral arrives at the conclusion that the petty bourgeoisie is the only class which is capable of playing a revolutionary role in the neo-colonial phase. He also concludes that this fact represents the greatest source of weakness of the anti-imperialist movements in Africa.

The colonial and the neo-colonial situations give to the petty bourgeoisie the opportunity to play a leading role as the force promoting radical change. In the colonial situation the petty bourgeoisie can lead the movement against foreign control, thereby bringing itself to the position of taking charge of the instruments of the state. Later, when independence has been achieved, elements of the petty bourgeoisie can again lead, only this time against those members of its own class which have become congealed into a pseudo-bourgeoisie. In order to retain the power which national independence puts into its hands the petty bourgeoisie has but one course to follow; it must attempt to become bourgeois. It must allow for the development of a bureaucratic and intermediary bourgeoisie in the commercial cycle in the hope, finally, of becoming a national middle class.[24] Unfortunately the pull exerted by imperialist capital means that the best this class can achieve is to elevate itself into a facsimile of a nationalist middle class; it must become a pseudo-bourgeoisie.

This account of the fall from youthful nationalism into neo-colonialism contains a significant paradox; within Cabral's theory the neo-colonial phase is important and progressive, because it brings the petty bourgeoisie to maturity. This occurs on two fronts: one section of the petty bourgeoisie is elevated into a pseudo-bourgeoisie while a second faction is radicalised into revolutionary action. In tandem with the peasantry and the small working class this latter group will lead the fight against imperialism. Consequently, the neo-colonial phase must be seen as bringing the petty bourgeoisie to maturity at the point of its conservative development and as a revolutionary class. It breaks off each of these strata and polarises the majority of the new middle class into one faction or the other. It is this change which marks the neo-colonial phase as revolutionary. Herein lies the main point of difference between Cabral's theory and that of other African socialists.

The career which Cabral maps out for the petty bourgeoisie, namely that it commit suicide as a class and ally itself with the peasants and small working class, depends upon the degree of social change which has taken place after independence. In the absence of a given level of political development and some transformation within the economic process, the petty bourgeoisie could never advance to the point of choosing between the two paths which political independence makes possible. The ability of the petty bourgeoisie to choose the path of revolution also depends upon a factor purely internal to the ranks of the petty bourgeoisie itself. This class, as Fanon pointed out with such effect, suffers above all else from an imperialist mentality which it inherits, at a discount, from the ruling colonial community. It is in its essence imitative. In the process of adopting the cultural style and values of the dominant community, this class ingests what Fanon believed to be the single most important characteristic of European culture - racial contempt for colonial peoples. The petty bourgeoisie learns to hate itself. In Cabral's theory it is in just this territory that the great weakness of the petty bourgeoisie and also its great potential for revolutionary action is assumed to lie. Cabral believed the petty bourgeoisie capable of committing class suicide because of the peculiar cultural situation in which it is placed. But he warns that only when the burden of its own peculiar psychological suffering is elevated from the level of a purely personal experience of racial and cultural contempt to that of a self-conscious class awareness can the members of the petty bourgeoisie develop as a revolutionary force.

The reason why Cabral can frame this career for the petty bourgeoisie is because, at the outset, he establishes a distinction between primary and secondary contradictions in the revolutionary process. Cabral assumes that for the duration of the colonial struggle the major contradiction would be between the Portuguese and international bourgeoisie on the one side and the peoples of Guiné on the other. This contradiction was dominant from the moment the struggle began in 1959. Once the PAIGC had been successful in expelling the Portuguese, the major contradiction would be between the indigenous ruling class (consisting of the petty bourgeoisie and semi-feudal ruling elements in the countryside) and those groups such as the Balanta which have no clearly defined social organisation. In the vanguard with this later group would be the working class which he expected to grow in numbers and political maturity during the neo-colonial period.[25] This line of argument emphasises the importance of those changes which Cabral believed would take place with political independence. In all of his writings on neo-colonialism, Cabral assumed that the principal difference between the colonial and the neo-colonial contexts lay in the higher level of the forces of production which would come after independence. This development would bring with it a sharpening of the class struggle.[26] It is this which Cabral claims gives reason for optimism. In fact, Cabral's main reason for believing in the obsolescence of neo-colonialism lies elsewhere.

There is an unhappy tension in Cabral's work between the two dialectics he identifies as promoting the movement towards genuine liberation. The first dialectic originates within the neo-colonial phase in the expansion which takes place as industry and commerce are, at least to a modest extent, nationalised. This brings that range of changes which Colin Leys and, earlier, Bill Warren identified as the source of real hope for the neo-colonial states of Africa. The second dialectic, which is implicit rather than explicit in Cabral's theory is in effect a restatement of a shibboleth common to the literature of African Socialism. Cabral assumes that the necessity for the African revolution comes from the egalitarian mode of social organisation characteristic of Black Africa. The point of escape from neo-colonialism is to be brought about by the ascendance of specific cultural values which originate in the communalist mode of production. It is here, as much as in Cabral's confessed faith in the immutable progressiveness of material development, that the optimism in his work originates. These two points of contradiction are quite divorced in Cabral's work and it is surprising that they should emerge within the same, apparently coherent theory. Their co-existence reverberates in various disguises throughout the design of Cabral's theory of imperialism.

5 CULTURE AND PERSONALITY

The Portuguese colonies differed in a number of important respects from the territories of British and Francophone Africa. Nowhere was this more apparent than in regard to the question of culture. In popular mythology, but also to a degree in fact, the Portuguese in Africa showed an ability for racial integration and a capacity for adaptation to local conditions. Salazar and his successor Caetano explained this by reference to the Portuguese genius for harmony. A better explanation, however, is found in the failure of Portugal to achieve the kind of material superiority which in other empires did so much to encourage ideas of racial superiority. In Angola and Mozambique this lack of obvious cultural tension was reflected in the non-racial quality of the indigenous colonial literature, and most especially in poetry which was the dominant form of artistic expression among the western educated elites. It was obvious, even in the creative literature of the 1950s, that the free mixing of poor Europeans with Africans, common to all the Portuguese colonies, had helped to frame the colonial experience in terms of class rather than of race. Behind the myth of racial equality and racial integration lay a reality of shared poverty which dampened the kind of hypersensitivity to racial questions which so preoccupied intellectuals in Francophone Africa.

The great strength of the writings of Cabral, Neto, Mondlane and Machel is that these men were more able to distinguish class forces from racial and ethnic movements than their counterparts in neighbouring colonies. However, this did not lessen the importance of cultural movements as harbingers of the nationalist struggles in Portugal's empire, nor did it diminish the role of national culture as a stimulus and as a goal of revolutionary nationalism. Most pertinent of all, despite the relative unimportance of the racial issue, Cabral was not entirely successful in his quest for an authentic class analysis of national culture.

In what was one of the central projects in his political theory, Cabral set out to clarify the relationship between national liberation and culture both in the specific case of Guiné, but also in the more general and abstract context of continental Africa. To this end Cabral set himself two tasks: he set out to define the relationship between culture and colonialism and to explore the relationship between culture and social class. In achieving the first of these objectives Cabral drew upon a variety of sources including the influential work of the West Indian Aimé Césaire. In pursuing the second aim he relied almost exclusively upon his empirical knowledge of Guiné. Both of these tasks drew Cabral

towards a preoccupation with an analysis of the mentality and
social experience of the petty bourgeoisie, for it is this class
which best illustrates the themes of cultural change and the
workings of colonial social influence. Cabral's success in not
falling prey to the temptation to subordinate class theory to that
of cultural determinism, so common among his contemporaries,
lends his work much of its strength.

In an oblique sense Cabral's analysis of culture confronted
him with the need to settle the score with African socialism and
especially those myths extolling Africa's cultural originality in
which the variety of African cultures were reduced in scope to
a single continental form.

In Cabral's theory the discussion of culture and identity is
in the most immediate terms a sociology of the petty bourgeoisie
by one of its own members. It is in this sense autobiographical.
But there is a difference between Cabral's 'autobiography' and
that of earlier nationalists, such as Nkrumah, Lumumba and
Kanza, each of whom was drawn from the same class. Invariably
these men wrote nothing but autobiography under the guise of
social history. Cabral's origins in the petty bourgeoisie did not
distort his political imagination in the same way.

In Cabral's writings there is virtually no discussion of the
problem of tribalism or of the peasant class in terms of beliefs
or culture or ideology.[1] As in the writings of his predecessors,
Fanon and Césaire, Cabral's analysis of culture and personality
takes the place of a discussion of ideology and political consciousness. This is so despite Cabral's declarations that it is the
absence of ideology that is the greatest danger facing the African
revolution.[2] This is an important omission, for where Cabral
writes of the revolutionary potential of the peasant or Lumpenproletariat the question of political consciousness is largely
ignored. Presumably this question is to be answered by reference to the position of these classes within the process of
production, but this in turn raises a further problem as to why
the ideology of these classes is determined in a crude sense
solely by economic forces when the outlook of the petty bourgeoisie is open to a wide range of influences. Within his theory
of class struggle and revolutionary nationalism Cabral's treatment of the peasant and Lumpenproletariat classes is inadequate.

Cabral's avowed aim in his writings on culture and identity
was to establish that in Africa as elsewhere culture is but one
aspect of the social reproduction of a community which has its
roots in the relationship between the satisfaction of human need
and the constraints placed on human behaviour by the natural
world. This approach contrasts with the usual practice found in
the literature of African socialism in which the spheres of culture
and class are seen as being entirely exclusive. Although at the
outset Cabral had intended to prove that the aspirations of the
petty bourgeoisie, like those of all other classes, derived from
their class position and were only subsequently refracted
through the medium of culture, his account of the petty bour-

geoisie becomes almost involuntarily an account of the pre-eminence of the force of cultural influence.

During the revolution the question of local and national culture was raised as a practical problem as to how the PAIGC should best approach the peasants given the ethnic diversity of Guiné. In the longer term this also raised the question as to the rate of change a peasant society could be expected to tolerate. Before Cabral's work on culture and national liberation, which was written towards the end of his life, this issue was avoided by political theorists and by governments alike. In theory it was answered, and then only obliquely, by the romanticisation of the peasant class which underlay African socialism. In practice the peasant was largely ignored once the question of political independence had been resolved.

The idealisation in theory of the peasant had an obvious parallel in the myth of narodism which Lenin took so much trouble in dismembering.[3] Lenin cites three guiding principles in narodnikist philosophy which also happen to be entirely consistent with the laws of African socialism; the first was the conviction that in Russia capitalism had been a degenerative force which should be resisted; the second was a belief in the exceptional character of the indigenous economic system in general, and in the peasant worker in particular. Together these characteristics were taken to hold the promise of an economic and social system more efficacious than any possible under capitalism. The final element in the narodnikist philosophy was a complete disregard for the relationship between the purposes of social and political institutions and the interests of particular classes. In the absence of a perception of how definite material interests gain political influence, the narodnikists believed that it was possible for Russian society to take an entirely new direction at will.

In the writings of the first generation of African nationalists capitalism was invariably condemned as an evil while the backwardness of African societies was seen by implication as virtuous. Consequently there arose a fiction about the remarkable and egalitarian pre-capitalist era in which equality and liberty were guaranteed. As with narodism this fiction was based upon a belief in the existence of an independent peasant owning and working his land under the blessing of bountiful earth. During the independence decade, this romantic vision of the past became so prevalent that it could only be challenged by a theory which attacked the idea of pre-colonial society from within the perspective of an authentic class analysis. This is the task Cabral set for himself.

Cabral defines culture as a product of the relationship between man and nature and the relationship between man and other men.[4] Nestling within these tensions culture is the result of economic and political activities as they appear on the idealistic and ideological planes. It is a continuing historical record of the physical achievements of a society. Although its principal basis lies in a society's level of productive forces and in the character of the dominant mode of production, culture is not tied in any qualitative sense to material production.[5] Cultural products cannot be understood as an appendage to economic forces. Therefore a people with only a simple economic life cannot be denied recognition of their cultural existence because of the technically rudimentary basis of their society. Culture can also exert an important influence either in a positive or a negative sense in the evolution of a people. As such it can be identified as the locus of a society's capacity for change and adaptability.

According to Cabral the primary function of culture lies in its role of fabricating a sense of individual identity.[6] A culture provides the individual with a sense of identity which signifies what a person is within his own social milieu in distinction from all other peoples. It is at the same time the purveyor of intimate information about the individual and his group's ethos and the manifestation of its most obvious and occasionally banal characteristics. Culture is therein a synthesis combining various elements and influences from within the society which Cabral aggregates under the heading of spiritual conditions.[7] Because these conditions cannot be deduced solely from class relations and Cabral concludes that the question of identity is a cultural rather than an economic problem.

Having distanced himself from what he believed to be a Marxist interpretation of culture, Cabral then makes the concession that a people's identity is tied to the maintenance and reproduction of the social system by a specific set of institutions and habits. Any change to those structures, the identity of which Cabral does not specify, would affect both culture as a whole and the people's intimate sense of selfhood. In discussing identity Cabral makes a distinction between biological factors (presumably including racial character) and social factors.[8] Of these two sets of factors the social element is by far the most important. Culture as a product of social history is itself a celebration of the conquest of nature and a recording of that victory among men. Identity is the central achievement of any culture and it serves to crystallise what is most distinctive and essential in each instance of the collective human experience.

Although Cabral attributes to culture a key position in the maintenance of any social system his account also carries the intimation that social reproduction is extremely fragile and vulnerable to sudden change. The presence of variations within the cultural whole, and even within a single sector of that whole, indicates why the colonial impact could never be uniform. It also indicates just why the colonial influence should be so disruptive. In allowing for the play of material, and what he calls spiritual elements, Cabral sought to account for the subtleties of the social landscape in Guiné in which peoples sharing identical levels of productive forces showed marked differences in the ways they ordered their daily lives and the ends to which their lives were directed.

Cabral discovered that in Guiné the profile of local cultures varied most where the social structure was itself most varied between levels of wealth and poverty, authority and subservience. Among the Balanta the variations in culture were slight in the absence of any clear divisions between higher and lower positions, while among the Fula they were more pronounced. Cabral saw in this further evidence of the interaction of economic influences and cultural characteristics especially where there was a clearly vertical social structure. Under Portuguese colonialism the political authority of Fula chiefs was nominal and, although the peasants were often aware of this fact, these rulers still managed to preserve their position as mediators of cultural practice. Despite the fact that these chiefs were the group most resistant to the idea of national liberation, their role as overseers of local culture was, in Cabral's view, constructive. And yet Cabral implies that where the Portuguese sought to utilise the existing structures of authority for their own purposes this drove a wedge within the social structure between the peasants and their genuine cultural aspirations which was socially and politically destructive. Unfortunately, there is no social psychology in Cabral's writings which explores the erosion of individual identity among the peasants and its effects upon the traditional authorities.

In his discussion of culture Cabral follows in the footsteps of Aimé Césaire in drawing an analogy between colonialism and Nazism.[9] He argues that, in denying the people of Africa their right to historical development, imperialism in a most intimate sense denied the African the right to cultural development and self-expression. This was to have a profound impact upon those who fell under colonial rule. Like the Third Reich, the colonial powers had understood that culture is an important element in sustaining resistance to foreign domination, and that complete domination can only be achieved where indigenous cultural life has been brought to a standstill. Although this may be a conscious policy of colonial regimes, indigenous cultural life also, in a more important sense, atrophies because of the very nature of the relationship between culture and economic activity. The vitality of the social formation is sapped whenever the indigenous economy is subordinated to external forces. If a strong cultural life survives, resistance may at any time erupt and take on the form of overt political dissent.[10] In their attempt to harmonise political and economic domination with the preservation of local cultures, the imperialist countries have set up what Cabral terms a 'state of siege'. They have usually sought to justify this siege with various theories about cultural assimilation. In the case of Portuguese Africa this led to the absurd claim that there were no Africans within the Portuguese empire, only peoples living in the 'overseas territories'. From this Cabral infers a law about cultural resistance and decolonisation, namely that the greater the difference between the cultures of the dominating and the dominated groups the greater is the possibility for a successful national liberation struggle.[11] Under conditions of extreme contrast the state of siege encourages cultural conflict

or resistance which in turn helps to preserve a people's sense
of originality. Cabral believes that this resistance is not found
among the petty bourgeoisie but is the prerogative of the
peasants. It is the ruling elements in the rural areas who are
the preservers of cultural integrity[12] and in consequence
indigenous culture is strongest where the social structure is
vertical.[13] As previously mentioned this line of argument is in
direct contradiction of Cabral's other comments connecting the
degree of opposition to colonial rule to the absence of such
vertical divisions.

This contradiction exposes a broader ambiguity in Cabral's
theory. This ambiguity lies in the contrast between his view of
culture as beleaguered and politically regressive where it is
allied to quasi-feudal social structures and his comments that
these same structures are conducive to revolutionary nationalism.
It also runs counter to the actual experience of the struggle in
Guiné in which the semi-feudal elements were least sympathetic
to the PAIGC. This contradiction would be resolved if Cabral
allowed for a distinction between culture and traditionalism (or
atrophied culture) which Fanon makes in his analysis in On
National Culture.[14] Cabral does not make this distinction and
therefore the contradiction remains.

In Cabral's theory the question of social paralysis is posed not
in terms of the impact of colonialism upon local culture or the psychological well-being of the individual or even community identity,
but appears rather in terms of the macro-historical development
of the society as a whole. Cabral endorses the positive influence
of the traditional institutions maintained by the colonial powers
as part of a policy of cheap administration and finds within them
the promise that the cultural struggle may easily pass over into
open political dissent. He also intimates that the problem of
identity is raised not only for the petty bourgeoisie, the most
obvious victims of colonial contact, but also for members of the
Lumpenproletariat. Most important of all, it is raised within
Cabral's analysis for those peasants whose cultural life is severed
from its sustaining spiritual values, values which Cabral deems
so important. However, Cabral has nothing to say about the
crisis of identity or the psycho-social welfare of the peasants,
for, like Césaire and Fanon, his analysis is confined to members
of the petty bourgeoisie.

In regard to the peasants there are two ideal forms of experience suggested in Cabral's theory; there are those peasants
who live within a stateless social structure and therefore are
more able to adapt to change brought by the intrusion of
colonial economic and political force. Secondly, there are the
peasants who live in a vertical social environment, who cling to
what they know, and are unable to adapt to change. Cabral
argues, in a highly contradictory way, that it is these peasants
who present the possibility for cultural opposition becoming
political and it is the stateless peasants who are naturally the
most sympathetic to revolutionary movements.

Cabral echoes a theme characteristic of African socialism where he argues that during the colonial period the strength of indigenous culture took refuge in the villages.[15] The peasants retained a rich and vibrant cultural life largely intact from the values and prejudices emanating from the European presence. In Cabral's view the richness of this cultural tradition is such that it can transform the mentality of the petty-bourgeois elements within the national liberation movement when they come into contact with it.[16] Contact with European culture is of course strongest among the urban classes and in particular the petty bourgeoisie, and it is within this group that the quest for identity and cultural authenticity usually first arises. Consequently the belief has developed that all national liberation movements are preceded by cultural renaissance movements,[17] of which negritude is the best known and the most typical. This error has tended to inflate the assumed cultural influence of imperialism which was in fact confined to a numerically small section of the indigenous society. It has also tended to encourage a dismissal of the peasantry as an actor in the colonial drama because this class lay outside of the area of cultural influence emanating from colonial rule.

In most nationalist literature there is an assumption that because the peasants did not suffer from cultural alienation, in the manner endemic to the urban middle classes, that they were inured to the colonial experience. It was for this reason that, from the first, questions about personality superseded questions about social class or political economy. In drawing an overt distinction between cultural contact among the peasants and the experience of the petty bourgeoisie, Cabral departs from the habits of his contemporaries, who invariably submerged categories of social class beneath those of race and racial identity. Yet ironically he remains faithful to that same tradition in viewing the peasantry as the repository of 'national values' and 'national culture' which elsewhere colonial contact had destroyed.

The cultural identity of the petty bourgeoisie is marked by its marginality as a class. Its members suffer from a number of socio-cultural conflicts which are played out against a background of relative affluence. But Cabral perceived that invariably these conflicts are experienced as individual fate rather than interpreted as being part of a collective existence.[18] In consequence the members of the petty bourgeoisie develop a frustration complex. Their sense of identity is seriously eroded by their exclusion from membership of either the European community or the indigenous society. It is among this class that the desire for a 'return to the source' is felt. This obsessive quest for a sense of identity is a reflection of an ambiguity experienced at the levels of social identity and economic opportunity that is the fate of members of the new middle class. Their desire for identity as members of a race is, according to Cabral, not a voluntary step, for it is the only avenue by which this class can escape from the psychological and social discomfort of its situation. When this need is transformed into collective action then it will move beyond the pre-political stage and become part of the prelude to the nationalist struggle. It is the variations in the levels of this response to the quest for identity which account for the instability or unevenness in the attitude of the petty bourgeoisie to the call for national liberation. The situation of urban intellectuals finds expression in the question of identity because only that ambitious quest can encapsulate the complexity of the social needs of this marginalised class.

The petty bourgeoisie in the colonial setting is like any petty bourgeoisie in that it always seeks for the impossible. It wants what it as a class cannot have and the social and material privileges which it employs are paid for by the diminution of its sense of identity. This loss of personal well-being is the subject matter of most of Frantz Fanon's writings, but Cabral, unlike Fanon, discovers in the search for identity the expression of a class interest which is often obscure and sometimes politically destructive. This at least was Cabral's intention.

Cabral's analysis of culture is essentially an account of the situation, experience and aspirations of the petty bourgeoisie. There is no coherent theory presented in either of the important essays, National Liberation and Culture or Identity and Dignity, of the cultural situation of the peasant or the Lumpenproletariat. The few references relating to the peasant are usually confined to practical questions arising directly from the struggle and are not taken up as posing problems of theory. When Cabral does address himself to the issue of peasant culture he produces a flagrant contradiction of which he appears unaware. In consequence it is only in his discussion of the petty bourgeoisie that Cabral's analysis of culture and, to a lesser extent, of class, reaches any heights of theoretical consistency. This failing is a serious one because for each of the classes in turn the discussion of culture is in fact a discussion of political and social consciousness. In this sense the petty bourgeoisie is the only class for which Cabral's analysis is adequate.

Whereas Fanon had written about the peasants and the Lumpenproletariat in a highly idealised way, and always from the perspective of the petty bourgeoisie, Cabral set out quite deliberately to write about the middle class from a perspective located from outside the boundaries of that class. And yet this covert preoccupation with the petty bourgeoisie and his clumsy response to the issue of political consciousness among the peasantry proves that in this he was not entirely successful. It is an irony consistent with the history of African socialism that the reason why Cabral could so easily identify the fears and aspirations of the indigenous middle class was because its fears and aspirations were once his own.

Cabral's writings on the subject of culture were intended to achieve a variety of aims, but he had hoped above all else to establish certain principles about the role of culture within national liberation movements. Attached to this was a second range of issues which concerned the place of culture within the wider historical context of imperialism and decolonisation. These secondary problems devolved in turn into a number of specific questions about the characteristics and potential of the petty bourgeoisie. Consequently from both corners of Cabral's enterprise he was driven in the direction of that marginalised class which is both the most typical and the least characteristic of colonial impact.

Cabral's analysis of the social structure of Guiné showed that culture could play an important role in defining the reaction of each group to colonialism and to the appeal of national liberation movements. This reaction proved that culture is not dependent upon class factors and that it can act as an independent determinant of a class's response to revolutionary action. Consequently Cabral based his theory on the assumption that the national liberation struggle has two foundations. The first is that of class which in turn is decided by the objective relation of each group to the ownership of the means of production. The second is culture itself, which is a complex outgrowth of a number of interdependent elements within the social formation but which finally concerns man's relations with other men and with nature. The interplay of the relative influence of cultural and class factors accounts for different responses to the appeal of nationalist politics. But according to Cabral's theory culture as a function of tribal identity is very much subordinate to that of class in deciding the issue of political allegiance. This at least is the implication in Cabral's account of culture and identity and it explains his dismissive comments on the issue of tribalism.

But Cabral is silent on the question of the relationship between tribalism culture and objective class interests. Unfortunately this leaves unresolved the problem of the possibility of allegiances being formed among members of the same cultural constellation in contradiction of class interests. This was in effect the situation Cabral describes among the Fula. The Fula peasants supported their chiefs' alliance with the Portuguese administration against the class interests which they shared with those other peasant communities which had joined the liberation movement. Cabral's failure to address himself to this question emphasises the shallowness of his work on tribalism. He dismisses the issue of tribalism out of hand for the same reason that he gets into difficulties in discussing the varied responses to cultural resistance between stateless tribes and those with a vertical structure. Cabral was so keen to establish class as the determinant of political behaviour that he drove a cleavage within the borders of his own theory between his account of culture and class. This cleavage was made possible by Cabral's preference, when writing of identity and culture, for employing a parody of a Marxist definition of class which is completely at odds with the definition he uses elsewhere. This established, in a mechanistic way, a separation between class and culture which Cabral had originally sought to avoid. In the end, because of his anxiety to demolish

Culture and personality

the prejudice that Africa is a continent without its own history, Cabral unbalances his theory from within.

Cabral saw very clearly that African societies are subject to the same general laws of evolution as other human communities. Therefore they are open to the same tools of political and economic enquiry. An acceptance of this principle should have ruled out the polarity Cabral finally establishes between classes and tribes as two exclusive modes of social organisation which demand two different types of social analysis. This was not an appropriate conclusion to draw from the principle that the laws governing the development of African civilisations are the same as those found in Europe. In the light of this ambiguity in Cabral's analysis of culture it is difficult to explain why he did not succeed in mythologising the peasant class, or else dismissing it as being unimportant.

It is ironic that Cabral's writings on culture and identity should be so obviously flawed without those flaws surfacing in his theory of class. The fact that these errors can co-exist with his compelling class analysis of Guiné indicates that the question of identity and culture are not critical to his theory in the way that Cabral, and his predecessors, thought them to be. In a practical sense these issues have been superseded in Cabral's work. The narodnikist philosophy is present in Cabral's writings, but only as a residue.

6 THE STATE

Amilcar Cabral's account of the state in colonial and post-colonial Africa is highly innovative, especially when his writings are viewed in terms of the direction which political theory has taken since his death. His analysis on the state and its function within the social structure of colonial Africa give an important insight into the true significance of nationalism and national liberation movements within a wider, if attenuated, historical framework. Eight years after his death Cabral's reflections on the state identify him as the forerunner of most contemporary theorising on post-colonial society.

As with the history of the idea of imperialism, Marxist theories of the state have been dominated by the figure of Lenin. In 'The State and Revolution' Lenin differed from Engels in concentrating exclusively upon the state as an instrument of repression and ignored the maintenance of class domination through other means. Lenin also had nothing of substance to say about the role of the state in the accumulation of capital, a process which was well documented in the writings of many of his contemporaries, including those of Hobson with whose work Lenin was familiar. During the past two decades the revival of interest in the state and its functions has come about through a recognition by Marxists of the importance of state intervention in contemporary capitalist economies. The publication of Ralph Miliband's 'The State in Capitalist Society'[1] was in this sense a landmark because it precipitated a rejection of the Leninist maxims about the state as a repressive apparatus.

Revival of interest in the analysis of the state in the setting of the metropoles has been paralleled by an upsurge of interest in the role of the state in colonial and post-colonial societies. In each instance the reason for this revival has lain in the failure of revolutionary transformations to materialise. In searching for the reason for this failure Marxist theorists have identified the importance of the role played by the state in harmonising class antagonisms in the capitalist nations. The bourgeoisification of the working class Herbert Marcuse perceived in Europe and North America is paralleled in the writings of underdevelopment theorists such as Samir Amin and Hamza Alavi,[2] in their formulations about political and economic stagnation orchestrated by the state in post-colonial societies. This supersession of Lenin's theory of the state has coincided with the supersession, in theory, of the revolutionary capacity of the proletariat. Theorists such as Alavi and Amin have hoped to find in an anatomy of the post-colonial state the hiding place of the class which could lead a revolutionary transformation of Third-World countries from the condition of perpetual stagnation.

The most popular and apparently original direction that Third-World theorists have taken is in the exposition on the concept of the semi-autonomous state. Because of the atypicality of the state in colonial and post-colonial settings, supposedly a consequence of the lopsidedness of colonial social structures and the effects of the imperialist economic relationship, the idea of an unhinged or semi-autonomous state has held great appeal. This idea of course originates in Marx's account of the Bonapartist state, and was re-echoed in Lenin's casual observation that in *certain circumstances* the activities of warring classes may temporarily achieve a balance, thereby allowing the state to assume a degree of independence.[3] Such formulations have become almost obligatory among those writers seeking to explain the oddness or pathological character of post-colonial societies.

In Africa the nationalist generation did not address itself at all to the question of the state, perhaps in part out of a sense of embarrassment. It was the administrative apparatus of the colonial and post-colonial states which allowed the petty bourgeoisie's dream of self-advancement to find expression. Fanon recognised this fact in 1961 but it was many years before the appearance of any detailed studies of the state in post-colonial Africa.

In all of Cabral's political writings, but in particular in those essays dealing with theoretical problems, there is considerable attention given to the role of the state in the transition from colonialism to independence. Most important of all, Cabral attempts to analyse the function of the state within the context of imperialism. Cabral's judgment on the role of the state underwent a major revision between 1964, when he wrote A Brief Analysis, and 1972. In the space of eight years Cabral apparently changed from viewing the state predominantly as a neutral instrument necessary to the functioning of any national polity to seeing it as an essentially repressive instrument devoted to the domination of one class by another. These contrary perceptions correspond to the individual sides of the crude dualism typical of Marxist theory in which the capital state is characterised alternately as a repressive or as an administrative apparatus. In the intermediate writings published between 1964 and 1972 there is no obvious tension in the way in which Cabral views the state, and therefore in a sense these alternate perceptions were reconciled for a time within his theory. One obvious explanation for Cabral's 'change of mind' is found in the experience of the national liberation struggle against the Portuguese which exposed the barbaric face of Portuguese fascism fighting to retain control of its vanishing empire. But a close examination of Cabral's writings shows that this hides a more significant dialogue taking place in Cabral's political theory as a whole. This dialogue has an importance far beyond the immediate questions concerning the functioning of colonial societies, questions which today are of only historical interest.

In A Brief Analysis Cabral begins his discussion of the colonial state with an examination of the social and historical conditions which existed prior to colonisation. With the arrival of the Portuguese the peoples of Guiné were forced to abandon their own history, that is, they were forced to abandon their own class struggle. This class struggle had already seen the partial dissolution of tribalism and had set the foundation for the emergence of a state among the Fula. However, the rudimentary state institutions of the Fula were gradually severed from the wider process of historical development as the Portuguese gained effective control of the country. Portuguese occupation brought with it a new history, a colonial history, in which the class struggle continued but in a different way.

The history of Guiné continued not as a struggle for ascendency among the various indigenous social groups but as a struggle between all the peoples of Guiné in a common front against colonialism. Understood in this way what is distinctive about the colonial situation is that all indigenous classes are the agents of history. Armed with this understanding, Cabral argues that under colonial conditions the class struggle cannot be said to be dominant since it continues only in a muted way.

Because the process of the development of indigenous class forces had been altered or mutated, it was not the class struggle but the state which came to command history. But in this context the state does not represent the interests of any particular class inside the social formation but rather acts on behalf of a class that is physically absent from the national territory. Therefore the problem set by the conflict between national history and colonial history is reflected in the function of the state. In the light of the asymmetrical character of the state the major problem which confronts nationalist movements concerns the identity of the class which at independence can control and manipulate the apparatus of this 'exotic' state. In Portuguese Africa the peasants' only contact with the state was through taxation or forced labour; there was no national bourgeoisie and the working class was embryonic. In Guiné only the petty bourgeoisie understood the working of the state apparatus. It was the only class with sufficient technical skill to utilise the instruments of daily administration.[4]

Cabral goes on to warn that, although the petty bourgeoisie is the only indigenous class capable of operating the institutions of the state, it cannot of its own accord wield state power. Its political limitations are imposed by the nature of state power and by its characteristics as a class. The African petty bourgeoisie cannot be successful as the servant of Portuguese or international capital. In consequence the post-colonial state is semi-autonomous.

In A Brief Analysis Cabral identifies a second quality of the state apart from its role as being the centre of social administration. Cabral argues that the possibility of socialism being established in the post-independence period depends upon the social instruments available to promote this transition, among which he refers specifically to the army and the police.[5] Much will depend upon who controls these institutions and how they are used. Presumably this problem is not to be resolved simply by the identity of the ruling class, since no single class has the capacity to rule effectively on its own and Cabral intimates that in the post-colonial context these instruments will assume a special significance. In a later essay Cabral refers again to the fundamental importance of the state in the process of transition from one mode of production to another,[6] although he makes no mention as to how he believes this will come about.

It is significant that in this essay Cabral should identify the repressive arms of the state with the state *per se* and that he should then break off the discussion at the point at which it holds wider implications. In these early essays Cabral does not in general identify the state with the repressive role which is characteristic of the Leninist conception of state power. Neither does he mention any necessity for the destruction of the state or its instruments as a prerequisite for a socialist revolution. At the same time Cabral does betray some concern that by its very nature the colonial state is designed for purposes quite contrary to those pursued by the nationalist movements. If this is in fact the case then the question of the design or purpose of the state must hold great importance for the theory and practice of national liberation struggles. Unfortunately these suspicions about the malleability of the colonial state are ignored and for a period of six years Cabral put aside the question of the state as an instrument of class domination.

In his account of the ascent of the petty bourgeoisie as heir to the post-colonial state Cabral presents the state as a body devoid of any inherent political purpose. Cabral's state is an instrument which has no function other than those practices, both visible and public, which are prescribed in its institutions. In short, Cabral characterises the state in much the same way as the developmentalists of the early and mid 1960s. Where Cabral differs from such writers as David Apter and Gabriel Almond is in associating the operation of the state with a class rather than with an elite.

Cabral again took up the problem of the state at an informal talk given in New York in October 1972.[7] The content of this talk is important because it brings to light a change in Cabral's assessment of the state which had gradually emerged in his writings in the previous three years. In answer to a question about the possibilities for genuine national liberation Cabral suggested that perhaps it was the nature of the state created after independence which accounted for the failure of African nationalism[8] and that in the case of Guiné the colonial state presented a special problem. Cabral argued that:

We don't accept any institutions of the Portuguese colonialists. We are not interested in the preservation of any of the structures of the colonial state. It is our opinion that it is necessary to totally destroy, to break, to reduce to ashes all aspects of the colonial state in our country, in order to make everything possible for our people.[9]

At this point Cabral identified the colonial state as being entirely synonymous with its repressive apparatus.

Unlike other colonial settings where the imperialist powers had succeeded in creating an elaborate state apparatus the economic backwardness of Portugal meant that the state in Guiné was quite rudimentary in character. This made the destruction of the colonial state a relatively easy task and it also removed the temptation to keep intact much of a state apparatus which would act as a hindrance to national development. Balanced against this advantage, however, was the possible retardation of future development that the absence of a basic administrative grid would mean for Guiné. Cabral argued that some nations have been successful in passing from social and economic conditions of semi-feudalism to socialism because they have possessed a state and a state apparatus which could oversee this transition.[10] The PAIGC had been successful in creating the foundations of an administrative apparatus during the period of armed struggle. This apparatus was fundamental to the achievement of social justice in the liberated areas and to the maintenance of daily life, the supply of goods and the provision of health and education services.

Despite his pride in the achievements of the state structures created by the PAIGC, Cabral did not presume that this embryonic state could in any way guarantee a successful national transformation. The state institutions in the liberated zones were rudimentary, and for as long as the war continued there could be no real possibility of development on a national scale. The problems of managing a national economy and the need to institute major programes for economic and social reconstruction could not be implemented during the war. Those challenges involving the management of an export economy and the development of infrastructure and industry, challenges which would decide the success or failure of the liberation struggle would only arise under the shadow of the post-colonial state.

In this later essay Cabral suggests that because the colonial state operates in contradiction of the interests of all indigenous classes it cannot be understood in the same terms which Marxists have used to characterise the state in European history. These differences hold true for both the colonial and post-colonial periods in which the state retains many of its distinguishing features. But in this formulation Cabral implies that during the post-colonial era the state and the state apparatus have no clear function or purpose as instruments of class domination. Accordingly the principal failure of imperialism can be seen in the type

of state it gives birth to; it creates a state without a function.
Where Cabral writes that under colonial conditions only the petty bourgeoisie can inherit state power, he does so in the belief that only this class possesses the technical facility to operate the institutions of the state. The lack of an economic base authorising its political ascendency is of only secondary importance since, for Cabral at least, the question of the operation of the state refers principally to maintenance and administration. Cabral fails to make a distinction between the state apparatus and state power, thereby exposing an ambiguity in his conception of the relationship between the state and class and class struggle. Cabral always characterises the colonial state as a break on the development of internal class contradictions. The contradiction between the nationalist movement and the imperialist ruling class which has been placed between the colonial peoples and their re-emergence as a people with their own history, is of a secondary order. The class contradictions which precede the setting up of the colonial state and its demise, are the prime forces for change. The national liberation struggle is merely a preparation for class struggle.

Subsequent writers have wrestled with these problems with varying degrees of success. In Issa Shivji's inventive studies of Tanzanian socialism[11] the concept of the semi-autonomous state is used to establish the principle that anyone who occupies the state apparatus thereby controls the state. Thus the idea of ownership of the means of production being the key to political power is replaced with the idea that those who manage the state apparatus are those who in fact rule. Although this type of analysis has often ended in blind pessimism (about the impossibility of change) or misconstrued radicalism (about social transformation), the benefit of works such as those of Alavi, Shivji and the earlier Leys lies in the recognition that it is in the structures of the state itself that is found one of the principal battlefields for class struggles in post-colonial societies. This perception has emerged at a time when First-World theorists have come to the same conclusion about the role of the interventionists' state in Western Europe and North America. In the former the underlying question is that of locating the ruling class, while in the latter the major issue is to identify the non-economic mechanisms governing the re-production of the dominating class.

One of the major benefits of the concept of the semi-autonomous state is that it represents a break away from dependency theory. In most of the dependency literature, as in the two recent volumes by Noam Chomsky on the New Imperialism,[12] the internal social and economic systems of the new states are assumed to be entirely subordinate to the purposes of an external ruling class. At the least the concept of the semi-autonomous state allows for the existence of indigenous class forces which have some capacity to act independently.

These debates about the state in First- and Third-World environments have taken place long after Cabral's essays on the subject were first written. Althusser's essay, Ideology and Ideological State Apparatus, was first published in early 1969 and there is no evidence that Cabral was influenced by this or any other work. This is not to claim that Cabral was unaware of contemporary Marxist or neo-Marxist scholarship. But the lines of development of Cabral's theory can more easily be identified as arising from his immediate experience within the national liberation struggle in Guiné than by reference to the contemporary European political theory.

The limitations of much recent literature on the autonomous or overdeveloped state can be linked with the vulgarity of Lenin's pioneering work. There is no profit in the argument that any capitalist state is a perfect instrument or mirror for the interests of a ruling class since this ignores the ideological function of the state and the equally complex question of the state as a locus for production and exchange. Much of the reason for the Marxist failure to see the state in these terms lies with Lenin. Lenin's work also encouraged later Marxists to suppose certain states to be unusual simply because he assumed the normal function of the state to be so narrow.

In the writings of Cabral, as in Fanon's 'The Wretched of the Earth', the colonial, as distinct from the post-colonial, state is depicted as a repressive apparatus displaying most of the characteristics laid out in Lenin's original work. But in the theories of both Cabral and Fanon this repressive face is seen as arising because of the atypicality of the colonial situation. Only in the colonies is the ideological role of the state underdeveloped. This line of argument was first suggested by Fanon in his thesis that in colonial conditions 'the infra-structure is the super-structure.' By this Fanon meant that in colonial Africa the ruling class made no attempt to cushion the reality of class domination. Colonial racism is a celebration of the inevitability of class rule rather than a justification for the power and material benefits enjoyed by the few.

In Cabral's work the question of the revolutionary nature of the nationalist movements is resolved, in part, into a secondary question concerning the character of the colonial and post-colonial state. In his earliest exposition on the theory of revolutionary nationalism (The Weapon of Theory) Cabral supports, with regret, the leading role of the petty bourgeoisie because he believes it to be the only class capable of operating the state apparatus. In the long term the petty bourgeoisie could create the conditions for the growth of an indigenous working class and thereby, against its own conscious interests, bring about a socialist revolution. But paradoxically Cabral also believes that the possibilities for just such a transformation are lessened by the character of the post-colonial state and its domination by petty-bourgeois elements.

In order to resolve this paradox Cabral employs the concept of an aborted or delayed history, thereby shifting backwards in time the idea of social pathology which is so important in Fanon's account of the national bourgeoisie. National liberation therefore promises the return to a pattern of social and economic evolution which had been waylaid by colonialism. In this sense even neo-colonialism is progressive. But Cabral's optimism is short-lived.

In his later writings Cabral tends to play down the threat posed by a petty-bourgeois-dominated state and only in the essay of 1970, National Liberation and Culture, is there any reference to the need to change the mentality of the petty bourgeoisie as a precondition to independence. Significantly on this occasion, Cabral refers to the psycho-social and psycho-cultural effects of colonialism upon this class, thereby substituting the question of personality in preference to that of political belief. This substitution tells us a great deal about the kinds of problems Cabral experienced in theorising about the state and state power.

Fanon had lain the blame for the failings of the African revolution squarely on the shoulders of the petty bourgeoisie. He believed that he had discovered the flaw in that class's peculiar and voluntary subordination to an essentially 'white way of seeing the world'. In so doing Fanon, in characteristic fashion, relocated the question of the uses of the 'state ideological apparatus' from the public to the private domains, from the arena of social theory to that of psychopathology. Ironically this is exactly the kind of perception which lies at the bottom of Cabral's discussion of the petty bourgeoisie in Identity and Dignity. Consequently Cabral's exposition on the state and his account of the petty bourgeoisie sit rather uncomfortably side by side. The threads which could join together these dimensions in his work are present, but because of the frailty of his account of ideology and class consciousness they remain separate.

7 THE FORCES OF PRODUCTION

Among European researchers the quest for a Marxist anthropology has been closely associated with the need to re-establish Marxism as a universal science. In failing to account for the enormous variety of human communities, many of which until quite recently were known as primitive, Marxism has been vulnerable to the criticism that it is Euro-centric in conception. The revolutions in the former colonial territories have heightened the importance of the question as to how pre-capitalist social formations can be accommodated within a Marxist historiography. It has also led in turn to an admission that anthropology has for some time posed questions to which Marxism could give no satisfactory reply. For Marxists the most important of these problems concerns the wide variety of social organisations which exist within a single, equivalent level of productive forces. The existence of this human diversity has exposed a basic weakness in traditional Marxist views on class analysis and the account they render of the interaction between the economic base and political institutions. Unfortunately for Marxist scholars Marx's and Engels speculations on primitive societies, as distinct from peasant societies, are often speculative and most inconclusive. This in part explains the frailty of Marxist theory.

Although towards the end of his life Marx became more interested in the different modes of pre-capitalist society and the various factors influencing the transition out of communalist forms, these considerations were always of secondary importance. Unlike many of his contemporaries, Marx never found primitive societies of interest in themselves. The reason Marx gives in explanation for the attractiveness of primitive society to nineteenth-century European intellectuals is both obvious and revealing. In 'The German Ideology' he writes that in the era of capitalism the world of primitives holds special appeal, for in a curious way it presents the vision of a superior life. However, he also believed that whatever the attraction of this earlier world, in reality it only offered a narrow satisfaction in comparison with the vast range of material and cultural benefits available under capitalism. Marx's successors have in fidelity to this prejudice remained faithful disciples.

The question as to how feudal and capitalist social formations emerge from simple communities has remained central to all subsequent theorising of pre-capitalist economic systems. Marxist anthropologists in particular have sought to uncover the points at which simple distribution of the product becomes transformed into a more complex system, thereby giving birth to class society.[1] Recent research by French anthropologists such as Meillassoux and Terray[2] has been particularly important in exploring the conditions under which simple distribution is transformed into more complex patterns.

In his research on the Mbuti of the Ituri Forest Meillassoux explores the transition between simple hunting bands and agricultural societies. The Mbuti appear quite deliberately to have chosen to remain hunters and gatherers despite their access to agricultural activities and the example of farming peoples living within their territory. Meillassoux argues that the presence of various modes of production within a single social formation may lead to the dominance of certain critical traits which prevent the positive transformation of the social whole. Such factors or traits may be exogenous or endogenous. The experience of the Mbuti, who by evading change achieved stagnation rather than preservation of their way of life, leads Meillassoux to conclude that there is no necessity for hunting bands to evolve into agricultural communities.

The results of Emmanuel Terray's research among the Guro, although formally in opposition to Meillassoux's findings, are in various respects complementary to the earlier work. Terray set out to define the elements in the dominant mode of production in a lineage-based society. Terray finally arrives at the conclusion that in such societies there are as many modes of production as there are forms of co-operation and in the case of the Guro he identifies two distinct modes. Terray reaches this conclusion because of the principle he adopts as necessary to any Marxist account of a social formation, namely, the multiplicity of the constituent modes of production. He also does this in order to account for the variations which exist between individual segmentary societies at the level of ideological, judicial and political organisation. However, this opens up a specific problem within Terray's analysis of the Guro since he identifies two distinct modes of production which share a single set of relations among producers. That is, Terray distinguishes between modes of production on the basis of a purely technical division of simple and complex distribution.

In their quest for a Marxist anthropology both Meillassoux and Terray manage to invert the Marxist formula on the relationship between material capacity, social relations and historical change. Meillassoux does this by claiming that the productive forces are the predominant element in the structure of the social formation, over and above relations among producers. Terray follows the same path through employing the assumption that a mode of production can be identified solely by reference to the forces of production regardless of the social relations between classes. Both anthropologists reduce the economic sphere to the dominance of technique. As we shall see, the parallel with the work of Cabral is formally quite striking. Meillassoux and Terray fall into the trap of abandoning Marxism in the process of seeking to apply a rigorous Marxist analysis to lineage-based societies. Cabral, on the contrary, endorses the productive forces thesis in the hope of gaining some respite from the pull of orthodox Marxism which he felt to be such a dead weight on the back of revolutionary theory in Africa. In Cabral's case the problem of transition was important because he believed it held the key to the question of Africa's lost history and the history that was yet to come.

The second major question which has preoccupied Marxist theory concerns the possibility that feudalist elements existed within traditional African societies. Supposedly, if the existence of such elements or traits could be established there would be overwhelming evidence that Africa's backwardness was accidental rather than inevitable. If this were the case, then in the period prior to the advent of imperialism such societies would have been in the process of establishing their own endogenous feudalist and capitalist formations. Walter Rodney's pioneering work on African underdevelopment[3] was motivated by an intention to discover evidence of just such a line of evolution. Samir Amin[4] has followed Rodney's lead and has coined the term the 'tributary mode of production' which, he argues, has the feudalist phase as one of a number of sub-types. Under this tributary schema, of which Amin finds numerous examples in pre-colonial Africa, the economic surplus was extracted through the imposition of tributes. Not only is the feudal mode a sub-type of a primary set but it is the least sophisticated or most primitive of the tributary schema. More recently the study of rural Tanzania by Hayden[5] is directed to answering the same question as to why African states have not developed. Hayden's analysis is largely confined to the post-colonial era but if one forgets the quest for attaching moral blame to European imperialism which Rodney and Amin are so anxious to establish, the search for a mechanism of non-sequential development places his work firmly in their company.

Whatever the merits of these varied and often inventive attempts to locate the mechanisms for change or for retarded development the preoccupation with feudalism bequeathed by Marx has not been very useful. The principal weakness in theories such as Rodney's and Amin's lies in the imprecision with which they employ the concept of feudalism. Perry Anderson[6] has given due warning that the concept of the feudal mode of production requires the presence of a variety of characteristics in terms of legal and property relations, and also in reference to the social division of labour, characteristics which have only ever existed in Europe and Japan. If the term is not applied with such rigour then there are numerous and totally dissimilar social formations ranging from the highly sophisticated to the quite rudimentary which may be termed feudal. Despite this warning there have been numerous studies addressed to discovering feudal modes of production in pre-colonial Africa.

Questions dealing with the grand design of historical change have always been popular with African political leaders, and Cabral was faithful to that tradition on at least two occasions. In his most important essay, The Weapon of Theory, Cabral set out to establish two basic propositions: firstly, he sought to prove that Africa has a history other than a colonial history, and secondly, that the national liberation movements are not in themselves revolutionary. These propositions represent particular facets of a question which intrigued Cabral for much of his intellectual career.

In his address given at the Tricontinental Conference at Havana in January 1966[7] Cabral argued that human history may be divided into three specific phases. The first period in human development corresponds to a low level of productive forces in which man's mastery over nature is quite tenuous. Private property does not exist and neither do classes. The social structure is horizontal. In the second phase there is a rise in the level of the productive forces which corresponds to the emergence of private property and the development of distinct social classes. During this phase social and economic change is achieved primarily through the means of class struggle. The social structure is characteristically vertical. In the third and final phase the level of the productive forces is highly advanced, private property is eliminated, social classes vanish and once again the social structure returns to a horizontal formation.[8]

In the language of political economy the first stage corresponds to the practice of communal agriculture and cattle-raising in which there is no state; the second corresponds to a wide range of social formations which Cabral admits to including feudal and industrial bourgeois societies. The final form refers solely to socialist or communist societies in which the means of production are essentially industrial and the state tends progressively to wither away. The major point of distinction between the first and the third phases lies in the higher level of the productive forces in the latter.

Having presented this schema of the three historical epochs, Cabral goes on to conclude that in any society the level of the development of the productive forces and the system of ownership of those forces defines the mode of production. The mode of production and the contradictions which arise within it and are manifested through the class struggle are the principal factors defining the history of any group. Within each particular mode it is the level of the productive forces that is the true and driving force of history. For every society the level of the productive forces indicates the stage of development.

Presumably these three stages are dialectically linked and once a certain level of transformation of the productive forces is reached the society will advance forward into the next stage. Given the potential for the development of the productive forces, which is in turn conditional upon the nature of the state structure, a society can advance rapidly. Moreover, the chronology of the three stages is not immutable.

The conclusions Cabral draws from his typology are far more interesting than is the delineation of the three phases themselves. There is history and historical change before the rise of classes and after their disappearance. Therefore the motive force of history is not, as Marxists suppose, class struggle, but the mode of production in which the force of production is the dominant term. It is here that the secret of change and social transformation lies. Only within a limited and quite specific historical phase is class struggle the determining element within the mode of production. Societies in which there are no classes and no state are dynamic entities capable of self-transformation. Cabral was quite consistent in adhering to this productive forces thesis, and later in the same essay he even differentiates between the colonial and neo-colonial situations on the basis of variations in the levels of the productive forces. He claims that the main point of difference between the colonial and post-colonial societies is found in the greater technical capacity of the latter rather than in variations in the composition of classes or class alliances.

Cabral's belief in the dominance of the productive forces as the wheel of history was designed specifically to refute the Marxist assumption that societies in which there is no state and no classes are retarded and lack a history of their own. But in doing this Cabral supposes that such diverse societies as the slave-owning states of ancient Egypt, the civilisations of classical antiquity, European feudalism and North American capitalism belong within a single historical phase. Unfortunately Cabral's schema also implies that if societies can best be identified according to the level of their productive forces, that is according to the level of their technical mastery over nature, then the peoples of Guiné, including the stateless Balanta, rank rather low in the human family.

Five years later in the essay National Liberation and Culture, presented originally as a speech on 20 February 1970, Cabral returned to the question of modes of production and productive forces. In this essay Cabral argued that in any society the level of the development of the productive forces and the system of the social utilisation of those forces (the pattern of ownership) determine the mode of production. The mode of production is the principal (determining) factor in the history of any group. Within each mode it is the level of the productive forces that is the true and permanent driving force of history. Because imperialism is founded upon the usurpation of the development of the productive forces, Cabral can define imperialism as the negation of the indigenous historical process.

For each society, as for each social group, the level of development of the productive forces indicates the stage of development of that society or group in relation to nature. It defines the society's capacity to act or react consciously in response to necessity, which in turn indicates the objective and subjective quality of relations among men. The level of the productive forces is the key to human history both as a causal agent and as a measure of human achievement.

The major difference between the arguments presented in The Weapon of Theory (1966) and National Liberation and Culture (1970) is Cabral's changed attitude to the role of class struggle. In the later essay Cabral has abandoned completely the role of class struggle as the motive force of history, as he calls dialectical materialism. This is a marked change from the earlier essay in which he conceded that class struggle is pre-eminent, if only for a specific range of historical experience. In the later essay Cabral draws perilously close to that strain in African socialism in which class theory is seen as being largely irrelevant to African history. The difference between Cabral and Nkrumah or Nyerere is that in Cabral's work this prejudice is expressed on a more theoretical plane by being couched in terms of productive forces and modes of production. Yet in each instance class struggle and class contradictions are seen to be of little importance in the movement of men and things. In Cabral's work this development is indeed curious since in the interim between writing The Weapon of Theory and National Liberation and Culture he had directed and experienced five years of an anti-colonial war, a war which in his practical writings he viewed exclusively in terms of class struggle.

It is very easy to attack Cabral's productive forces thesis simply because of the clumsiness of the formulation. We know that the issue of productive forces and modes of production was raised by Cabral because of his intellectual involvement with Marxist theory and in particular because of his agronomic practice. It was also raised for a less obvious reason, namely his subliminal involvement with negritude. In this sense the formulation on productive forces offered Cabral a solution to a problem of which he was not entirely aware.

Cabral was not concerned in any academic sense with typologies of modes of production or with sequences of pre-capitalist economic formations. He was concerned with the impact of imperialism upon pre-capitalist societies and the changes that such an impact brought. It was for this reason that he became involved with questions of higher theory including the place of the various factors influential in historical development. In order to uncover why Cabral should at several points of his political life refer to such problems, and what importance this has within his general theory, it is necessary to explore three particular questions: why did Cabral resort to his productive forces thesis apart from the obvious reason, that is, to attack Marxism; is the productive forces thesis connected in any way with Cabral's refusal to adopt the perspective of underdevelopment theory in his approach to the neo-colonial era; and finally, how does the productive forces thesis fit in with Cabral's class theory and his theory of imperialism as an historical force?

Even without reading Cabral's agronomic writings, it is obvious that he recognised the presence of a variety of levels among the forces of production in Guiné. These variations were present within the agricultural sector where indigenous patterns of cultivation existed side by side with mixed cash and subsistence cropping and even a few commercial holdings. The great change the Portuguese brought to agriculture was not in the techniques used in cultivation, for these remained largely static, but in the social relations surrounding production.

In Guiné the whole subject of productive forces was diffused because of the dominance in the final instance of imperialist economic relations. According to Cabral's own analysis imperialism in the colony operated through the Portuguese government which acted as an intermediary for a select few commercial monopolies. This gives the first condition which limits the operation of the productive forces thesis which Cabral outlines in The Weapon of Theory. The second is presented in Cabral's account of national liberation and culture. Although the productive forces are presumed to be the dominant term within any specific mode of production, the productive forces do not define culture. Cabral is careful to explain that the positive or negative influences of a national or local culture are not synchronised with the level of the productive forces, and that one cannot be deduced from the other. The relationship between the level of material production and the cultural production characteristic of a people is extremely complex and cannot be reduced to any single formula. However, this formulation appears to run counter to Cabral's repeated claims that it is the level of the productive forces which defines the social formation. This suggests that Cabral had finally identified a series of contradictions or lapses between different aspects of the national culture and the aggregate of material production in the community. Alternatively, it could suggest the presence of a contradiction between Cabral's own work on productive forces and the account of class and class struggle which runs throughout his work.

Cabral's productive forces thesis does not work in the way in which Cabral hoped it would. In The Weapon of Theory he argues that the productive forces are only dominant where social classes have yet to evolve, but at other points he places the influence of productive forces above that of class factors. Certainly the class struggle in Guiné was complicated by the embryonic level of the social structure as a whole and by the presence of a wide diversity of cultures. In places adherence to local culture reinforced class alliances among the peasantry in favour of the PAIGC, while at others it loosened or even negated class solidarity. It is apparent that for Cabral the problems posed by this complex and diffuse social formation were easier to resolve in practice than in terms of his political theory.

It is obvious from Cabral's productive forces thesis that he views every increment to the level of technology or to the productive forces in general as progressive and liberative. This is in complete contradiction of underdevelopment theory in which high but uneven levels of technology are seen as being tied overall to a degenerative pattern of economic and social change.

The forces of production 107

In various ways the hybrid social formations taken as characteristic of underdevelopment represent a reversal to an earlier and more archaic form of capitalist exploitation. Although the possibility of just such a pattern of pathological growth is suggested in Cabral's agronomic writings, he treats as anathema any idea of regression at a higher level of production. Like Marx, but unlike so many contemporary neo-Marxists, Cabral views technology and liberation as being inexorably linked. Since 1945 this attitude has been progressively abandoned in neo-Marxist theories because of a growing concern with the inherent destructiveness of technology. Although far removed from Marxism, the work of Ivan Illich has served to distil a fear which first found expression on the left among Marxist meta-psychologists such as Reich, Fromm and Marcuse. While the original suspicions of technological development arose in the realms of culture and personality, Illich shifted the emphasis from the realm of psychic malaise to a critique of the instruments of production in a manner which has profound implications for Marxist theory.

Cabral's conviction that imperialism has a progressive influence in the colonial countries grew in parallel with his thesis on the dominance of productive forces in the social process. Therefore in formal terms at least Cabral adopts a mechanistic stance in which the growing sophistication of the means by which man transforms nature for his own ends is seen of necessity to forward the cause of man's liberation. But, in pursuing this line of argument which led away from both underdevelopment theory and from neo-Marxism, he encountered a new range of problems.

In any discussion which employs the terms productive forces and mode of production it is necessary to distinguish between the extent to which the forces of production themselves encourage or institute social change and the degree to which the productive forces are constrained or stimulated by the social relations of ownership and use. The productive forces alone cannot define or determine the level of production. In the case of communalist societies any surplus can easily be consumed in potlatches without leading to a further social division of labour. In such societies it is the absence of a social division of labour which is itself the major impediment to increased output. Cabral proposes to invert this relationship. He argues in effect that an increase in the level of the productive forces arises autonomously from within the society and it is this which moulds the relations of production. Therefore social structure or class structure is a function of the level of the productive forces. Presumably every society which shares a common level of technology displays the same type of social structure. Of course this line of argument is hopelessly muddled as any reading of Cabral's own account of the social structure of Guiné readily shows.

It makes no sense if one is using the terminology of modes of production and forces of production to separate these categories one from the other in the way in which Cabral does. The productive forces can only be defined in the final instance by their articulation within a particular mode of production, that is, in concert with a specific set of relations of production. The key to this Marxist formulation is not the mode of appropriation of nature but rather the social division of labour and the way in which the surplus is apportioned. All this of course takes place within the context of a specific set of productive forces. By persevering with his eccentric interpretation of the 'motor force of history' Cabral ends by embracing a line of argument which is completely at odds with the rest of his analysis. In this sense the productive forces thesis is an anomaly. By employing this model of change Cabral succeeded in achieving what he set out to do but for reasons other than those he supposed.

Prior to the creative work of French anthropologists during the later 1960s the categories of successive modes of production had really proved an excuse to render much of Marx's work useless. For more than two generations Marxists clung to a few peripheral passages in 'The German Ideology' in the hope of discovering a secret which did not exist. It is now clear that in Marx's theory there are no definitive categories of modes of production exposing an inexorable advance of history. For far too long the entire debate about productive modes led into a *cul de sac*. In Cabral's work the typology of modes of production is revived in response to the previous neglect of Africa's history. He also employs this concept to account for the gains made by African and Asian peoples during the era of decolonisation. In both instances the mode of production thesis is tied to the problem of transition and to two specific questions that this in turn raises: why was it that the communalist societies of Africa did not evolve autonomously toward a capitalist social formation, and how is it now possible to invent a socialist society? In theory the dividing line between these two problems is marked by various theories of imperialism.

It was not until the early 1970s that studies devoted to exploration of *the concept* of the mode of production began to proliferate. This new work promised to reconcile the two branches to the theory of imperialism, as circulation and as production, and thereby bring together an analysis of the lower levels of the imperialist relationship (within the productive process) with the higher schemas concerning distribution on a world scale. Within the confines of his own work Cabral was not able to achieve this accommodation. This is particularly obvious in Cabral's class analysis which does not mesh at all with his higher level discussions of imperialism. However, at the lower level of material production Cabral's productive forces thesis does agree with the work of contemporary anthropology even though it is highly unlikely that Cabral would have read the work of Meillassoux or Terray. It is really a matter of coincidence that Meillassoux and Terray, like Cabral, adopt a technocratic interpretation of the mechanism of change in the communalist mode of production. But the purposes of Cabral's theory and those of the modern anthropologists were quite opposite. Meillassoux, Terray and

Godelier were all keen to prove that Marxism applies to lineage-based societies, that is, to pre-class societies. Cabral, on the other hand, was anxious to show that Marxism does not apply in such contexts.

Cabral arrived at his productive forces thesis subliminally or even accidentally. It does not fit in directly with his general theory of imperialism nor with his analysis of the class struggle in Africa. If it did then it would satisfy a number of questions which Cabral's theory as it stands cannot answer. The reason for this gap is in part due to the fact that Cabral's writings pose a number of problems concerning historical change, the nature of the imperialist relationship and the possibilities for post-colonial development which fall beyond the scope of Cabral's own work.

8 IMPERIALISM

FIRST- AND THIRD-WORLD THEORIES OF IMPERIALISM

The theory of imperialism is the one area of Marxist scholarship which has been truly influential among non-Marxists. So successful has this enterprise been that today, more than sixty years after the publication of Lenin's syncretic work, it is possible to identify numerous theories of imperialism, and to distinguish between those theories which may be deemed to belong to First- and Third-World schools.

It is now part of conventional wisdom that neither Marx nor Engels had very much of significance to say about the backward countries of Asia and Africa. Nor did they pay attention to the question as to whether these regions could avoid the capitalist stage in the process of their development. Although there are a number of select references in Marx's work, which admit the possibility that a people may skip particular historical phases, there is no convincing discussion in Marx or Engels of what have proved to be the two principal forces in the developing countries, that is, the role of the peasantry and the impact of nationalism. Such silences have been important in stimulating a wide range of works by Third-World theorists on the subject of peasant revolutions and the influence of national self-determination as a world historical force.

Despite controversy on the left as to what the theory of imperialism should be about, there are two elements that are common to most theories: the first is that capitalist development in Europe and its world-wide expansion has created a single world economy. That process, although held to be incomplete, is assumed to carry strategic implications for the proletarian revolution in Europe. The second element is that, within this world economy, convulsions in the non-western sector could help to provoke the conditions for a revolutionary situation in Europe. This possibility, which is usually associated with Lenin, was first intimated in the writings of Marx. The question as to the relative balance between the European and the non-European political systems in the global revolutionary process has become one of the principal grounds for the divergence between First- and Third-World theories of imperialism.

Marxists have vacillated in their use of the term imperialism. It has been used to describe the capitalist system as a whole and has even on occasions been employed as a synonym for capitalism; it has been used as a device to define the relations between the advanced and economically backward countries; and most recently it has become a label for the mechanism associated with the creation of underdevelopment. These three usages have not fallen into any specific chronological order and it is not uncommon to discover all three present in an individual work on international political economy, where the usages have been helpful in deciding the point at which classical Marxism and contemporary theories of underdevelopment have parted ways.

Marxist theories of imperialism have for over thirty years suffered from a separation between class analysis and the analysis of national units. The effect of this can be seen in the popular interpretations of Lenin's essay. Lenin's 'Imperialism' was conceived as a study in the class theory of later capitalism for, although it contains little overt reference to class structure and to the role of the bourgeoisie, Lenin's principal concern throughout the work is with class conflict. Unfortunately subsequent readers and, in particular, Marxist admirers of 'Imperialism' have tended to see nothing in the work but a line of argument which Lenin himself would have ridiculed as economistic. Lenin did not equate imperialism exclusively with colonialism for he was only too aware that the expansion of imperialist forces in the final decade of the nineteenth century followed, and did not precede, colonial partition. Nor did Lenin believe that the establishment of agreed colonial boundaries would mean the end to conflict between the major powers. In his view there was no possibility of collusion among the imperialist states.

Today the term imperialism is used to refer most commonly to the capitalist system as a whole and to the process of dominance of the advanced countries within that system. Consequently, there has been a slackening of interest in the relations among the advanced capitalist states and a disavowal of the importance of class relations within the dependent countries. This development within Marxist scholarship came about in part as a result of the dominance of particular elements within the theory of imperialism itself.

The classic theories of imperialism raised one important question which remained largely unanswered; was it possible for capitalism to lead to the development of a fully independent industrial development in the colonial or post-colonial environment? Lenin had believed that the export of capital would greatly accelerate the growth and spread of capitalism in the colonial territories, even if that export subsequently retarded the same process in the domestic economies. Like Marx, he assumed that it was possible that capitalism would develop to the point of growing most quickly in the colonies. This assumption can be found also in the writings of the other classic theorists such as Kautsky, Luxemburg, and Nicholai Bukharin. The work of each of these theorists suggested that, by spreading capitalist relations of production and the material accomplishments of European civilisation to the colonies, imperialism was playing a progressive role. There has been general agreement among Third-

World socialists for some time that capitalism has played anything but a revolutionary role in the countries of exploitation, and it is only recently that the question has been revived as worthy of serious discussion.

After 1945 African intellectuals following in the footsteps of Asian nationalists such as Ho Chi Minh suddenly felt the need to make a new beginning in assessing the colonial relationship.[1] Initially this meant coming to terms with the subjectivity of the colonial experience, but it soon came to imply a complete revisioning of the understanding of imperialism itself. These innovations came about through the workings of factors endogenous to the colonial world and they cannot really be deduced from the contemporary failings of Soviet or European Marxism. The questions which so troubled Césaire and Ho Chi Minh could not have occurred to individuals standing geographically on the opposite side of the imperialist relationship.

Third-World theorists in general and African theorists in particular have identified imperialism with the immediate and visible effects of colonial occupation and the terms colonialism and imperialism soon came to be entirely interchangeable. With the end of the colonial era in Africa in the 1960s, the need arose for a category to describe what its users always insisted was the unchanged relationship between the former colonial powers and the new states. In the writings of two of the most influential Third-World theorists, Aimé Césaire and Frantz Fanon, there is no distinction made, in effect, between colonial and post- or neo-colonial environments, even though their work is associated with the critique of neo-colonial domination.

In his 'Discourse on Colonialism',[2] first published in 1950, Césaire drew together the principal elements which were later to become characteristic of Third-World theories of imperialism. Césaire defined colonialism in terms which were in deliberate contradiction of European accounts of the colonial experience; he explains that colonialism is nothing other than 'appetite and force'.[3] It acts as a poison which trickles back into the society of those who gain benefits from its practice. In essence, colonialism is fascism exported aboard and in it is found the same reliance upon racism and violence and the same motivation of squalid greed that characterised Nazism.

Césaire, like Fanon after him, was angered by what he perceived as the massive psychological damage done to individuals by European colonialism and he soon arrived at the conviction that colonialism could only be understood by reference to the subjective experience that it entailed. An adequate theory of imperialism had, before all else, to be empathetic through option of the cause of the oppressed and through an understanding of the real suffering of people's colonialism rendered racially inferior. Césaire believed that a European could never achieve the kind of imaginative understanding that this task required.

The second element in Césaire's definition is that European society is essentially bankrupt because civilisation in Europe has wandered into a blind alley. All of bourgeois society is doomed and its claims to moral and spiritual superiority over the people it dominates are a sham and a fraud. The spiritual decay of Europe is final proof that there is no positive connection between a people's material capacity and dominance over nature and the quality of its civilisation. In fact, Césaire assumes that the relationship is inverse. Although he rightly perceived that the power of the nations of Europe was declining, Césaire feared that Europe would be replaced by America which could prove to be even more destructive than its predecessor.

The third element in Césaire's theory contains an idealisation of pre-colonial societies. Césaire views this world as virtuous because it is both pre-capitalist in time and anti-capitalist in its ethos. According to Césaire, prior to the intervention of the European powers in Africa, pre-colonial societies had already embarked on achieving an autonomous line of development which eventually could have seen the invention of a civilisation as powerful as that which came into existence in Europe. However, this endogenous reflex to development was smashed by colonial conquest.

In summary, Césaire's work was intended to attack the central myths which accompanied colonial rule: the myth of Europe's civilising mission, the myth of Africa's incurable cultural and material backwardness, and the myth that without European intervention the colonial countries could never have achieved anything of significance. Above all else, Césaire's work carries a number of implications about the nature of the colonial relationships, which now can be seen to be typical of African and Caribbean visions of European domination of the Third World. Like his successors, such as Nkrumah,[4] Césaire invariably employed the term colonialism in preference to imperialism, thereby stressing the physical and cultural aspects of the relationship.

The preoccupation among Third World nationalists with the perceived de-humanising effect of colonialism called forth a new social psychology, thereby stunting research into the class analysis of the colonial world. The preoccupation with the psychological impact of colonialism encouraged the belief that the most important social contradiction in the colonial context lay between the interests of the metropoles and those of the colonised or neo-colonised societies as a whole. This contradiction was usually presumed to overshadow the play of all internal factors within each individual society, including those contradictions arising specifically from class relations. In African theories of imperialism the primacy of the contradiction between the First and Third Worlds was on occasions conceived in terms of racial characteristics which seemed to counterpose two separate ontologies. Most importantly this contradiction could not be deduced from the class antagonism between bourgeoisie and proletariat. Consequently, the Marxist belief in the necessary solidarity between the working class of the European states and the colonial peoples was jettisoned. In aggregate, these individual modifications to the theory of imperialism moved towards the conclusion that in the struggle for national independence the colonial peoples could experience the joy of regaining the historical initiative from all sections of European society, and of supplanting one type of man with another.

The various themes and elements in Césaire's 'Discourse on Colonialism' were woven together in different ways by different theorists so that at times one thread would predominate and then another. The most important effect or legacy established by these theories is that all too often they replaced a crude Marxist economism with an equally crude cultural determinism.

Since Cabral's death developments in the fields of anthropology and political theory have opened up new ground in the literature on imperialism which were largely foreshadowed in Cabral's own work.

Whereas previous theories of imperialism had been largely or even exclusively addressed to the question of distribution, the new anthropology has laid the foundation for a comprehensive analysis of production. Marx wrote little of substance on the subject of the Asiatic mode of production of which African societies were for so long presumed to be examples. The absence of a centralised state apparatus discouraged any great interest in societies which appeared to be rather modest in their design and achievements. These societies simply did not seem to warrant the kind of sophisticated analysis that the category of the mode of production implies in terms of ideological systems and class and economic structures. This lack of interest had as much to do with the limited tools of analysis then available as with blind prejudice.

The reason for the great popularity of theories focusing upon modes of production is that the associated concepts have allowed Marxists to do research in territory which previously lay beyond their reach. Marxists were now able to break away from the idea of rigid and successive sets of modes of production which were invariably unhelpful as well as being Euro-centric in temper.

In the context of post-colonial Africa this frantic activity in identifying the dominant forces of production has led, at each successive turn, to the question of the relationship between African and European states. Anthropology has explored this question at the level of culture and more recently production; underdevelopment theory has followed the trail at the level of the political economy of commodity exchange; and the national liberation movements have hoped to attack imperialism in the most mundane terms at the level of political practice.

These then are the sets of environments in which Cabral's writings on imperialism were framed. At the highest level lie the problems which have been tackled by grand theories of imperialism and at the lowest lie the problems of production and class creation with which anthropologists have busied themselves. These two points of reference present the two poles within Cabral's own theory. In tackling the question of class struggle in Guiné, it was likely that Cabral would, through preoccupation with immediate events, have left the question of imperialism as a blur on the edge of his theory. Alternatively, if he had focused his attention upon the imperialist relationship (with Portugal as the intermediary for the imperialist states), then the theory of class conflict would have become abstract and emaciated. This later tendency is all too obvious in the writings of earlier African and Third-World nationalists such as Fanon, Nkrumah, and Touré. The fact that Cabral managed to erect a theory of imperialism which embodies an attempt to reconcile these two main lines of drift is an indication of the extent of his achievements.

CABRAL'S THEORY OF IMPERIALISM

Within Cabral's writing the re-thinking of the theory of imperialism begins with the question as to the status of pre-colonial history. The period, prior to colonial expansion, had for so long been neglected or trivialised or simply dismissed as insignificant, because the colonial societies so little resembled the societies from which the Europeans had come. Cabral deliberately chose to approach the analysis of the pre-colonial societies, not as examples of lineage-based or tribal communities, which suggested an earlier phase of human history, but rather to use the concepts and vocabulary of class formation and class contradictions. He believed that these tensions existed in numerous African societies before the final onslaught of colonial conquest, but that the fact had been obscured by the unfamiliarity to western eyes which class formation took in such instances. These tensions were also well hidden behind the edifice of the colonial state.

The existence of classes and class contradictions, however misshapen, demands of the observer two things. Firstly, it means that African societies must be treated in the same general way and accorded the same status as European social formations. This ends at one blow the subordination in reference to political theory which colonial societies had suffered in tandem with their subordination in terms of political liberties. The second implication runs directly counter to the first and it is that colonial and postcolonial societies must not be treated as equivalents of European societies because each lies at the opposite end of the imperialist relationship. In its most obvious expression this can be seen in the alternate characteristics of the state and in the composition of the social class structure in the two settings.

In the case of Guiné the effect of imperialism was evident in the paucity of economic development in which all but the most rudimentary industries were absent. Cabral treats this particular set of characteristics arising from imperialism as the minor term in the new theory. At a second and more important level, the new theory would have to take account of the individual history of each separate colonial territory prior to the colonial conquest

which, in the case of Guiné, can be dated as late as the 1930s.
It is in the understanding of this history, rather than the
ephemeral history of the colonial period, that the real story
of the country's future must be seen to lie. The phase of the
colonial or imperialist period, terms which Cabral tends to use
interchangeably, belongs rightfully to the history of the colonising powers.

Although Cabral's desire to take indigenous history into
account in this way may now seem trivial and obvious, it was at
the time a radical step. Before Cabral's important essays on the
periodisation of colonial history, the romanticisation of precolonial Africa in most nationalist literature had made indigenous
history irrelevant to contemporary political analysis.

In Cabral's writings there are a large number of references to
the subject of imperialism. In describing Cabral's position there
are three specific works which best represent his overall view.
The first is found in the essay, The Death Pangs of Imperialism,
which was originally published in July 1961. The second comes
in the important article The Weapon of Theory, written in 1965,
and the last is presented in the article Is Portugal Imperialist?[5]
which is taken from a speech Cabral gave in Helsinki in 1971. In
terms of their historical point of reference these three articles
appeared in reverse order, with the last containing the most
explicit material on the subject of nineteenth-century imperialism.
The most striking feature, however, about the three essays is
that in each case the account rendered of imperialism is based
upon identical assumptions. Imperialism was one subject about
which Cabral never changed his mind.

Although in all of his writings on the subject Cabral supports
the classic Marxist view of imperialism as an outgrowth of
capitalist relations of production, he takes great care to distinguish between the situation of Portugal and the other imperialist powers. Because of its history, Portugal could not be
classified in the same way as Britain or France in regard to
her colonial empire. Portugal had been pushed into imperialism
by circumstance. From the beginning of the eighteenth century,
with the signing of the treaty of Metheun, Portugal became to
all intents and purposes a client of Britain in the colonial exploitation of Africa. In each of Portugal's African territories the
imperialist relationship was mediated by the dominance of British
capital and political favour, which after 1885 was the means by
which Portugal managed to hang on to its colonial possessions.
By the turn of the century over half of the total exports from
Angola and Mozambique were directed to Britain, France, and
Germany which in turn provided the bulk of investment in the
territories. Guiné and the Cape Verde Islands alone remained
genuine colonies of Portugal because only there was foreign
capital largely absent.

Cabral viewed the relationship between the imperialist powers
as being highly competitive and invariably destructive, since
the primary aim of each of the imperialist states was to exclude

its competitors in the pursuit of its own exclusive interests. The
Conference of Berlin was in this sense unusual because it
indicated that the individual powers jostling for territory in
Africa could reconcile their differences in pursuit of common goal.
But this fraternity was essentially illusory. In The Death Pangs
of Imperialism Cabral argues that it was the influence of imperialism and, in particular, the exclusion after 1918 of Germany from
the colonial enterprise which brought about the Second World
War. However, as a result of the 1939-45 conflict the destruction
of the old imperialist world order had begun, for the war
strengthened the socialist camp, and it awakened the colonial
peoples to the possibility of political freedom.

At various points, Cabral explains that imperialism, by which
he means the economic relations existing between colonies and
metropoles, is the result of the growth of monopoly capitalism
in the capitalist nations.[6] The domination of the economies of the
capitalist states by a small number of giant monopolies was the
factor which led these countries into imperialist expansion. The
need for new markets and raw materials was the principal motive
for the articulation of capital on a world scale and the Conference
of Berlin of 1885 was convened in order to satisfy the needs of
these monopolies. Cabral argues that the Conference also served
the purpose of making public the fact that the colonialist countries had now become imperialist. Imperialism is domination by
capitalism for the purpose of capital. This is the reality behind
the idea of imperialism as a civilising mission which was used to
justify the exploitation of the peoples of Asia and Africa in the
name of a higher order. Imperialism has various guises, and its
appearance can take the forms of colonialism, neo-colonialism,
and even semi-colonialism, as was the case in Cuba and in pre-
revolutionary China.

The fact that Portugal was not itself an imperialist state but
rather an intermediary in the imperialist exploitation of Africa
made Cabral sensitive to the distinction between economic and
political power. But Cabral's major complaint against the
Portuguese was that, unlike the other colonial powers, Portugal
failed completely to bring about constructive change in its
colonies. There were few schools, few roads, and only the most
elementary kinds of light industry. In short, Portugal faithfully
transposed the condition of backwardness from the metropolitan
setting to Black Africa.

These then are the immediate themes of a theory of imperialism.
But, within this set of relationships, Cabral discovers a grander
design created by the changing processes of material production
and human purpose. In this sense imperialism is an historical
necessity. It is a consequence of the impetus given to the
ambitious nations by the expansion of their productive forces
and by the transformation of the means of production under the
sway of capitalism working as a world order. The historical
significance or purpose of this expansion is found in the acceleration of the process of development. Imperialism must increase

the complexity of the means of production and of man's mastery over nature. It will inevitably increase the difference between various social strata, thereby creating the conditions for the emergence of a bourgeoisie. In the rich countries imperialist capital has heightened the creative capacity of man through progress in the domains of science and technology. Imperialism should be capable of achieving creative change in the two contexts in which it operates; that is, in the countries of accumulation and in the colonies themselves.

There is a second facet to Cabral's theory which is far more important than this essentially conventional account of imperialist intervention in the colonial world. In The Weapon of Theory Cabral argues that for imperialism as an historical force to achieve its mission it must follow with fidelity its own self-interests, and it must reflect the strength and vitality of a young capitalism. But in order to do this, above all else, it must have time. In the absence of this combination of factors it was common that, in a number of colonial countries, imperialism served to block the historical process.

Although it may still have imposed new relationships upon the social fabric, encouraged the development of internal and external markets, introduced a money economy and given birth to new nations from among peoples living at greatly varied stages of historical development, this in itself did not constitute revolutionary change.

The national liberation movements opposing colonial rule were fighting against imperialism which is the basis of every colonial holding. This explains why Cabral employed the terms imperialism, colonialism, and capitalism as synonymous, whenever writing of either Europe or Africa. But by doing so Cabral draws away from the growing trend among theorists then working on the subject of relations between First- and Third-World countries. Cabral equates colonialism directly with capitalism, although he views capitalism as inherently revolutionary and yet paradoxically degenerative. This is why Cabral can incorporate into his work elements synonymous with notions of pathological development and can still manage to avoid joining that fraternity of underdevelopment theorists whose work always begins with the dictum that capitalism is itself an historical dead end.

At a number of places in his collected writings Cabral makes reference to blocked development[7] by which he appears to mean two quite different things. In the first instance, blocked development refers to the truncating of the process of endogenous change brought about by colonial occupation. This aspect of the colonial impact is given sufficient detail in Cabral's work to form part of an overall view of the twin histories of colonialism. The significance of the second aspect of blocked development is anything but clear for, although Cabral refers to the failure of imperialism to bring about the growth of productive forces and the birth of a proletariat, there is no reason given anywhere in his work to explain why this should be the case. Cabral's major complaint against colonialism is that in the countries of Africa imperialism did not do enough to bring about change. In a Marxist sense it was not sufficiently exploitative. Although Cabral does make a distinction between the old and a new imperialism, which helps to extend the differences between the first and the second points of historical blockage, this does not explain the failure of imperialism as a revolutionary force in the colonial world.

After 1945 there was a major relocation among the imperialist states as the older powers, namely, Britain and France, were replaced by the United States as the dominant force. Imperialist exploitation now took the guise of preferential investment at home in the countries of the First World, coupled with the export of capital through programmes to the developing nations. Cabral explains that this pattern of investment was intended to stimulate the growth of a labour aristocracy in Europe and simultaneously to enlarge the field of action of imperialism within the colonies.[8] It is this strategy which connects the national liberation struggles in the Third World with the internationalist working-class movements.

Although in terms of theory the struggles of the working class and the national liberation movements are unified in that they confront the same enemy (especially under neo-colonial conditions), this does not imply that there can be any operational unity between the two. Cabral conceded that it is not practicable to hope for any effective alliance between these separate parts of the revolutionary struggle.

In contrast to Fanon, who believed the emergence of the parasitic national bourgeoisie to be an outgrowth of a pathological historical process, Cabral identified the emergence of the reactionary classes of post-independence Africa as a consequence of a specific policy by the imperialist powers. The programmes of foreign aid directed to the countries of the Third World were given with the specific purpose of warping the social structures of the recipient states by encouraging the growth of a local petty bourgeoisie. In the colonial setting this strategy was intended to liberate those reactionary forces previously stifled by colonialism, thereby creating a pseudo-bourgeoisie with which an alliance of interests could be formed. In the light of this strategy Cabral concludes that: 'This rise of the bourgeoisie in the new countries far from being at all surprising should be considered absolutely normal.'[9] By employing this policy the imperialist powers could continue to dominate the working-class movements in the First World and smother the national liberation movements in the Third. Neo-colonialism is a rationalised form of imperialism which represents more a defeat for the metropolitan proletariat than for the colonial peoples.[10]

Cabral argues that under conditions of classical colonialism the historical process appears to be frozen while neo-colonial dictatorships give the illusion of progress adorned as they are with the trappings of political autonomy. In reality, however, the degree of change is not so great as it appears since the local elites are incapable of breaking their subordination to the dominance of metropolitan interests. Cabral explains that in the concrete conditions of the world economy this dependence is fatal for it means that the indigenous pseudo-bourgeoisie is prevented from directing the development of the local productive forces. Cabral employs Marx's argument that for the process of development to be effective there must be complete freedom for the advancement of the forces of production. This of course, in Marxist literature, always carries with it the conclusion that in those circumstances in which the productive forces are prevented from gaining free expression then a revolutionary transformation of society is inevitable.

In assessing the long-term future of African states existing under neo-colonial rule, Cabral draws a parallel with Latin American countries which he identifies as having a more clearly defined set of contradictions and a far higher level of social and economic development.[11] Cabral is optimistic that in the near future these countries will reach out for a genuine independence. Presumably Latin America presents an image of the future awaiting Black Africa.

As early as 1964 Cabral had arrived at a highly sophisticated understanding of the principal differences between the colonial and the neo-colonial situations and he describes in some detail the variations in the spheres of social structure, economic formation, and popular culture which separate these two epochs. Yet, in distinguishing between the two periods, he ignores completely the influence on the new states of forces within international capitalism or imperialism. In what is an extraordinary omission Cabral gives no explanation whatsoever as to the connection between neo-colonial social structures and the interests of international capital. The only response of any kind he makes is to assume the presence of an abstract quest for political advantage by the metropolitan bourgeoisie. This omission places Cabral in opposition to most Marxists who, in their analysis of the post-colonial states, so readily discovered a total subordination of the political process to economic influence and writers, such as Fanon, who sought to uncover the *raison d'être* of neo-colonialism within the realm of psychology and personality. In contrast to both of these schools Cabral maintains that political factors are dominant in the creation and maintenance of neo-colonial regimes. Not surprisingly, this lack of precision leads Cabral into a *cul de sac* when his theory approaches the issue as to how imperialist forces operate in the Third-World environment. This weakness is expressed in the form of a paradox: on the one hand, Cabral argues that, because of the contradictions inherent in imperialism, the evolution of capitalism has led directly to the growth of African nationalism. Yet, counterbalanced against this, he also presumes that neo-colonialism is a necessary and logical outgrowth of classical colonialism. Therefore imperialism is simultaneously highly adaptive to change and self-destructive. This leaves unanswered the most important question as to how and under what specific conditions nationalist movements can avoid the trap of neo-colonial dependence.

As early as 1961 Cabral was convinced that the final stage of imperialist as distinct from colonial domination of the Third World had been reached. The transformation of the colonial states would take a greater or lesser period of time, but the process was irreversible.[12] In concurrence with Fanon and Césaire he discovered in the national liberation movements the dominant political force in contemporary history replacing in importance the class struggles in the capitalist states and even the conflict between the capitalist and the socialist blocs. The class struggle between European labour and European capital has been superseded as an historical force.[13] In the writings of such people as Césaire this shift in balance from class forces to nationalism was seen to have its origins in factors which pre-date colonialism itself. This contradiction is traced as arising out of the fundamental differences between European and non-European civilisations. It is these kinds of differences, rather than an historical development such as presented in Mao's proletarian and bourgeoisie nations thesis, which are important in most Third-World theories of imperialism. Cabral was faithful to this myth and the idea of the primacy of the nationalist movements which he first outlined in 1961 surfaces again in the important essay The Death Pangs of Imperialism, published in 1963. In this later essay Cabral identifies even the struggle among the imperialist states for advantage, like the class struggles within the nations of Europe, as being of secondary importance to the national liberation movements. The colonial peoples are alone in occupying the stage of history.

These two lines of argument in Cabral's writings in which he claims that imperialism can be overthrown and that neo-colonialism is the fate of African nationalism are not reconcilable. The incongruity of this facet of Cabral's theory is a reflection of the ambiguity in his response to the question as to whether imperialism is itself revolutionary in the way Rosa Luxemburg and Lenin had believed it to be. Cabral answers no to this question by contrasting the pretensions of imperialism with the achievements of the nationalist movements which it brought to life. Imperialism is not a revolutionary force because it has not brought forth a revolutionary response from the colonial peoples. Cabral concludes from this that the decline of nationalism into neo-colonialism was both necessary and inevitable. This failure is indicative of the *cul de sac* into which the two sides of capitalism, its First- and Third-World faces, has sunk. This at least is the conclusion to be drawn from reading Cabral's early writings on the subject of imperialism and revolution. However, this contradiction tends to become less severe in his later writings, particularly after the publication of his study of the social structure in Guiné. In order to explore this conflict between the alternate judgments of imperialism in Cabral's theory it is necessary to examine how this contradiction is resolved, at least formally in his class theory.

In The Weapon of Theory Cabral discovers the point of exit from neo-colonial domination in the suicide of the petty bourgeoisie which voluntarily relinquishes its social and economic advantages in order to throw its weight behind the peasantry and forge a genuine national revolution.[14] This extraordinary formulation opens up the questions as to why factions within the petty bourgeoisie would choose to follow such a path and what it is in the experience of this class which led Cabral to believe that it could willingly abandon its own interests as an incipient bourgeoisie.

In reading Cabral's writings in chronological order, it becomes clear that he could discover only one possible means of exit from the neo-colonial phase and that lay with the achievement of particular structural changes during the post-independence period accompanied by the voluntarist action of certain sections of the petty bourgeoisie. Cabral arrived at this conclusion because he felt that he had identified two special characteristics of the indigenous petty bourgeoisie which lent a unique aspect to that class. The position of the petty bourgeoisie under colonial and semi-colonial conditions made it a competitor for state power simply because of the absence of any other class with knowledge of the workings of state apparatus. But, above all else, Cabral believed that certain cultural factors peculiar to the petty bourgeoisie endowed it with the capacity to destroy itself as a class. It is here in the arena of cultural affiliation and social psychology that the revolutionary potential of Cabral's petty bourgeoisie is found. Paradoxically, it was in just this same territory that Fanon, writing less than six years earlier in 'The Wretched of the Earth', believed he had discovered the reason why in Africa the national bourgeoisie was reactionary and self-seeking in the extreme. Cabral's petty bourgeoisie is revolutionary for the very same reasons that Fanon's national bourgeoisie is atavistic.

The central problem in Cabral's revolutionary theory arose because of the absence in Africa of an indigenous bourgeoisie. In both the colonial and neo-colonial contexts the only classes which can rule are the petty bourgeoisie and the incipient proletariat. Cabral argues that for the petty bourgeoisie to retain the power, which nationalist revolution has invariably placed in its hands, it must follow only one path; the petty bourgeoisie must ally itself directly with the interests of imperialist capital. This is of course the path which Fanon feared would be characteristic of African nationalist regimes, while Cabral, on the contrary, views such a development without apparent concern. But this scenario raises the problem as to why the indigenous petty bourgeoisie cannot transform itself into an authentic national middle class. There is no indication anywhere in Cabral's work that he believed in the existence of a structural barrier blocking the creation of a national middle class. Most certainly his por-

trayal of the metamorphosis of the petty bourgeoisie into a
pseudo-bourgeoisie is not presented as an unavoidable fate
awaiting nationalist regimes, that is, as a consequence of structural
barriers in the spheres of production and exchange. Cabral
simply fails to explain the absence of a national bourgeoisie in
post-colonial Africa. Cabral's theory allows for the emergence of
a small working class but not a national middle class. This
absence is all the more puzzling when Cabral presupposes the
emergence of such a class through the successful elevation of a
segment of the pseudo-bourgeoisie.

Despite its limitations, Cabral's description of the colonial and
neo-colonial phases is far closer to the reality of the past two
decades and it is far more subtle in account for the changes
which have subsequently become obvious in social structure
and economic formations than anything suggested in the writings
of his contemporaries. Yet in other ways Cabral's theory appears
to be less advanced than even Fanon's and in certain respects it
is even antiquated. There is no concept of underdevelopment in
The Weapon of Theory, despite Cabral's assertion that there can
be no national bourgeoisie in Africa, which indicates the presence
of a distortion in the development of the local forces of production. That this has in fact been the case during both the colonial
and the post-colonial periods suggests that capitalism operates in
a rather atypical fashion in Third-World situations.

The confusion surrounding Cabral's account of the national
middle class spills over and muddies the conclusions he arrives
at on the question of escape from imperialism. In concluding his
discussion of the nationalist and post-independence struggles
Cabral proposes that, if the struggle for independence is essentially a political problem, then the liberation of the national
productive forces is essentially a question of morality. The class
suicide of the petty bourgeoisie comes about for reasons of moral
sensitivity which may prove dominant, although they run directly
counter to class interest. This conclusion flies in the face of
Cabral's otherwise careful description and analysis of the
development of contradictions within the post-colonial phase. One
obvious reason for Cabral's erratic response can be found in
the fact that The Weapon of Theory was written four years after
'The Wretched of the Earth', and therefore is bound to reflect
the growing pessimism to which the first years of independence
soon gave rise. But the major reason is found in the character of
Cabral's own theory.

When Cabral was writing his most important essays on social
structure, the site of theories about imperialism was shifting
from the First to the Third Worlds. It was also shifting simultaneously from an analysis of social classes to a macro-historical
mode of discourse in which class analysis was being largely
abandoned. This work was synthesised into what we now know
as underdevelopment theory and today we can identify it in its
various guises, whether it be that of Fanon's national bourgeoisie
or Emmanuel's expanded labour aristocracy, or most obliquely

of all where it finds a refuge in Cabral's self-destructing petty bourgeoisie.

Like most Third-World socialists, Fanon defines imperialism principally according to its external characteristics, that is, according to the variety of features which touched most intimately upon the lives of the évolué class. Cabral by contrast sought to define imperialism as the relationship between the metropole and the colony, according to the impact that the relationship had upon the methods and purposes of production. This is the reason why, until his essay of 1970, there is so little in Cabral's work on that cluster of questions associated with changes to the superstructure. This is indicative of the advance that Cabral's work represents upon that of his predecessors. Third-World socialists before Cabral were, above all else, concerned with the flagrant injustices of the colonial relationship and therefore they were preoccupied with such issues as racism and violence. These particular questions are almost entirely absent from Cabral's work, even though he had far better credentials than either Fanon or Césaire to discuss the darker side of colonialism.

In totality, Cabral's essays and speeches on the subject of imperialism coalesce into one major problem and that concerns the connection between the failure of imperialism in Africa to achieve its historical mission and the emergence of neo-colonialism as a rationalisation of imperialist domination. There are references in his work which indicate that Cabral believed that the imperialist states had themselves suffered a loss of impetus by preventing the expansion of productive forces in dependent countries. Unfortunately Cabral gives no indication that this loss of vitality could be due to structural characteristics of imperialism such as the method of the extraction of the economic surplus, or the manner of exchange between First- and Third-World economies. His definition of imperialism as the 'ever increasing accumulation of surplus values by monopoly finance capital centred in Europe'[115] is a faithful recapitulation from Lenin's essay of 1917. But in contrast to Lenin, Cabral's theory carries the conclusion that only under neo-colonial conditions will imperialism be able to achieve what it found impossible during the eighty or so years of classical colonial domination.

Cabral discovered in the neo-colonial situation the possibility for the expansion of the forces of production and the differentiation of the social structure into a nascent working class and an embryonic bourgeoisie. In this context favourable political conditions would allow for all those developments which classical colonialism had hitherto prevented from coming to fruition. Therefore, the blockage to development lies in colonialism and in the colonial period, and not in the machinery of imperialism which has borne the brunt of attack from the left for the past two decades. Under colonial conditions imperialist capital was not allowed the necessary freedom of expression. Therefore, we can now understand that when Cabral employs the term underdevelopment he simply means non-development.

This characterisation exaggerates, slightly the distinctions Cabral draws between the colonial and neo-colonial situations by underplaying the emasculated nature of the indigenous ruling class he portrays as coming to power at independence. Even so, he found sufficient grounds for optimism to expect eventually the kinds of important changes which Colin Leys was finally to discover in Kenya.[16] However, there are also elements in Cabral's theory which indicate that, in contrast to Leys, he feared that the changes between the colonial and neo-colonial situations would lessen rather than grow over time. It is this hidden pessimism which accounts for Cabral resorting to the thesis of self-immolating petty bourgeoisie.

TOWARDS A NEW THEORY OF IMPERIALISM

The theory of underdevelopment grew readily out of previous theories of imperialism in response to a number of specific phenomena which the old theories appeared unable to explain. The most obvious of these were the successes of revolutions in the colonial world and the lopsidedness of the economies which appeared in Asia and Africa soon after independence. These developments indicated that the new nations could not adequately be characterised in the maxims of the old theory.

More than a decade after the invention of underdevelopment theory, it is now even more obvious that capitalism has left in its wake some truly grotesque regimes and some hideous societies which are in every way more unjust than the colonial regimes they have replaced. Underdevelopment theory was in many respects a creative response because, for the first time, it explained how the Third World had come into being. The undevelopmentalist did this without reference to such familiar prejudices as the absence of occidental values blocking the development of a vigorous capitalism. In brief, the undevelopmentalists were able to show that poverty among the new states was the result of neither accident nor fate. And yet soon after these early successes in applying insights into the political economy of poverty on a global scale, drawn invariably in the first instance from Latin America, underdevelopment theory began to attract from the left its first serious critics.

In numerous African states the underdevelopmentalists seemed to have discovered the reason for the endemic poverty of these new nations relying upon a single export crop. Their theory seems also to apply fairly accurately in the case of those southern African states, such as Botswana and Malawi, which are suffocated by their proximity to the Republic of South Africa. But underdevelopment theory does not seem appropriate in such instances as Kenya or Nigeria or Zaire in which independent capitalist strata have evolved.

This limitation in the theory has been used to justify the return to a more orthodox, and in many ways an antique, Marxist position by such people as Bill Warren.[17] Warren had launched a fierce attack upon underdevelopment theory because he felt it to be based upon the presumption that, in the Third World, development cannot take place within a capitalist framework. Warren adopted the position that capitalism and the productive forces disseminated by it are inherently revolutionary and that the importance of the exotic capitalism associated with colonialism and imperialism does not prevent the spread of indigenous capitalism. Therefore, it is quite wrong to suppose, as various influential writers have, that the bureaucratic class which is so common in African states is derived primarily or even principally from the operation of centre-periphery relations.

A second and probably even more important challenge to underdevelopment theory came from the work of French anthropologists. Whereas people such as Wallerstein, Amin, and Emmanuel were primarily concerned with the circulation of goods, rather than with the question of the condition of their production, Marxist anthropologists such as Terray and Meillassoux concerned themselves with the identification and classification of various modes of production.

Although this school cannot boast of having a theory of imperialism of its own, the work of Meillassoux and Terray has been immensely important in demonstrating the complexity of productive relations within the so-called dependent sector. Unfortunately these two sides to the debate on underdevelopment have been separated and consequently theories have been about either production or circulation but rarely both. The productionists demonstrated the complexity of the social fabric of precolonial African societies, and they also indicated that these societies had considerable capacity for endogenous development.

Cabral predicted the appearance of these two new threads in the theory of imperialism. He did this by accepting that capitalism is revolutionary in a way that the underdevelopmentalists would never allow, and, by studying the foundations of Guinéan agriculture to a depth that had for so long been alien to Marxist theories.

In a superficial sense many of the weaknesses in Cabral's work demonstrate that theories of class struggle sit uncomfortably with theories about imperialism. Running in tandem with this, Cabral also claims that, although imperialism has failed to fulfil its creative vocation in the countries of exploitation, it has managed to change its guise into a neo-colonialist form in order to survive the tide of nationalism. But why this should be the case and to what ends the imperialist states have subsequently sought to control the Third World are not explained.

The early agronomic studies which Cabral carried out in Guiné hold the key as to how in his mature writings Cabral managed to escape from the seduction of underdevelopment theory. Although much of Cabral's work is held back or landlocked by the various influences within his intellectual environment through the force of intuition, he was able to steer clear of the pitfalls to which

Fanon so readily succumbed. No better candidate for underdevelopment could be imagined than a country such as Guiné-Bissau dominated by a groundnut economy. The country is small with no obvious natural resources, and groundnuts are an unprofitable crop which deplete the soil, bring a declining living standard, and worsen the natural diet of the cultivator. As early as 1955, Cabral had knowledge of all those factors which subsequent writers would identify with 'terminal development'. And still Cabral chose not to side with then or later with the prophets of underdevelopment. Cabral knew from first-hand experience that the intrusion of capitalist agriculture did not directly replace peasant subsistence cultivation. On the contrary, the switch to cash cropping began a process which is vastly complex and includes a range of factors which may either accelerate or retard change within the wider social formation. Cabral identified indigenous culture as a major element determining the points at which these varied reactions would take place.

The term underdevelopment does not appear in Cabral's agronomic writings because they were published even before Paul Baran's 'Political Economy of Growth'. However, the experience contained in the agronomic researches drew Cabral away from the pull of underdevelopment theory rather than towards it for the rest of his intellectual life. Despite this fact, all current debates on the left concerning the state in Africa, the designation of modes of production, and the significance of the neo-colonial period have antecedents in Cabral's work. This is so because Cabral was more orthodox than a writer such as Frantz Fanon.

Throughout the 1960s and at the height of the popularity of underdevelopment doctrines, Cabral held steadfastly to a position on centre-periphery relations which had been abandoned by all but the most retrograde and apparently unimaginative Marxists. And yet curiously this is not reflected at all in his broader theorising on imperialism. Where writing on the subject of the grand historical design of imperialist relations, Cabral devoted most of his attention to exploring the question of the growth of a national middle class. Much current debate on Africa likewise centres on the possible emergence of a national bourgeoisie in countries such as Nigeria, Kenya, and Zaire. Beneath this theme, Cabral also poses the question of a possible drift towards the creation of such a class in Black Africa as a whole. Cabral brings his analysis to this point then suddenly abandons it. He identifies the importance of changes which took place at independence and discusses how these changes are far more substantial than is usually conceded under the term neo-colonialism. Cabral even allows for the emergence of a pseudo-bourgeoisie which is far more vigorous and independent than Fanon's national bourgeoisie. Yet the only route he can foresee out of the neo-colonial situation is to come about through the mass class suicide of the national middle class which acts in direct violation of its own class interests.

There is no resolution to these problems in Cabral's writings but his theory does indicate correctly the direction in which theories on the radical left have taken over the past decade.

Cabral's theory of imperialism, in as much as it is new, is presented in the guise of a metaphor. The outlines of that metaphor can be found in his discussion of modes of production, his typology of historical epochs, and his invention of the concept of an aborted history. When combined, these elements suggest a new direction which the discussion of relations between the First and Third World should take. These new prescriptions for a theory of imperialism arrived as it were prematurely in Cabral's writings and he can do no more than suggest the form a new theory should take.

9 CONCLUSION

In the writings of Marx and in the theory of classic Marxism there is no suggestion that development and inequality are of necessity tied together. Certainly under the conditions of capitalist economic and social relations they have gone hand in hand. But the project of Marxism has always been to prove that this was unnecessary. Yet so much of the literature which nowadays goes under the name of Marxism has drawn away from the belief in the liberative capacity of technology and presents theories which are based upon the assumption that the relationship is in fact inverse. In consequence a reactionary reading of Marx and a faithful interpretation of Weber have grown together to establish a collusive unity between underdevelopment and modernisation theories. The ghost of the Asiatic Mode of Production has found a home in both schools. Underdevelopment theorists have clung as tenaciously to the idea of an inherently backward orient as Marx and Hegel did to the myth of oriental despotism. The devaluation of the non-west which was for so long conceded to be one of the errors in Marx is now one of the major achievements of underdevelopment theory.

The unwillingness of many Third-World socialists to take account of unpleasant problems in the realms of political theory and political practice has been due not so much to ideological blindness as to a lack of faith. African socialists have always been plagued with the pervasive self-doubt that in substance the new states were houses built on sand, and that the just societies they sought to bring into being had no real hope of survival. In consequence when questions of higher theory were raised it became obvious that the new socialists were trapped in a web created by the confluence of pessimism, prejudice, faith and naivety. The absence of a convincing theory was therefore due not to a lack of seriousness but to a fault of imagination.

The irony of the decade of the African revolution is that the decade lasted for twenty years, yet it managed to produce hardly a revolutionary government. Guiné's revolution came late, but it was a genuine revolution, and like all genuine revolutions it was accompanied by its own theory. That theory is found in the writings of Amilcar Cabral. Because of the conjunction of a wide range of factors the revolution in Guiné assumed an importance far out of proportion to the size or economic significance of the country. Consequently Cabral's theory has come to take on an historical importance.

Cabral is in many ways a prototype of his age; his work represents a return to a human scale in recording the victory of a small and apparently powerless people over a giant opponent. His work also contains a vision which opposes a world of crushing misery, with a vision of a society based upon the dignity of the individual. But unlike the memoirs of innumerable African nationalist politicians whose work is invariably infected with frustrated ambition, there is no suggestion in Cabral of personal vanity or a will to power. There is nothing self-conscious or elegant in Cabral's writings and, as in the prison notebooks of Gramsci, there is a complete absence of the argot of the super-left.

There is obviously a close connection between the conditions of Cabral's life and his intellectual preoccupations as the biography of the writer and philosopher were refracted back into the theory. And yet Cabral was an involuntary theorist; his life demanded the need for a theory but he theorises without apparent enthusiasm and he would most probably have assessed his own work in a very different light to that which it has assumed since its death. Possibly he would have viewed his practical writings as his most important intellectual achievement because they served to propagandise the revolution and now stand as a verbal record of the struggle of the peoples of Guiné in the process of becoming a nation. The macro-historical writings such as The Weapon of Theory were a sideshow to the more pressing concerns of the liberation struggle.

Cabral's intellectual legacy comes to us in a series of fragments. This ephemeral quality is due to two causes: the writings were peripheral or, more correctly, preparatory to the struggle, and they were never written for the purpose of intellectual or abstract enquiry. Therefore they take the form of short articles, scattered essays, speeches and memoranda.

The physical aspects of Cabral's work make it necessary to distinguish between what is reflexive and what is substantive in his theory. More importantly this fragmentary quality is reinforced by Cabral's near obsessive pursuit of the truth; his work was fragmented by the very nature of its subject - a national liberation struggle fought under the most trying conditions and motivated by the dual purpose of freeing a colonial people from foreign domination and of creating a social revolution. Ironically Cabral was the best read of all the African nationalists or revolutionaries. He was at the same time the individual who was most knowledgeable about the specific social and economic conditions of his country. That is, at the two extremes of political discourse, in his capacity for abstract theorising and in his sensitivity to social process at the village level, Cabral was the most gifted member of his generation.

Cabral's work is apparently weak in the absence of an encompassing conceptual view and it is divided by a sharp contrast between the intricate and detailed observations of social formations and the casual and even on occasions incoherent quality of his arguments when the farther reaches of the empirical world

are approached. What holds the work together is a vision of
liberty which is as dominant in the agronomic papers as in the
purely theoretical essays. It is also held together by Cabral's
largely intuitive skills as a political theorist. Cabral was always,
even in the earliest essays, a political theorist who was not in
the least interested in theory. In his work there is an implicit
distinction between *theory* and *knowledge;* knowledge he identifies with practice and the changing of re-shaping of the world,
while he tends to identify theory with Marxism, that is with
useless intellectualising. His rejection of Marxism was motivated
at the base by what he believed to be its impractical quality.

Cabral's intellectual world was fundamentally ambiguous; it
was a world which was at once essentially visible and tangible
but it was also a world which was moved by abstract principles
in which material interests were not an adequate guide to felt
needs or beliefs or behaviour. Each sphere of this cleavage was
an effect on Cabral's life of his social experience as a member of
the Guiné assimilados transposed into his intellectual world. It
is at this point that Cabral's theory is refracted from his biography and it is here that he differs from his contemporaries.
Cabral's theory is a penumbra of his class experience as a
member of the indigenous petty bourgeoisie. This is why on the
surface of his work there appears to be no guiding scientific
theory.

At the heart of Cabral's theory lies a *practical idealism* which
is the greatest legacy Cabral has left us. That idealism is
founded upon a mundane reverence for human life and a passion
for social justice which is the cornerstone of his revolutionary
nationalism. This practical idealism is anti-Marxist in the sense
that Cabral defined Marxism. Because of his ability to discuss
highly complex concepts and arguments in simple language,
Cabral's writings are characterised stylistically by their *decep-
tive simplicity*. This is true of all his writings, including the
agronomic essays which otherwise would hold no appeal to the
non-specialist reader. The final lasting quality of Cabral's work
is found in his *uncompromising honesty*. Cabral is never evasive
and never polemical and his truthfulness lends his work an
imaginative quality which alone is sufficient to distinguish his
writings from those of his contemporaries. This is also seen in
his refusal to seek to disguise, for his own advantage, his
essential beliefs. Nowhere is this more obvious than in Cabral's
appearance before the US Congress Foreign Relations Committee
when his disarming honesty was maintained in the face of outright hostility. In combination these individual qualities of
Cabral's writings give his work its particular character, and
they explain why his work should have an air of incompleteness
or failure.

In his theory of imperialism Cabral arrives at a number of
apparently contradictory conclusions. He begins his intellectual
career by providing a model of agriculture in which the future
of Guiné is paradigmatically one of underdevelopment; he accepts

the plain Marxist thesis that in the colonial world imperialism is a revolutionary force; he goes on from this point to argue that neo-colonial formations are inevitable (presumably even under conditions where an armed struggle has taken place) because of the nature of the colonial state and the earlier failure of imperialism to create an indigenous bourgeoisie; and he arrives at the conclusion that imperialism has failed its historical mission in the colonial world, although he can find no reason for this within the structure of imperialist relations.

Woven within this set of paradoxical propositions is a single dominating question which Cabral does not really pose in its essential terms; that is the problem of whether or not the progressive forces in the nationalist movements could manage to implant their own design on the revolution so that the anti-colonial movement could carry within it the seeds for the development of a new class and a new class struggle. In the case of Guiné, existing economic conditions and the level of class consciousness made immediate liberation from capitalist relations of production impossible. There is a strong suggestion in Cabral's work that the nationalist movements in Africa could only hope to express the need for capitalist development and broaden and deepen the foundations of the national middle class. But it was at this exact point of his analysis that Cabral moved toward pessimism. He was confident of the success of the national liberation movement against the Portuguese, but he was all too aware of the failure of so many progressive movements on the continent which had been blessed with more favourable circumstances than those in Guiné. Cabral hoped that the experience of the war would have sufficiently changed the men and women who fought in it and that such change would find sanctuary in the institutions of the new state. And yet Cabral also feared that this would not be enough.

This uncertainty is paralleled by a wider tension in Cabral's theory in his account of the post-independence state. That tension is created by the contrast between Cabral's enthusiasm for the changes which had taken place during the period of armed struggle in the spheres of education and health and his prescriptions on the development of the state and the rise of a pseudo-bourgeoisie once independence had been achieved. This tension is not confined to Guiné where the war had taken such a long time to come to an end, but it applies to the whole of Black Africa. It is a recognition on Cabral's part of the extent of the transformation of the social whole necessary to return the people of Guiné to their 'own history'. The national liberation struggle merely begins the process, it cannot complete it.

There is a second level of tension in Cabral's theory which centres on the role of leadership and the party within the process of struggle. Many of Cabral's writings suggest the importance of strong leadership without which success in the struggle would have been impossible. In the same essays and speeches there is also the imperative that all men are philosophers and political actors, an idea which is seen most clearly in Cabral's view of culture. Therefore there is a tension between those constraints on individual initiative and responsibility which Cabral felt necessary to the prosecution of the struggle and the ethos of his theory which has its nucleus in the idea of individual autonomy. In his practical history of the struggle, the activities of the party are not predominant in the sense in which they always are in Leninist histories. What is predominant is the activity of the peoples of Guiné not under the party but rather through the party, which is nothing other than the repository of their aggregate interests. Unlike the work of any Marxist with the exception of Gramsci, the spirit of Cabral's work is egalitarian and the tension between leadership and participation exposes Cabral's tendency to view political action as necessarily unsuccessful or tragic. He tends to believe that political action directed to achieving greater freedom will in the short term lead to repressive ends; in the contemporary setting the drift of history is weighted against the peoples of the colonial countries. Through the expulsion of the colonial powers the nationalist movements may only be able to achieve a fatal repetition. However, this pessimism is largely repressed within Cabral's theory and he maintains his confidence that the peasants of Guiné would be able to re-fashion their lives at the same time as they came to understand how the forces of economic necessity and political influence shaped their world.

The aspect of Cabral's work which has attracted most critical attention concerns the question as to whether or not he is a Marxist. The record of nearly every interview Cabral gave contains some reference to this issue which so preoccupied western audiences sympathetic to the PAIGC. Over time Cabral became less and less tolerant of what he perceived to be an irrelevant issue. In one such response to this question Cabral answered that the ideological aim or project of the PAIGC was for justice and 'If you want to call it Marxism you may. Am I a Marxist? Judge from what I do in practice. Labels don't concern us (the PAIGC). People here are preoccupied with this question. The only issue is, are we doing well in the field?'[1] Today as during Cabral's lifetime, the PAIGC, unlike FRELIMO and the MPLA is not nominally a Marxist-Leninist party. And yet what happened in Guiné during the decade of the national liberation struggle approximates in every respect to a revolution. We are then left with the problem as to how such a revolution can be non-Marxist in the context of our time when all the revolutions of this century (with the exception of the most recent events in Iran and Libya) have been Marxist if only for the superficial reason that they were perceived as such by the United States.

It is worth remembering that much of the non-Marxist left, and this has been especially true in nationalist Africa, is either ridiculous or merely eccentric and Cabral was neither of these. Cabral knew and understood more about conventional Marxism than any other nationalist of his generation and yet he is the

Conclusion

least conventional of all. The major reason why Cabral was not a Marxist, and it is the reason which Cabral himself gives, is that Marxism was not adequate to the task confronting the struggles in colonial Africa. The situation in the Portuguese territories, as in the rest of Black Africa required a new theory and a new practice and the struggle could not be fought along lines used in the Soviet or Chinese revolutions. Consequently Cabral rejected Marxism first of all on practical grounds. The basis for political mobilisation and the theme of the political action of the PAIGC as well as the mode of organisation of the movement had to be created according to the dictates of the situation in Guiné and in the light of the social structure of the country. Neither Fanonian, nor Soviet Marxist, nor Chinese Maoist theories could give the people of Guiné the means to re-establish themselves as the creators of their own history. Cabral's explanation for the irrelevance of Marxism was simply that Marx was not a member of a tribal society, therefore Marxism was not the tool of the people of Guiné.

It is quite easy to trace out the exact points at which Cabral consciously rejected a Marxist approach. Cabral felt very strongly that European-derived categories of class and class analysis were inappropriate in the context of Africa. He went even further than this in rejecting the primacy of class struggle as the motive force of historical change, thereby deliberately distancing himself from the very heart of Marxism. Not only is the model of class inappropriate, so also is the European notion of a political party. In doing this Cabral was exposing his anger at the European left which had, he believed, pushed the question of political struggle further and further into the realm of obtuse theory-making. Although the class struggle in Europe had been in obvious decline for so long, it was European Marxists who insisted both on the primacy of the class conflict and that Cabral as the representative of the PAIGC explain his party's position in terms of such orthodox categories. This is why Cabral insisted that the PAIGC was not a Marxist-Leninist party. Like the issue of class struggle, the social foundations of the party and the historical context in which the struggle was being fought made such terminology meaningless.

The one notable omission in Cabral's attack upon Marxism is his failure to refer to the implicit racism of the European left which Fanon had felt so acutely. The errors of the Marxist left were, for Cabral, the result of overt social and historical factors and not the machinations of a negrophobic culture. Cabral was, however, sensitive to the ethnocentrism of the Marxist tradition which denied the non-west an important and independent place upon the stage of world history. So it was that he was anxious to impress upon his readers the fact that at least one major ethnic group in Guiné had a feudal mode of production and were capable of embarking upon an endogenous line of development. Therefore it was in order to anticipate Marxist critics that Cabral employed the concepts of the mode of production and the productive forces.

Conclusion

Leaving aside the work of academic Marxists and the writings of Fanon, who was uncritically anti-Marxist, Cabral is the first truly important African socialist. In its rigour and its imaginative quality, his work is in accord with the best of the Marxist tradition. He rejected underdevelopment theory because he admired the transformative quality of modern technology, and he never lost sight of the meaning of history as the liberation of man from the slavery to need. In his essays and his early research papers both human society and the natural world are treated as historical categories. Like the work of imaginative Marxists, his theory is grounded in a recognition of the materiality of social conflict.

Cabral approached the problems confronting the liberation struggle at three interdependent levels: at the most abstract level he explored the problems of the macro-historical development which he perceived as arising from the colonial and nationalist phases; at the intermediate level lies his class analysis and his theory of revolutionary nationalism; at the third and final level is Cabral's analysis of the economic horizons which Guiné's agriculture set as the parameter for future development. Despite the proximity of this approach to that of Marxists working subsequently on African sociology, Cabral's dismissal of himself as a Marxist is indicative of his disregard for the abstract theorising which he felt Marxism had become preoccupied with since the end of the Second World War.

Remembering the qualities which are found in the best of Marxist theory, Cabral's writings have a certain fidelity to the Marxist tradition, but in his most important essays he quite deliberately broke away from the crushing conformity of Marxist strictures on the subjects of class, nationalism and historical development. Cabral's work therein represents a dis-Europeanisation of revolutionary theory long after the peoples of Africa had rid most of the continent of European colonialism. But Cabral's work differs from that of European Marxists for a wider range of reasons than are contained in tactical or strategic necessity. At the core of his work Cabral veers away from Marxism on those questions which relate to the interaction of man, society and nature. One of the few important characteristics Marxist philosophy shares with bourgeois ideology is a triumphant vision of man's domination and final conquest over nature. Marxism contains the same brutal and dominative approach to the physical world that has been the hallmark of European civilisation since the Enlightenment. There is quite simply no ecological dimension in the writings of Marxism. The figure of Prometheus is the correct symbolic representation for Karl Marx and for those who have chosen to work in the tradition he founded.

In the vision of Marx the world is to be changed through the force of human activity which above all else entails the transformation of nature into an historical category to be continuously modified by the accretions of human labour. No matter how convoluted it appears in terms of its methodology there is always the Promethean dream in Marxism and such ideas as harmony and balance are quite alien to it. Yet in truth the destructive impact of industrial civilisation upon the natural world is not tied to the pattern of ownership. The same negative features associated with industrial civilisation in the United States are also present in the Soviet empire. Many Third-World states are also making their own modest contribution to the destruction of the biosphere. Marxism has not been dragged unwillingly into ratifying the destruction of the physical world through the accident of having to serve as a doctrine for industrial modernisation. The treatment of the natural world is the same in the Soviet Union as in the United States because both political systems are founded upon the self-same wish. There is nothing in the literature of Marxism which questions in any fundamental way the necessity for the total subordination of nature to human purpose. The only question with which Marxism is concerned is to the identity of the beneficiaries. In this respect Marxism is as teratogenic as the bourgeois philosophies it seeks to replace. It is also at this point that by dint of historical accident African and Third-World revolutionary nationalism has launched a most important challenge to Marxism.

It is now evident that there are strict limits to the Third World's capacity to duplicate the industrial civilisation of the western capitalist states. Because of the depletion of world resources the foundation upon which the development of the First World was largely based is gone for ever. It is now also obvious that the environmental damage associated with high-consumption societies is not supportable in the long term, either politically or ecologically. The major truth in underdevelopmental theory is that the development of Europe, and in particular the older colonialist states, was accelerated by the penetration of the continents of Africa, Asia and Latin America. Although they must be accepted as fixing the future options for the development of the former colonial territories, none of these factors appears in Cabral's theory. In 1972 when Cabral wrote his final important works the limits to growth were not as certain as they now are. It was not clear at that time how cartels among resource producers would affect states such as Tanzania or Malawi. Therefore Cabral's rejection of the ideal of a limitless material development as a model for Africa is correct, but not for the reasons that are now accepted as indisputable.

In all the literature of African socialism there is a strong ecological element which supposes that in African civilisation man has been able to achieve a balance among the members of traditional society and between that society and nature or the natural order. Unfortunately there is little besides this theme in African socialism, so that it has tended to strangle what was essentially a worthwhile project. In Cabral's theory the use of the productive forces thesis seems to indicate that Cabral stands in the company of plain Marxists on the issues of technology, change, labour and nature, and that he could rightfully be called a Marxist if one were able to ignore that range of methodological issues which for Marxists separate Marxism as a science from pseudo-science. But Cabral's productive forces thesis is not integrated into the rest of his theory, a fact which is proven by his attitude towards the impact of labour on nature in the agronomic writings. Those writings carry the warning that the rate of change is dictated finally by the ecological balance between the needs of human society and the capacity of the natural world to support such change. This argument is reinforced in Cabral's history of the revolution in which the ideals of harmony and balance are predominant. Cabral's theory highlights the fearless and dominative attitude of Marxism toward nature and the natural world which has on occasions been mirrored in the behaviour of socialist regimes in the management of human society. Perhaps this will eventually render Marxism obsolete for the second time.

Unlike Fanon, who never came to terms with Marxism and, unlike that huge congregation of African nationalists who, through indolence or lack of imagination rejected Marxism without ever understanding it, Cabral was quite aware of the significance of his choice. Cabral employed the Marxist tool of class analysis against negritude in order to show the meaning of the cultural renaissance movements which were so important in the development of African nationalism. Having done this, he was able to reject Marxism from a position established outside that of the petty bourgeoisie from which all previous African socialist theory had come. In his writings on personality Cabral emphasises the ideals of dignity, community, responsibility and creative productive work. Largely gone is the myth of the uniqueness of the African world because in Cabral's materialism all peoples are unique.

Since 1976, with the steadily declining fortunes of the revolution in Guiné, the immediate response upon reading Cabral's work has changed. Now the reader tends to look for a ghost in the machine in order to discover reasons in the history or the theory of the struggle to explain the withering of the revolution. Cabral however, would not have viewed the coup of November 1980 as the end of the revolution, but rather as an episode in the unfolding of Guiné's independent history in which various class contradictions were being resolved. But the coup does emphasise the fact that Cabral's work contains in its essence a body of knowledge which may be termed tragic.

Each of Cabral's essays points to the conclusion that the nationalist movements could have only modest pretensions even in those situations in which nationalism had been violent and ostensibly revolutionary. The period of anti-colonial struggle could not constitute, in Cabral's terms, a revolutionary movement; it was simply the price paid by the peoples of Africa for the colonial experience. Even those important changes instituted during the struggle in Guiné did not constitute a revolutionary break with the past in the sense that the new health services or the schools or the literacy programmes could not guarantee a post-independence liberation. It is at exactly this point of his analysis that Cabral arrives at the idea that the petty bourgeoisie must commit class suicide. Cabral's theory is not an instance of underdevelopment theory and yet he arrives at the only conclusion which underdevelopment theory can rightfully carry - that of a self-destructing petty bourgeoisie.

Cabral's work is a battleground on which there is no final victory, either for Marxism or for African socialism. The conflict in his work between the account of class analysis and class struggle and the wider theory of imperialism indicates that there is a certain irresolution or immaturity within the theory. Fanon's work is not such a battleground because in 'The Wretched of the Earth' the conflicts between the demands of African socialism and the tradition of Marxism are so impure. In Fanon the question of a new revolutionary theory is interleaved with exotic problems concerning personality, psychopathology and existential authenticity which generate all manner of secondary skirmishes on the borders of the work. In the writings of Cabral, the conflict is more pure and in consequence his achievements in advancing the cause of socialist theory are more substantial. And yet Cabral's work is reminiscent of Fanon's in that the best and most stimulating aspects of his theory are presented in effect as a battle of shadows. In Cabral these shadows were cast by the myths of the African personality and the classlessness of pre- and post-colonial societies, and by the suffocating weight of centre-periphery relations on the development of an independent polity. Where these shadows meet they tend to obliterate what is otherwise most illuminating in Cabral's theory. The major point of difference between Fanon and Cabral is that the identity behind the shadows has changed with the success of the independence decade.

In total, the effect of Cabral's political career was to help bring down the last of the great colonial empires in Africa, and in the realm of theory to dismantle the central shibboleths of African socialism. As such Cabral's intellectual legacy, like his bequest to the people of Guiné, does not represent so much a conclusion as a new beginning freed from the fears, prejudices and superstitions of the past.

NOTES

CHAPTER 2 THE STRUGGLE FOR GUINÉ

1. A. Cabral, 'Our People are our Mountains', (London: Committee for Freedom of Mozambique, Angola and Guinea, 1971).
2. A. Djassi, 'The Facts about Portugal's African Colonies' (London: Union of Democratic Control, June 1960).
3. S. Amin, 'Neo-Colonialism in West Africa' (New York: Monthly Review Press, 1973).
4. See A. Cabral, 'Our People are our Mountains', pp. 11, 12.
5. The PAI did not adopt the initial PAIGC (Partido Africano da Independência da Guiné e Cabo Verde) until four years later in October 1960. Initially the PAIGC was only one of a number of nationalist organisations. However, it was from the beginning the most unified and the most successful of all these movements. For further detail on the other nationalist movements in Guiné including FLCC, FLC and FLING, see L. Rudeback, 'Guiné-Bissau: A Study in Political Mobilization' (Uppsala: Scandinavian Institute of African Studies, 1974) and R., Chilcote (ed.), 'Emerging Nationalism in Portuguese Africa (Stanford: Hoover Institute Press, 1972).
6. A. Cabral, Determined to Resist, 'Tricontinental' (Sept./Oct. 1968), pp. 114-26.
7. A. Cabral, Memorandum to the Portuguese Government, in Chilcote, ed., Documents, Dec. 1, (1960).
8. A. Cabral, PAIGC Minor and Major Programmes, in Chilcote (1960).
9. A. Cabral, Frente al Ultra Colonialisme Portugues, 'Pensamiento Crítico', no. 36 (Jan. 1970), pp. 186-97.
10. See A. Cabral, 'Revolution in Guinea', (New York: Monthly Review Press, 1969), p. 59.
11. A. Cabral, Guinea: The Power of Arms, 'Tricontinental', vol. 12 (Jan. 1969), pp. 5-16.
12. A. Cabral, The National Fight for Liberation, in Chilcote, ed., 'Documents', pp. 374-6.
13. See A. Cabral, The Battle of Como and the Congress of Cassaca, in 'Unity and Struggle' (London: Heinemann Educational Books, 1980), pp. 175-9.
14. Cabral, Determined to Resist.
15. Cabral, Guinea: The Power of Arms, p. 13.
16. Ibid., p. 16.
17. Cabral, Frente al Ultra Colonialismo Portugues, p. 196.
18. Cabral, Determined to Resist, p. 117.
19. For a report on the political and military achievements of the PAIGC during this year, see A. Cabral Developments in the Struggle for the National Liberation of 'Portuguese' Guiné and the Cape Verde Islands in 1964, in Chilcote (ed.) 'Documents', pp. 377-81.
20. See A. Cabral, Guinea: Political and Military Situation, 'Tricontinental', no. 37 (April, 1969), pp. 25-34.
21. A. Cabral, Dez Anos Despois do Massacre de Pidjiguiti, in 'Unidade e Luta': (Vol. 1) 'A Practica Revolucionaria' (Lisbon: Seara Nova, 1977), pp. 69-76.
22. A. Cabral, A Brief Report on the Situation in the Struggle, Jan./Aug. 1971, 'Ufahamu', vol. 11 (1972), pp. 4-28.

23 A. Cabral, New Year's Message, in 'Return to the Source' (New York: Monthly Review Press, 1973), pp. 93-106.
24 Ibid., p. 97.
25 Cabral, Dez Anos Despois do Massacre de Pidjiguiti.
26 Cabral, A Brief Report on the Situation of the Struggle.
27 See A. Cabral, Report on Portuguese Guinea and the Liberation Movement, 'Ufahamu', vol. I, no. 2, (Fall 1970), pp. 69-95.

CHAPTER 3 THE AGRONOMIC WRITINGS

1 A. Cabral, Recenseamento Agricola da Guiné, 'Boletim Cultural da Guiné Portuguesa', vol. XI, no. 43, (July 1956), pp. 7-243.
2 All of the peoples of Guiné practise some form of crop consociation, that is the simultaneous use of two or more crops on the same piece of land. Because of this there was some difficulty in determining the true area under cultivation. However, a formula was finally arrived at which gave an accurate figure of the true area cultivated. This formula was based upon knowledge of the proportions of specific crops used by each ethnic group.
3 Amilcar Cabral, Acerca da contribuicao dos 'povos' guineenes para produçao agricola da Guiné, 'Boletim Cultural da Guiné Portuguesa', vol. IX (October 1954), pp. 771-7 (On the Contribution).
4 Amilcar Cabral and Maria Helena Cabral, Breves notas acerca da razão de ser, objectivos e processo do execução do recenseamento agricola da Guiné, 'Boletim Cultural da Guiné Portuguesa', vol. IX (January 1954), pp. 195-201. (Brief Notes on The Objectives and Methods of the Survey).
5 Amilcar Cabral, A propos du cycle cultural Arachide-Mils en Guinée Portugaise, 'Boletim Cultural da Guiné Portuguesa', vol. XIII (April 1958), pp. 149-56. (On the Cultivation of Groundnuts and Millet in 'Portuguese', Guiné).
6 A. Cabral, Feux de brousse et jachères dans la cycle cultural arachide-mils, 'Boletim Cultural da Guiné Portuguesa', vol. XIII (July 1958), pp. 257-68. (Burning Off and Fallow in the Cultivation of Groundnuts and Millet).
7 Amilcar Cabral, Queimadas e pousios na circunscrição de Fulacunda em 1954, 'Boletim Cultural da Guiné Portuguesa', vol. IX (July 1954), pp. 627-43 (Burning and Fallow in the Circle of Fulacunda in 1954).
8 Amilcar Cabral, Em defensa da terra, 'Cabo Verde: Boletim de Propaganda e Informação', vol. I (1 November 1949), pp. 2-4 (In Defence of the Land).
9 Amilcar Cabral, Para o conhecimento do problema da erosão do solo na Guiné. I Sobre o conceito de erosão, 'Boletim Cultural da Guiné Portuguesa', vol. IX (January 1954), pp. 163-94. (Understanding the Problem of Soil Erosion in Guiné).
10 A. Cabral, On the Cultivation of Groundnuts and Millet in 'Portuguese' Guiné, p. 155.
11 Samir Amin, 'Neo-Colonialism in West Africa', pp. vii-xviii.
12 Ibid., pp. 3-40.
13 Amilcar Cabral, Acerca da utilização da terra na Africa negra, 'Boletim Cultural da Guiné Portuguesa', vol. IX (April 1954), pp. 401-16.
14 Amilcar Cabral, A. propósito de mecanização da agricultura na Guiné Portuguesa, 'Boletim Cultural da Guiné Portuguesa', vol. IX (April 1954), pp. 389-99. (On the Mechanisation of Agriculture in Guiné).

CHAPTER 4 THE CLASS ANALYSIS OF AFRICAN SOCIETY

1 Issa Shivji, 'Class Struggles in Tanzania' (London: Heinemann, 1976), in discussing the fashionability of elite theory makes the wry comment that western capitalism has seen fit to export elite theory along with underdevelopment. The unintended irony of Shivji's comment is that underdevelopment theory has itself become an important export. See esp. pp. 13-26, for a discussion of the merits of Marxist class analysis in contemporary Africa.

2   See J. Nyerere, The Purpose is Man, in 'Uhuru Na Ujamma: Freedom and Socialism' (London: Heinemann, 1974), pp. 315-26. In a similar vein Walter Rodney, 'How Europe Underdeveloped Africa' (Dar es Salaam: Tanzanian Publishing House, 1972), argues that in pre-colonial Africa there was no evidence of class conflict as the motive force of change; rather the process or change can only be understood through an examination of the forces of production as a whole. Rodney proposes that prior to the fifteenth century most African societies were in a transitional phase between the practice of agriculture in family groups and the emergence of neo-feudal states and societies. Rodney's transitional phase indicates that African societies had begun a process of autonomous development before European penetration of the continent. See Rodney, esp. pp. 40-57. A parallel line of argument is found in Samir Amin's, Underdevelopment and Dependence in Black Africa, 'Journal of Modern African Studies', vol. 10, no. 4 (Dec. 1972), pp. 503-24 where he argues that up until the seventeenth century African societies had begun a process of autonomous development in that various modes of production and, by implication, various class divisions were already present. Unlike Rodney, Amin makes little comment on the relationships between social cleavage and historical development that is so important both in relationship to the contemporary use of class analysis and the myth of a classless pre-colonial Africa.
3   A. Cabral, A Brief Analysis of the Social Structure in Guiné, in 'Revolution in Guinea' (New York: Monthly Review Press, 1969), pp. 56-75.
4   Ibid.
5   A. Cabral, The Weapon of Theory, in 'The Revolution in Guinea', p. 93.
6   Ibid., p. 93.
7   Ibid., p. 67.
8   Ibid., p. 57.
9   A. Cabral, Determined to Resist, in 'Tricontinental', no. 8 (Sept./Oct. 1968), pp. 114-26.
10 A. Cabral, Towards Final Victory, in 'Revolution in Guinea', p. 158.
11 F. Engels, 'The Peasant War in Germany' (Moscow: Progress Publishers, 1956), pp. 12-24.
12 A. Cabral, A Brief Analysis, p. 58.
13 A. Cabral, At the United Nations, in 'The Revolution in Guinea', p. 36.
14 Ibid., p. 105.
15 A. Cabral, National Liberation and Culture, in 'Return to the Source', (New York: Monthly Review Press, 1973), p. 54.
16 Ibid., p. 47.
17 A. Cabral, The Weapon of Theory, p. 100.
18 A. Cabral, A Brief Analysis of the Social Structure in Guiné, p. 66.
19 Ibid., p. 62.
20 Gerard Chaliand, 'Armed Struggle in Africa' (New York: Monthly Review Press, 1969), pp. 20-1.
21 See Nicos Poulantzas, 'Classes in Contemporary Capitalism' (London: New Left Books, 1975), esp. pp. 193-208.
22 A. Cabral, The Weapon of Theory, p. 101.
23 Ibid., p. 105.
24 Ibid., p. 100.
25 Ibid., p. 106.
26 Ibid., p. 107.

CHAPTER 5 CULTURE AND PERSONALITY

1   Cabral generally avoids using the term tribalism, preferring instead the more neutral term ethnicity. He justifies this on the grounds that in Africa the tribal system was already in a state of disintegration before the colonial era began and that all that now remains of that system are certain remnants in the mentality of the people. The economic foundations of the system have quite disappeared. For Cabral's comments on tribalism, see Frente al Ultra Colonialisme Portugues, 'Pensiamento Critico', vol. 36 (Jan. 1970), pp. 186-97.

2   A. Cabral, Guinea and Cape Verde against Portuguese Colonialism, 'Revolution in Guinea' (New York Monthly Review Press, 1969), p. 17.
3   V. Lenin, The Heritage We Renounce, in 'Selected Works', vol. I (Moscow: Progress Publishers, 1963), pp. 57-91.
4   A. Cabral, National Liberation and Culture, in 'Return to the Source' (New York: Monthly Review Press, 1973), p. 41.
5   Ibid., pp. 42, 44.
6   A. Cabral, Identity and Dignity, in 'Return to the Source', p. 65.
7   Ibid., p. 50.
8   Ibid., p. 65.
9   A. Cabral, National Liberation and Culture, p. 39.
10 Ibid., p. 40.
11 Ibid., p. 48.
12 Ibid., p. 47.
13 Ibid., p. 61.
14 Frantz Fanon, On National Culture, in 'The Wretched of the Earth', pp. 166-99.
15 A. Cabral, National Liberation and Culture, p. 49, and Identity and Dignity p. 61.
16 A. Cabral, Identity and Dignity, p. 54.
17 Ibid., p. 59.
18 Ibid., p. 61.

CHAPTER 6   THE STATE

1   R. Miliband, 'The State in Capitalist Society' (London: Weidenfeld & Nicolson, 1969).
2   Samir Amin, Underdevelopment and Dependence in Black Africa: their Historical, Origins and Contemporary Forms, 'Journal of Social and Economic Studies', vol. 10, no. 4 (Dec. 1974), pp. 177-96.
3   V. Lenin, 'The State and Revolution' (Peking: Foreign Languages Press, 1970), p. 14.
4   A. Cabral, A Brief Analysis of the Social Structure, in 'Revolution in Guinea', (New York: Monthly Review Press, 1969), p. 69.
5   Ibid., p. 72.
6   A. Cabral, The Weapon of Theory, in 'Revolution in Guinea', p. 97.
7   A. Cabral, Connecting the Struggles, in 'Return to the Source', (New York: Monthly Review Press, 1973), pp. 75-92.
8   Ibid., p. 85.
9   Ibid., p. 83.
10 Ibid., p. 89.
11 Issa Shivji, 'Class Struggles in Tanzania' (London, Heinemann, 1976); et al. 'Silent Class Struggle' (Dar Es Salaam: Tanzanian Publishing House, 1974).
12 N. Chomsky and S. Herman, 'The Political Economy of Human Rights', vols 1 and 2 (Boston: South End Press, 1979).

CHAPTER 7   THE FORCES OF PRODUCTION

1   In 'The Family, Private Property and the State', Engels presents an argument that is essentially an adjunct to that found in 'The German Ideology' in accounting for the rise of class society. Engels argues that the breakdown of communalist society is brought about by a combination of population growth (to which Marx also refers in 'The Grundrisse') and by the development of specialised labour processes which necessitates exchange among producers. The development of a system of complex distribution accelerates the social division of labour and allows for a rapid advance in the level of the productive forces. Engels also shares with Marx the assumption that the disintegration of Gentile society is brought about by demographic factors

and the separation of part of the population from its original territory. Paradoxically this same process is also supposed to result from the appropriation of the surplus by a particular class.
2 Claude Meillassoux, From Reproduction to Production: A Marxist Approach to Economic Anthropology, 'Economy and Society', vol. 1 (1972), pp. 93-105; Claude Meillassoux, On the Mode of Production of the Hunting Band, in P. Alexandre, (ed.), 'French Perspectives in African Studies' (London: OUP, 1973); Emmanuel Terray, 'Marxism and "Primitive Societies"' (New York: Monthly Review Press, 1972).
3 Walter Rodney, 'How Europe Underdeveloped Africa' (Dar Es Salaam, Tanzanian Publishing House, 1972).
4 Samir Amin, The Third World Today and the International Division of Labor, 'AMPO', vol. II, no. 1 (1979), pp. 19-37.
5 Goron Hayden, 'Beyond Ujama in Tanzania: Underdevelopment and the Uncaptured Peasantry' (London: Heinemann, 1980).
6 Perry Anderson, 'Lineages of the Absolutist State' (London: New Left Books, 1974).
7 A. Cabral, The Weapon of Theory, in 'Revolution in Guinea' (New York Monthly Review Press, 1969.
8 Ibid., p. 97.

CHAPTER 8 IMPERIALISM

1 See Ho Chi Minh, 'On Revolution: Selected Writings 1920-66', ed. Bernard Fall (New York: Frederick A. Praeger, 1967), esp. pp. 23-9.
2 Aimé Césaire, 'Discours sur le colonialisme' (Paris: Présence Africaine, 1950).
3 Ibid., p. 12.
4 Nkrumah's stance on the question of imperialism is erratic and this can be seen clearly in his vacillations on the question of the existence of classes in Africa. In his early essay 'Conscientism' (London: Heinemann, 1964) he denies the presence of class divisions in African states, while six years later in 'Class Struggle in Africa' (London: Panaf, 1970) he sets out to construct a class analysis of post-colonial Africa. In both works Nkrumah supports a belief in the efficacy of traditional society as a model for future development because this society has remained untouched by imperialism or the colonial experience. The most grandiose attempt to integrate Lenin's theory of imperialism into the literature of African nationalism is found in Nkrumah's 'Neo-Colonialism: The Last Stage of Imperialism' (London: Nelson, 1965). Unfortunately this work is far too self-conscious to add anything of value to the debate about imperialism.
5 Amilcar Cabral, The Death Pangs of Imperialism, in Chilcote, ed., 'Documents', pp. 318-22; The Weapon of Theory, in 'Revolution in Guinea' (New York: Monthly Review Press, 1973), pp. 90-111; Portugal e imperialista? in 'Unidade e Luta', vol. II, pp. 203-6.
6 See 'Revolution in Guinea', pp. 13, 73, 98, 99.
7 Ibid., pp. 68, 76, 78, 99, 102, and 'Return to the Source', pp. 41, 43, 58.
8 See Amilcar Cabral, Brief Analysis of the Social Structure in Guinea, in 'Revolution in Guinea', p. 73.
9 Ibid., p. 75.
10 Ibid., p. 75.
11 Amilcar Cabral, Practical Problems and Tactics, in 'Revolution in Guinea', p. 150.
12 Amilcar Cabral, Guinea and Cape Verde Against Portuguese Colonialism, in 'Revolution in Guinea', p. 14.
13 Ibid., p. 14.
14 Amilcar Cabral, 'Revolution in Guinea', pp. 70, 72, 109, 110 and 'Return to the Source', p. 69.
15 Amilcar Cabral, The Weapon of Theory, p. 98.
16 See Colin Leys, 'Underdevelopment in Kenya' (London: Heinemann, 1975), and The 'Overdeveloped' Post Colonial State: A Revaluation, 'Review of

African Political Economy', no. 5 (Jan/April, 1976), pp. 39-48.
17 Bill Warren, Imperialism and Capitalist Industrialisation, 'New Left Review', vol. 81 (Sept.-Oct. 1973), pp. 3-44.

CHAPTER 9 CONCLUSION

1 Amilcar Cabral, Our People are our Mountains, p. 22.

BIBLIOGRAPHY

COLLECTED WRITINGS OF CABRAL

The most readily available sources of Cabral's writings are:
'Revolution in Guinea: Selected Texts' (New York: Montly Review Press, 1969).
'Return to the Source: Selected Speeches' (New York: Monthly Review Press, 1973).
'Unity and Struggle: Speeches and Writings', trans. Michael Wolfers (London: Heinemann, 1980).
To date the most complete compilation of Cabral's writings is to be found in 'Unité et lutte': vol I, 'L'Arme de la théorie', and vol. 2, 'La Pratique révolutionnaire' (Paris: Maspero, 1975). Unfortunately this edition is now out of print, as is the Portuguese edition of the same volumes, 'Unidade e Luta' (Sera Nova, 1977).
The most extensive bibliography of Cabral's writings and speeches is found in R. Chilcote's Amilcar Cabral: a Bio-Bibliography of his Life and Thought, 1925-1973, 'Africana Journal', vol. V, no. 4 (Winter 1974-5), pp. 289-307. Chilcote's bibliography contains reference to most of Cabral's agronomic writings as well as to numerous ephemera written for the PAIGC.

ARTICLES BY CABRAL
Acerca da utilização da terra na Africa negra, 'Boletim Cultural da Guiné-Portuguesa', vol. IX (April 1954), pp. 401-16. The first two sections of this article are available under the title Original Writings in 'Ufahamu', vol. 3, no. 3, (1973), pp. 31-41.
Acerca da contribuição dos 'povos' guineenes para a produção agrícola da Guiné, 'Boletim Cultural da Guiné Portuguesa', vol. IX (October 1954), pp. 771-7; reprinted in Chilcote, ed. 'Documents', pp. 352-5.
Acerca de uma classificação fitossanitária do armazenamento, 'Ministerio do ultramar', (Lisbon, 1958), pp. 1-95.
Anonymous Soldiers for the U.N. (Extracts, Declaration to 4th. Commission to the U.N. Dec. 1962), in 'Revolution in Guinea', pp. 50-2.
At the United Nations (Extracts, Conakry statement to U.N. Committee on the Portuguese Territories, June 1962), in 'Revolution in Guinea', pp. 24-49.
(With Maria Helena Cabral), Breves notas acerca da razão de ser, objectivos e processo do execução do recenseamento agrícola da Guiné, 'Boletim Cultural da Guiné Portuguesa', vol. IX (January 1954), pp. 195-201.
A Brief Analysis of the Social Structure in Guinea, in 'Revolution in Guinea', pp. 56-75. Originally published as Breve análisis de la estructura social de la Guinea 'Portuguesa', 'Pensamiento Crítico', vol. 2-3 (March/April 1964), pp. 24-48. This article has been reprinted in various forms and under various titles. See also The Struggle in Guinea, 'International Socialist Journal', vol. I (August 1964), pp. 428-46.
A Brief Report on the Situation of the Struggle, 'Ufahamu', vol. II (1972), pp. 4-28 (a report on the struggle covering the period Jan/August 1971). This is also available under the title Fruits of a Struggle in 'Tricontinental', no. 31 (July/Aug. 1972), pp. 61-77.
Connecting the Struggles: An Informal Talk with Black Americans, (African Information Serivce, Oct. 1972), in 'Return to the Source', pp. 75-92.

146 Bibliography

Creation of the People's National Assembly in Guiné, 'Unity and Struggle' (8 Jan. 1973, communiqué), pp. 277-87. Also in 'Unidade e Luta', pp. 209-16.
The Death Pangs of Imperialism, in Chilcote (ed.) 'Documents', pp. 318-22. A cannibalised version of this article appeared under the title The War in 'Portuguese' Guinea, in 'Revolution' (Paris) vol. I (July 1963), pp. 103-8. Further fragments from this article have also been published under the title Guinea and Cape Verde Against Portuguese Colonialism, in 'Revolution in Guinea', pp. 11-23.
Declaration on the Present Status of the Fight for Liberation in 'Portuguese' Guiné and in the Cape Verde Islands, in Chilcote, (ed.), 'Documents, pp. 372-4. Originally published as Déclaration sur la situation actuelle de la lutte de libération en Guinée 'Portugaise' et aux Iles du Cap Vert, Conakry (Jan 20, 1962).
Determined to Resist, 'Tricontinental', no. 8 (Sept./Oct. 1968), pp. 114-126, reprinted as Practical Problems and Tactics, in 'Revolution in Guinea', pp. 134-51.
The Development of the Struggle (Extracts, Declaration to OSPAAAL, Dec. 1968), in 'Revolution in Guinea', pp. 112-26.
Developments in the Struggle for the Liberation of 'Portuguese' Guiné and the Cape Verde Islands in 1964, in Chilcote (ed.), 'Documents', pp. 377-81. Originally published as Le dévelopement de la lutte nationale en Guinée 'Portugaise' et aux Iles du Cap Vert en 1964, Conakry, 1965(?). This also appears as The Battle for Como and the Congress of Cassaca, in 'Unity and Struggle', pp. 175-9. See also 'Unidade e Luta', pp. 40-4.
Dez anos depois to massacre Pidjiguiti, in 'Unidade e Luta', vol. II, pp. 69-75. An abridged version of this article appeared under the title PAIGC: On the Situation of our Armed Struggle for National Liberation, 'Ufahamu', vol. I, no. 2 (Fall 1970).
The Eighth Year of the Armed Struggle for National Liberation, (report on the situation of the struggle, Jan. 1971), in 'Unity and Struggle', pp. 180-210; also in 'Unidade e Luta', pp. 77-100.
Em defensa da terra, 'Boletim de Propaganda e Informação' vol. I (November 1949), pp. 204. Also available in Chilcote (ed.), 'Documents', pp. 350-2.
(Pamphlet under pseudoynym Djassi, Abel) The Facts About Portugal's African Colonies, introduction by Basil Davidson (London: Union of Democratic Control), June 1960, p. 20, reprinted in 'Unity and Struggle', pp. 17-27.
Feux de brousse et jachères dans le cycle cultural arachidémils, 'Boletim Cultural da Guiné Portuguesa', vol. XIII (July 1958), pp. 257-68.
On Freeing Captured Portuguese Soldiers-II (Declaration made at Dakar, 19 Dec. 1968), reprinted in 'Revolution in Guinea', pp. 131-3.
Forward, in B. Davidson, 'The Liberation of Guiné (Harmondsworth: Penguin, 1969), pp. 9-15.
On Freeing Captured Portuguese Soldiers-I (Declaration made at Dakar, 3 March 1968), reprinted in 'Revolution in Guinea', pp. 127-30.
Frente al ultra colonialisme portugues, 'Pensamiento Crítico', vol. 36 (Jan. 1970), pp. 186-97.
General Watchwords, in 'Unity and Struggle', pp. 224-50. The eight directives included under this title were written by Cabral after the First Party Conference of the PAIGC held at Cassaca in February 1964, and were published in Portuguese in November 1965. An excerpt is also available under the title Tell No Lies: Claim No Easy Victories, in 'Revolution in Guinea', pp. 86-9.
Guinea and Cape Verde against Portuguese Colonialism, (Speech 3rd Conference African Peoples, Cairo, 25-31, March 1961) in 'Revolution in Guinea', pp. 11-23.
Guinea: Political and Military Situation, 'Tricontinental', no. 37 (April 1969), pp. 25-34.
Guinea: The Power of Arms, 'Tricontinental', vol. 12 (Jan. 1969), pp. 5-16. A condensed version of this interview appeared under the title Towards Final Victory in 'Revolution in Guinea', pp. 156-64.
Homage to Kwame Nkrumah, in 'Unity and Struggle', pp. 114-18 (a speech given at Conakry on 13 May 1972). It was first published under the title Cabral on

Nkrumah (Newark: Iihad Productions in co-operation with the PAIGC 1973), p. 8.

Identity and Dignity in the Context of the National Liberation Struggle, is the text of an address Cabral gave at Lincoln University on 15 October 1972, published in 'Return to the Source', pp. 57-69. The text of this speech was based wholly on Le Rôle de la culture dans la lutte pour l'independence, which Cabral presented at the Réunion d'Experts sur les Notions de Race, d'Identité et de Dignité, UNESCO, Paris 3-7 July 1972, pp. 1-15. The text from the conference was originally published by the UN organisation for Education, Science and Culture.

Liberation Movement in Portuguese Guinea, in 'Voice of Africa', vol. 2 (March 1962).

Liberating Portuguese Guiné from Within, 'New African', vol. 4 (June 1965), p. 85.

Mankind's Path to Progress, 'World Marxist Review' vol. X (Nov. 1967), pp. 88-9.

(With others), Message to the Portuguese Colonists in Guiné and Cape Verde, in Chilcote, (ed.), 'Documents', pp. 355-7. Originally published in 'Frente de Libertacao da Guiné e Cabo Verde, Partido Africano da Independência', np (Oct. 1960). Part of this statement is reprinted in 'Unity and Struggle', p. 162 and it is also available in 'Unidade e Luta', pp. 19-24.

(With others), Memorandum to the Portuguese Government, in Chilcote, (ed.), 'Documents', pp. 367-9. Originally published as Memorandum enviado ao govérno peol Partido Africano da Independência, (Conakry 1 Dec. 1960). This article has been reprinted under its original title in 'Unity and Struggle', pp. 166-71. It is also available in 'Unidade e Luta', pp. 26-33.

Memorandum to the United Nations General Assembly, in Chilcote (ed.), 'Documents', pp. 369-71. Originally published as Memorandum à Assembleia Geral da Organização das Nações Unidas, (Conakry, 26 Sept. 1961).

A Message to Guinean and Cape Verdean Civil Servants and Employees in Commerce, for the Political Bureau of the PAI, Oct. 1960, in Chilcote (ed.), 'Documents', p. 315, reprinted in 'Unity and Struggle', pp. 157-9. It is also available in 'Unidade e Luta', pp. 11-14.

Message to the People of Portugal, (Declaration made at Khartoum, Jan. 1969), in 'Revolution in Guinea', pp. 152-5.

The Minor Programme and the Major Programme, in Chilcote (ed.), 'Documents', no date available, but this statement was certainly issued near to November 1960.

The National Fight for Liberation, in Chilcote (ed.), 'Documents', pp. 374-6. Originally published as Le peuple de la Guiné 'Portugaise' devant l'organisation des Nations Unies, (Conakry, June 1962), pp. 64-5.

National Liberation and Culture (Eduardo Mondlane Memorial Series Lecture, Syracuse University, 20 Feb. 1970), p. 18, in 'Return to the Source', pp. 39-56. Also available in a slightly longer version under the same title in 'Unity and Struggle', pp. 138-56.

National Liberation and Peace: Cornerstones of Non-Alignment (Extracts from Speech, Congress of Non-Aligned Countries, Cairo 1964), in 'Revolution in Guinea', pp. 53-5.

The Nationalist Movements of the Portuguese Colonies (Address at CONCP conference, Dar-Es-Salaam, 1965), in 'Revolution in Guinea', pp. 76-85. Also available under the title The Options of the CONCP, in 'Unity and Struggle', pp. 251-61.

New Year's Message (Delivered to the PAIGC: Jan. 1973), in 'Return to the Source', pp. 93-106. Also in Wolfers (trans.), 'Unity and Struggle', and in 'Unidade e Luta', pp. 127-36.

An Open Note to the Portuguese Government (Conakry, 13 Oct. 1961), in 'Unity and Struggle', pp. 172-3. Also available in 'Unidade e Luta', pp. 33-4.

Our People are our Mountains (London: Committee for Freedom for Mozambique. Angloa and Guinea, Oct. 1971).

Message to the Soldiers, Officers and NCO's of the Portuguese colonial Army (23 Jan. 1963), reprinted in 'Unity and Struggle', pp. 163-5, also available

in 'Unidade e Luta', pp. 23-6.
PAIGC: Optimistic and Fighter, 'Tricontinental', vol. 19/20, (July/Oct. 1970), pp. 167-74, report presented before OSPAAL.
Para o conhecimento do problema da erosão do solo na Guiné. I. - Sobre o conceito de erosao, 'Boletim Cultural da Guiné Portuguesa', vol. IX (January 1954), pp. 163-94.
Party Principles and Political Practice, in 'Unity and Struggle', pp. 28-113. This consists of a series of nine lectures given by Cabral to PAIGC cadres during Nov. 1969.
Portugal e imperialista? in 'Unidade e Luta', vol. II, pp. 203-6. This is an extract of a speech Cabral presented at Helsinki on 20 October 1971.
Poems, in 'Unity and Struggle', p. 3. Originally published in 1946 and 1949.
(With others), Proclamation, in Chilcote (ed.), 'Documents', pp. 258-60. Originally published as Movimento de Libertação da Guiné e Capo Verde - proclamação, (Conakry, Nov. 1960).
Proclamation of Direct Action (Conakry, 3 August 1961), reprinted in 'Unity and Struggle', p. 174, and in 'Unidade e Luta', pp. 35-6.
A Propos du cycle cultural Arachide-Mils en Guinée Portugaise, 'Boletim Cultural da Guiné Portuguesa', vol. XIII (April 1958), pp. 149-56. This is the next of a speech first presented at the Conférence Arachide-Mils at Banbey, Senegal in September 1954.
A propósito de mecanização da agricultura na Guiné Portuguesa, 'Boletim Cultural da Guiné Portuguesa', vol. IX (April 1954), pp. 389-99.
Queimadas e pousios na circunscrição de Fulacunda em 1954, 'Boletim Cultural da Guiné Portuguesa', vol. IX (July 1954), pp. 627-43.
Realities, 'Tricontinental', no. 33 (1973), pp. 97-109 (interview held in 1972 shortly before Cabral's death).
Recenseamento agrícola da Guiné, 'Boletim Cultural da Guiné Portuguesa', vol. XI no. 43, (July 1956), pp. 7-243. A fragment from this important survey is reprinted under the title Agricultural Census of Guinea: estimate 1954, in 'Unity and Struggle', pp. 4-16.
A Report to Our Friends, 'Africa Today', vol. 20, no. 1 (Winter 1973), pp. 7-14. Excerpts of a public statement by Cabral made on 19, October 1972 in New York.
Report on Portuguese Guinea and the Liberation Movement, 'Ufahamu', vol. I, no. 2 (Fall 1970), pp. 69-103. This includes Cabral's statement before the US Congress House Committee on Foreign Affairs, 26 February 1970.
The Rise of Nationalism, in Chilcote (ed.), 'Documents', pp. 301-5. Originally published as Rapport général sur la lutte de libération nationale, (Conakry, (?) July 1961), p. 7.
Second Address Before the United Nations (27th. Session of 4th. Committee, Oct. 16 1972: Questions on Territories under Portuguese Admin.), p. 19, in 'Return to the Source', pp. 15-33. Also available as The People of Guinea and Cape Verde before the UN, in 'Unity and Struggle', pp. 261-76. A fragment of this statement was reproduced under the title Support of the People's Legitimate Aspirations to Freedom, Independence and Progress, in 'Objective: Justice' vol. 5 (Jan./March 1973), pp. 4-7.
New Year's Message, in 'Return to the Source', pp. 93-106. This was intended to be part of a dossier prepared by Cabral for presentation before an extraordinary session of the OAU scheduled for February 1973 at Addis Ababa. It was in fact Cabral's final statement as he was assassinated only hours after its completion on 20 January 1973. Also available in 'Unity and Struggle', pp. 288-98.
Statutes of the PAIGC (Conakry, 1962) in Chilcote (ed.), 'Documents', pp. 327-32.
The Struggle Has Taken Root, 'Tricontinental', vol. 84 (1973), pp. 41-9. Text of a statement made at a Conakry press conference in Sept. 1972. Also in 'Black Scholar', vol. 4 (July/August 1973), pp. 28-31.
The Weapon of Theory, (address First Tri-Continental Conference, Havana, Jan. 1966), in 'Revolution in Guinea', pp. 90-111. Also in 'Unity and Struggle', under the title Presuppositions and Objectives of National Liberation

in Relation to Social Structure, pp. 119-37.

ARTICLES ON CABRAL

Andelman, David, Profile: Amílcar Cabral: Pragmatic Revolutionary shows how an African Guerrilla War can be Won, 'Africa Report' (May 1970), pp. 18-19.
Andrade, de, Amilcar Cabral, 'Présence Africaine' (1973), pp. 3-19.
Anon., Tussles Among Guerrillas in Guinea, 'The Star Johannesburg' (3 Feb. 1973), p. 13.
Bienen, Henry, State and Revolution: the work of Amilcar Cabral, 'Journal of Modern African Studies', vol. 15, no. 4 (Dec. 1977), pp. 555-95.
Blackey, Robert, Fanon and Cabral: A Contrast in Theories of Revolution for Africa, 'Journal of Modern African Studies', vol. 12, no. 2 (1974), pp. 191-209.
Chaliand, Gerard, The Legacy of Amilcar Cabral, 'Ramparts', vol. XI (April 1973), pp. 17-20.
Chaliand, Gerard, The PAIGC without Cabral: An Assessment, 'Ufahamu', vol. III, no. 3 (Winter, 1973), pp. 87-111.
Chilcote, Ronald, The Political Thought of Amilcar Cabral, 'Journal of Modern African Studies', vol. 6, no. 3 (1968), pp. 373-88.
Dadoo, Yusuf, Amilcar Cabral: Outstanding Leader of African Liberation Movement, 'African Communist', vol. 53 (Second Quarter 1973), pp. 38-43.
Davidson, Basil, Cabral's Monument, 'New Statesman' (26 Jan. 1973).
Fernandes, Gil, Talk with a Guinean Revolutionary, 'Ufahamu' vol. I, no. 1 (Spring 1970), pp. 6-21.
Goldfield, Steve, Amilcar Cabral and the Liberation Struggle in Portuguese Guinea, 'Socialist Revolution', 13-14 (Jan.-April 1973), pp. 127-30.
Hubbard, Maryinez, Culture and History in a Revolutionary Context: Approaches to Amilcar Cabral, 'Ufahamu', vol. III (Winter 1973), pp. 69-86.
Magubane, Bernard, Amilcar Cabral: Evolution of Revolutionary Thought, 'Ufahamu', vol. II, no. 2 (Fall 1971), pp. 71-88.
McCollester, Charles, The African Revolution: Theory and Practice. The Political Thought of Amilcar Cabral, 'Monthly Review', vol. XXIV (March 1973), pp. 10-21.
'Newsweek', Freedom Fighters (5, Feb. 1973), pp. 44-9 (an account of the assassination of Cabral).
Nyang, S.S., The Political Thought of Cabral, 'Africana Research Bulletin', vol. 5, no. 2 (1975), pp. 48-77.
'Ufahamu', vol. III, no. 3 (Winter 1973). The whole issue is devoted to Cabral and his assassination.

ARTICLES - GENERAL

Adam, Hussein, M.; Black Thinkers and the Need to Confront Marx, 'Pan-African Journal', vol. 4, no. 1 (Winter 1971), pp. 75-102.
Alavi, Hamza, Imperialism Old and New, 'Socialist Register' (1964), pp. 104-26.
Alavi, Hamza, Peasants and Revolutions, 'Socialist Register' (1965), pp. 241-77.
Alavi, Hamza, The State in Post Colonial Societies: Pakistan and Bangladesh, 'New Left Review', vol. 74 (July/Aug. 1972), pp. 59-81.
Allen, V.I., The Meaning of the Working Class in Africa, 'Journal of Modern African Studies', vol. 10, no. 2 (1972), pp. 169-89.
Amin, Samir, Development and Stagnation in Agriculture, in Gutkind and Waterman (eds), 'African Social Studies' (London: Heinemann, 1977), pp. 154-8.
Amin, Samir, The Third World Today and the International Division of Labor, 'AMPO; Japan/Asia Quarterly Review', vol. II, no. 1 (1979), pp. 19-37.
Amin, Samir, Underdevelopment and Dependence in Black Africa: Their Historical Origins and Contemporary Forms, 'Journal of Modern African Studies', vol. 10, no. 4 (Dec. 1972), pp. 503-24.
Anderson, Perry, Portugal and the End of Ultra-Colonialism, 'New Left Review',

vol. 4 (Winter 1962), pp. 85-114.
Armah, Ayi Kwei, African Socialism: Utopian or Scientific, 'Présence Africaine', no. 64, 4th quarter (1967), pp. 6-30.
Bailey, A.M. and Llobera, J., The Asiatic Mode of Production: An Annotated Bibliography, 'Critical Anthropology', vol. 4/5 (1975), pp. 165-76.
Bender, G., The Limits of Counter-Insurgency: an African Case, 'Journal of Comparative Politics', vol. IV, no. 3 (1972), pp. 331-60.
Berman, Sanford, African Liberation Movements: A Preliminary Bibliography, 'Ufahamu' (Los Angeles, Spring 1970), pp. 107-28.
Biggs-Davison, John, The Current Situation in Portuguese Guinea, 'African Affairs' (Oct. 1971), pp. 385-94.
Braundi, E.R., Neo-Colonialism and Class Struggle, 'International Socialist Journal', no. I (Jan/Feb. 1964), pp. 48-68.
Cabral, Luis, Portuguese Guinea: United Front against Imperialism, 'Tricontinental', vol. 15 (Nov.-Dec. 1969), 141-6.
Cabral, Luis, et al., Ways of the Anti-Imperialist Struggle in Tropical Africa, 'World Marxist Review', vol. XIV (Aug. 1971), pp. 83-93.
Cabral, Vasco, Guinea-Bissau: Free Territory of Africa, 'Tricontinental News Service', vol. I, no. 2 (1, Jan 1973), pp. 20-3.
Cabral, Vasco, We Build as We Fight, 'World Marxist Review', vol. X (Feb. 1967), pp. 30-1.
Casals, R., The New Battle for PAIGC, 'Tricontinental', vol. 95 (1975), pp. 53-60.
Césaire, Aimé, L'Homme de culture et ses responsibilités, 'Présence Africaine', no. 24/25 (1959), pp. 116-22.
Chodak, Szymon, The Birth of the African Peasantry, 'Canadian Journal of African Studies', vol. 5, no. 3 (1971), pp. 327-48.
Cohen, Robin, Class in Africa: Analytical Problems and Perspectives, 'Socialist Register' (1972), pp. 231-55.
Davidson, Basil, The African Peasants and Revolution, 'Journal of Peasant Studies', vol. 1, no. 3 (April 1973/4), pp. 269-89.
Davidson, Basil, Growing From Grass Roots: The State of Guinea-Bissau, (London: London Committee for Freedom of Mozambique, Angola and Guiné, 1973), p. 20.
Davidson, Basil, The Liberation Struggle in Angola and 'Portuguese' Guinea, 'African Quarterly', vol. X, no. I (1970), pp. 25-31.
Fallers, L.A., Are African Cultivators to be 'Peasants'? 'Current Anthropology', vol. 2, no. 2 (1961), pp. 108-10.
Ferreira, E., Portugal and her Former African Colonies, 'Ufahamu', vol. 5, no. 3 (1975), pp. 159-70.
Foster-Carter, Aidan, Neo-Marxist Approaches to Development and Underdevelopment, 'Journal of Contemporary Asia', vol. 3, no. 1 (1973), pp. 7-33.
Franklin, Burce, The Lumpenproletariat and the Revolutionary Youth Movement, 'Monthly Review', vol. 21, no. 8 (Jan. 1970), pp. 10-25.
Glantz, M.H., Portugal vs PAIGC, 'Pan African Journal', vol. 6, no. 3 (1973), pp. 285-96.
Grundy, Kenneth W., African Explanations of Underdevelopment: The Theoretical Basis for Political Action, 'Review of Politics', vol. 28, no. 1 (January 1966), pp. 62-75.
Grundy, Kenneth W., The 'Class Struggle' in Africa: An Examination of Conflicting Theories, 'Journal of Modern African Studies', vol. 2, no. 3 (1964), pp. 379-93.
Grundy, Kenneth W., Nkrumah's Theory of Underdevelopment, 'World Politics', vol. 15, no. 3 (April 1963), pp. 438-54.
Hill, Polly, The Myth of the Amorphous Peasantry: A Northern Nigerian Case Study, 'Nigerian Journal of Economic and Social Studies', vol. 10, no. 2 (1968), pp. 239-60.
Hobsbawm, Eric J., Peasants and Politics, 'Journal of Peasant Studies', vol. I, no. 1 (1973), pp. 3-21.
Hodgkin, Thomas, Some African and Third World Theories of Imperialism, in Owen, R. and Sutcliffe, B. (eds), 'Studies in the Theory of Imperialism'

(London: Longman, 1972), pp. 93-116.
Irele, Abiola, Literature and Ideology in Martinique: René Marin, Aimé Césaire and Frantz Fanon, 'Research Review Monography', vol. 1, no. 3 (Ghana University: Institute of African Studies, 1969), pp. 1-32.
Kiernan, V.G., The Peasant Revolution: Some Questions, 'Socialist Register' (1970), pp. 9-37.
Kitching, Gavin N., The Concept of Class and the Study of Africa, 'African Review', vol. 2, no. 3 (1972), pp. 327-50.
Land, Thomas, Western Investment in Portugal's African Wars, 'East African Journal', University College Nairobi (June 1971), pp. 27-9.
Ledda, Romano, Social Class and Political Struggle, 'International Socialist Journal', no. 22 (August 1967), pp. 560-80.
Leys, Colin, Capital Accumulation, Class Formation and Dependency – The Significance of the Kenyan Case, 'Socialist Register' (1978), pp. 241-66.
Leys, Colin, The 'Overdeveloped' Post Colonial State: A Revaluation, 'Review of African Political Economy', no. 5 (Jan./Apr. 1976), pp. 39-48.
Leys, Colin, Underdevelopment and Dependency: Critical Notes, 'Journal of Contemporary Asia', vol. 7, no. 1, pp. 92-107.
Lobban, R., Guiné-Bissau, 'Africa Today', vol. 21, no. 1 (1974), pp. 15-24.
Martin, Charles, Nkrumah's Strategy for Decolonization: Originality and Classicism, 'Présence Africaine', no. 85, 1st, quarter (1973), pp. 74-105.
Meillassoux, Claude, On the Mode of Production of the Hunting Band, in P. Alexandré (ed.), 'French Perspectives in African Studies', (London; OUP, 1973).
Meillassoux, Claude, From Reproduction to Production: A Marxist Approach to Economic Anthropology, 'Economy and Society', vol. I (1972), pp. 93-105.
Miller, Robert A., Elite Formation in Africa: Class, Culture and Coherence, 'Journal of Modern African Studies', vol. 12, no. 4 (1974), pp. 521-42.
Mintz, Sidney W., A Note on the Definition of Peasantries, 'Journal of Peasant Studies', vol. I, no. 1 (1973), pp. 91-106.
Mohan, Jitendra, Varieties of African Socialism, 'Socialist Register' (1966), pp. 220-6.
MPLA, 'Revolution in Angola' (London: Merlin Press, 1972).
Obichere, B., Reconstruction in Guinea-Bissau, 'Current Bibliography of African Affairs', vol. 8, no. 3 (1975), pp. 204-19.
Omewale, Matteos, The Cape Verdeans and the PAIGC. Struggle for National Liberation, 'Ufahamu', vol. III (Winter 1973), pp. 43-8.
Oudes, Bruce, The Not So Much Fable of Bissau Desh, 'Africa Today' (Fall 1972), pp. 48-53.
Petras, James, Neo-Fascism: Accumulation and Class Struggle in the Third World, 'Journal of Contemporary Asia', vol. 10, no. 1/2 (1980), pp. 119-29.
Pinto, Cruz, Guinea-Bissau's Liberation Struggle against Portuguese Colonialism, 'Freedomways', vol. 3 (1972).
Rudebeck, Lars, Political Mobilization in Guinea-Bissau, 'Journal of Modern African Studies' (May 1972), pp. 1-18.
Sarrazin, C., The State of Guiné-Bissau, 'Tricontinental', vol. 34, no. 5 (1974), pp. 46-87.
Sarte, Jean-Paul, Orphée Noir, in L.S. Senghor (ed.), 'Anthologie de la Nouvelle Poésie Négre et Malgache de Langue Francaise' (Paris: Presses Universitaires de France, 1948, 4th. edn. 1969).
Saul, John, The State in Post Colonial Societies: Tanzania, 'Socialist Register' (1974), pp. 349-71.
Taylor, John, Neo-Marxism and Underdevelopment – A Sociological Phantasy, 'Journal of Contemporary Asia', vol. 4, no. 1, (1974), pp. 5-23.
United Nations, Report to the United Nations, Special Mission to Guinea (Bissau) (New York 1972), p. 14, reprinted from Objective Justice' (Sept. 1972).
Urdang, S., Women's Struggle in Guinea-Bissau, 'African Studies Review', vol. 18, no. 2 (1975), pp. 29-34.
Wallerstein, I., The Lessons of the PAIGC, 'Africa Today' (July 1971), pp. 62-8.
Warren, Bill, Imperialism and Capitalist Industrialisation, 'New Left Review', vol. 81 (Sept.-Oct. 1973), pp. 3-44.

152 Bibliography

Williams, Olu, The Test of Pan-Africanism: The Invasion of Guinea and Aftermath, 'Mazubgumzo' (Michigan: Winter 1972), pp. 27-51. Source 'Ufahamu', vol. 3, no. 3 (1973), p. 159.
Wiseberg, L.S. and Nelso, G., Mini-state with Maxi-problems, 'Africa Report', vol. 21, no. 2 (1976), pp. 15-17, 21-5, 48-9.
Zartman, I.W., Africa's Quiet War: Portuguese Guinea, 'Africa Report', vol. IX (Feb. 1964), pp. 8-12.
Zartman, I.W., Guinea: The Quiet War Goes On, 'Africa Report' (Nov. 1967), pp. 67-72.

BOOKS

Amin, Samir, 'Accumulation on a World Scale', vols 1 and 2 (New York: Monthly Review Press, 1974), trans. by Brian Pearce.
Amin, Samir, 'Neo-Colonialism in West Africa' (Harmondsworth: Penguin Books, 1973).
Anderson, Perry, 'Lineages of the Absolutist State' (London: New Left Books, 1974).
Anon., 'Eduardo Mondlane' (London: Panaf Books, 1972).
Arrighi, Giovanni and Saul, John, 'Essays on the Political Economy of Africa' (London, Monthly Review Press, 1973).
Baran, Paul, 'The Political Economy of Growth' (New York: Monthly Review Press, 1957).
Baran, Paul and Sweezy, Paul, 'Monopoly Capital' (Harmondsworth: Penguin Books, 1966).
Bascom, William and Herskovits, M. (eds), 'Continuity and Change in African Cultures' (Chicago: University of Chicago Press, 1959).
Bateson, Gregory, 'Steps to an Ecology of Mind' (London: Paladin, 1972).
Blair, Thomas L., 'The Land to Those who Work it: Algeria's Experiment in Workers' Management' (New York: Doubleday, 1970).
Bukharin, N., 'Imperialism and World Economy' (London: Merlin Press, 1972).
Césaire Aimé, 'Discours sur le Colonialisme' (Paris: Présence Africaine, 1950).
Cadbury, W.A., 'Labour in Portuguese Africa' (London: Routledge, 1910).
Chaliand, Gerald, 'Armed Struggle in Africa' (New York: Monthly Review Press, 1969).
Chilcote, Ronald H. (ed.), 'Emerging Nationalism in Portuguese Africa: A Bibliography of Documents, Ephemera, Through 1965' (Stanford, Hoover Institute, 1969).
Curtin, Phillip (ed.), 'Africa and the West: Intellectual Responses to European Culture' (Wisconsin: University of Wisconsin Press, 1972).
Davidson, Basil, 'In the Eye of the Storm' (Harmondsworth: Penguin Books, 1972).
Davidson, Basil, 'The Liberation of Guiné: Aspects of an African Revolution' (Harmondsworth: Penguin Books, 1969).
Debray, Regis, 'Revolution in the Revolution?' (Harmondsworth: Penguin Books, 1967).
Deutscher, Isaac, 'Marxism in Our Times' (San Francisco: Ramparts Press, 1973).
Duffy, James, 'Portugal in Africa' (Harmondsworth: Penguin Books, 1962).
Duffy, James, 'Portuguese Africa' (Cambridge, Mass: Harvard University Press, 1959).
Engels, F., 'The Origin of the Family, Private Property and the State', 4th. ed. (1884; reprinted Moscow: Progress Publishers, 1948).
Engels, F., 'The Peasant War in Germany' (Moscow; Progress Publishers, 1956).
Fanon, Frantz, 'The Wretched of the Earth' (Harmondsworth: Penguin Books, 1967).
Ferreira, E. de Sousa, 'Portuguese Colonialism: From South Africa to Europe' (Germany: Druckerei Horst Ahibrecht, 1972).
Figueiredo, Antonio de, 'Portugal: Fifty Years of Dictatorship' (Harmondsworth: Penguin Books, 1975).

Fitzgerald, Francis, 'Fire in the Lake: The Vietnamese and the Americans in Vietnam' (New York: Random House, 1972).
Fortes, M. and Evans-Pritchard (eds), 'African Political Systems' (London: Oxford University Press, 1940).
Frank, André Gunder, 'Lumpen-Bourgeoisie, Lumpen-Development: Dependence Class and Politics in Latin America' (trans. M. Berdecio, London: Monthly Review Press, 1972).
Frank André Gunder, 'Sociology of Underdevelopment and Underdevelopment of Sociology' (London: Pluto Press, 1971).
Freire, Paulo, 'Cultural Action for Freedom' (Harmondsworth: Penguin Books, 1970).
Freire, Paulo, 'Pedagogy of the Oppressed', trans. M. Ramos (Harmondsworth: Penguin Books, 1972).
Friedland, W.H. and Rosberg, L.G. (eds), 'African Socialism' (California: Stanford University Press, 1964).
Gerassi, John (ed.), 'Venceremos: The Speeches and Writings of Che Guevara' (London: Panther Books, 1972).
Gibson, Richard, 'African Liberation Movements' (London: Oxford University Press, 1972).
Grundy, Kenneth W., 'Guerrilla Struggle in Africa' (New York: Grossman, 1971).
Guevara, E., 'Guerrilla Warfare' (Harmondsworth: Pelican Books, 1969).
Gutkind, P. and Waterman, P. (eds), 'African Social Studies' (London: Heinemann, 1977).
Hayden, Goron, 'Beyond Ujamaa in Tanzania: Underdevelopment and the Uncaptured Peasantry' (London: Heinemann, 1980).
Hindess, B. and Hurst, P., 'Mode of Production and Social Formation' (London: Macmillan Press, 1977).
Hindess, B. and Hurst, P., 'Pre-capitalist Modes of Production' (London: Routledge & Kegan Paul, 1975).
Hobsbawm, Eric J., 'Primitive Rebels' (Manchester: Manchester University Press, 1959).
Hobsbawm, Eric J., 'Revolutionaries: Contemporary Essays' (London: Weidenfeld & Nicolson, 1973).
Hobson, J., 'Imperialism: A Study', 3rd. ed. (London: Allen & Unwin, 1938).
Ho Chi Minh, 'On Revolution: Selected Writings, 1920-1966', ed. by Bernard Fall (New York: Frederick A. Praeger, 1967).
Humbaraci, Arslan and Muchnik, Nicole, 'Portugal's African Wards' (London: Macmillan, 1974).
Ionescu, Ghita and Gellner, Ernest (eds), 'Populism: Its National Characteristics' (London: Weidenfeld & Nicolson, 1969).
Jahn, Janheinz, 'Muntu: An Outline of Neo-African Culture', trans. by M. Grene (London: Faber & Faber, 1958).
Kiernan, V.G., 'Marxism and Imperialism' (London: Edward Arnold, 1974).
Krader, Lawrence, 'The Asiatic Mode of Production: Sources, Development and Critique in the Writings of Karl Marx' (Assen: Van Gorcum & Corp. B.U., 1975).
Lenin, V.I., 'Imperialism: The Highest Stage of Capitalism', 2nd edn (1917: rpt. Moscow: Progress Publishers, 1971).
Lenin, V.I., 'Selected Works' (Moscow: Progress Publishers, 1971).
Lenin, V.I., 'The State and Revolution', 2nd edn. (1917; rpt. Peking: Foreign Languages Press, 1970).
Leys, Colin, 'Underdevelopment in Kenya' (London: Heinemann, 1975).
Lichtheim, George, 'Imperialism' (London: Allen Lane, 1971).
Lumumba, Patrice, 'La Pensée Politique de Patrice Lumumba' (Paris: Présence Africaine, 1963), selected and edited by Jean Van Lierde.
Machel, Sandra, 'Mozambique - Sowing the Seeds of Revolution' (London: Committee for Freedom in Mozambique, Angola and Guinea: undated).
Magdoff, Harry, 'The New Imperialism: The Economics of US. Foreign Policy' (New York: Modern Reader Paperbacks, 1969).
Marcum, John, 'The Angolan Revolution', vol. I: 'The Anatomy of an Explosion' (Cambridge, Mass.: MIT Press, 1969).

Marx, Karl, 'The Class Struggles in France 1848 to 1850' (Moscow: Foreign Languages Publishing House, 1952).
Marx, Karl, 'On Colonialism and Modernization', ed. by Shlono Avineri (New York: Anchor Books, 1969).
Marx, Karl, 'A Contribution to the Critique of Political Economy', ed. by Morris Cobb (New York: International Publishers, 1970).
Marx, Karl, 'Critique of the Gotha Programme' (New York: International Publishers, 1973).
Marx, Karl, 'The 18th Brumaire of Louis Bonaparte', 2nd edn. (1869: rpt. New York: International Publishers, 1966).
Marx, Karl, 'Pre-Capitalist Economic Formations', trans. by Jack Cohen, ed. and intro. E.J. Hobsbawm (New York: International Publishers, 1966).
Miliband, Ralph, 'The State in Capitalist Society' (London: Weidenfeld & Nicolson, 1969).
Miller, N. and Aya, R. (eds), 'National Liberation' (New York: Free Press, 1971).
Minogue, M. and Molloy, J., 'African Aims and Attitudes: Selected Documents' (Cambridge: Cambridge University Press, 1974).
Minter, William, 'Portuguese Africa and the West' (Harmondsworth: Penguin Books, 1972).
Mondlane, Eduardo, 'The Struggle for Mozambique' (Harmondsworth: Penguin Books, 1969).
Nkrumah, Kwame, 'Class Struggle in Africa' (London: Panaf Books, 1970).
Nkrumah, Kwame, 'Neo-Colonialism: The Last Stage of Imperialism' (London: Nelson, 1965).
Owen, Roger and Sutcliffe, Bob (eds), 'Studies in the Theory of Imperialism' (London: Longman, 1972).
Pomeroy, William, 'Guerrilla Warfare and Marxism' (New York: International Publishers, 1968).
Poulantzas, Nicos, 'Classes in Contemporary Capitalism' trans. David Fernbach (London: New Left Books, 1975).
Poulantzas, Nicos, 'The Crisis of the Dictatorships: Portugal, Greece, Spain', trans. David Fernbach (London: New Left Books, 1976).
Poulantzas, Nicos, 'Political Power and Social Classes', trans. Timothy O'Hagan (London: New Left Books and Sheed & Ward, 1973).
Rodney, Walter, 'How Europe Underdeveloped Africa' (Dar Es Salaam: Tanzanian Publishing House, 1972).
Rudebeck, Lars, 'Guinea-Bissau: A Study of Political Mobilization' (Uppsala: Scandinavian Institute of African Studies, 1974).
Sandbrook, R. and Cohen, R. (eds), 'The Development of an African Working Class' (London: Longmans, 1976).
Schultz, A., 'The Concept of Nature in Marx' (London: New Left Books, 1972).
Scott, James C., 'The Moral Economy of the Peasant: Rebellion and Subsistence in South East Asia' (New Haven: Yale University Press, 1976).
Shivji, Issa, 'Class Struggles in Tanzania' (London: Heinemann, 1976).
Shivji, Issa, et al., 'The Silent Class Struggle' (Dar Es Salaam: Tanzanian Publishing House, 1974).
Spinola, Antonio, 'Portugal and the Future' (Johannesburg: Perksor, 1974).
Strunik, W.A.E. (ed.), 'African Political Thought: Lumumba, Nkrumah, and Touré (Denver: University of Denver Monograph Series in World Affairs, nos. 3 & 4, 1968).
Taber, Robert, 'The War of the Flea: Guerrilla Warfare, Theory and Practice' (London: Paladin, 1970).
Terray, E., 'Marxism and Primitive Societies', trans. Mary Klopper (New York: Monthly Review Press, 1972).
Wauthier, Claude, 'The Literature and Thought of Modern Africa' (London: Pall Mall, 1966).
Woddiss, Jack, 'New Theories of Revolution: A Commentary on the Views of Frantz Fanon, Regis Debray and Herbert Marcuse' (New York: International Publishers, 1972).
Wolf, Eric, 'Peasant Wars of the Twentieth Century' (London: Faber & Faber, 1978).

INDEX

African artists, influence upon Europe, 13
African socialism, 5-6, 7, 8, 10, 59; and negritude, 61-2; and problems of, class theory, 62, 137, 138
Agriculture in Guiné: absence of land alienation, 67; groundnuts, disadvantages to grower, 38-9; groundnuts and the Fula, 38; groundnuts in Fulacunda, 43-5; impact of mechanisation upon agriculture, 51-5; production of Balanta perennial crops, 39; production of Fula, 38, 39; rice cultivation, 39
Agronomic writings: Burning off and Fallowing of Groundnuts and Millet, 43, 45-6; Burning off and Fallowing in the area of Fulacunda, 43, 44-6; Census of agriculture in Guiné, 36-41 (see also model of census); On the Contribution of the peoples of Guiné to the agriculture of Guiné, 41-3, 47-8; On the Cultivation of groundnuts and millet in 'Portuguese' Guiné, 43, 45, 47-9; In Defence of the Land, 46; On Land Utilisation in Black Africa, 49-51; On the Mechanisation of Agriculture, 51-4; Understanding the Problem of Soil Erosion, 46-7, 55
Alavi, Hamza, 76, 92, 97
Algeria, 15, 22; Lumpenproletariat, 73, 75; peasants, 67; struggle for independence, 8, 67
Almond, Gabriel, 95
Althusser, Louis, 98
Amin, Samir, 15, 49, 56, 59, 92, 95, 102, 126
Anderson, Perry, 102
Angola, 1, 2, 3, 13, 14, 15, 16, 20, 21, 24, 26, 28, 30, 35, 116
Animists, 65, 66
Apter, David, 95
Arusha Declaration, The, 61
Asiatic mode of production, 3, 4, 5, 129
Assimilados, 16-17, 131; see also Cape Verde Islands
Azores, 1, 31

Balanta, 14, 55; agricultural production among, 38; class structure of, 57, 66; rice growing of, 38-9, 57
Bananas, 39
Baran, Paul, 'The Political Economy of Growth', 127
Bauxite, 26
Belgium, 30
Benin, artists of, 13
Berlin, Conference of, 14, 116
Bissagos archipelago, 14, 34
'Black Skin, White Masks', 77
Blyden, Edward W., 6
Botswana, 126
A Brief Analysis of the Social Structure of Guiné, 63-4, 94-5
Brief Notes on the Objectives and Methods of the Survey, 41-3
Britain, 1, 15, 26, 31, 116, 119
Burning off and Fallowing in Fulacunda, 43, 44-6
Burning off and Fallowing of Groundnuts and Millet, 43, 45-6
Bukharin, Nikolai, 111

Cabora Bassa, 27
Cabral, Amilcar: appointed head of agricultural census, 36; before US Senate Foreign Affairs Committee, 30-1; birth, 2; career, 2, 36; expelled from Guiné, 3; and foundation of PAIGC, 3
Cabral, Luis, 33, 34
Caetano Marcelo, 26, 28, 82
Cape Verde Islands: assimilados, 16, 131; droughts, 46; famines, 16; military conditions in, 34; post independence problems, 33-4; and revolution in Guiné, 24, 25, 30-1; social conditions in, 16-17
Cassaca, Congress of, 20-2, 29
Census of Agriculture in Guiné, 36-41
Census: census model, 36-7; commissioned by the FAO, 36-7; problems of data collection, 37-8
Césaire, Aimé: colonialism and nazism, 86; culture and national liberation, 121; Discourse on Colonialism, 9,

156 *Index*

86, 114; and national liberation, 121; theory of imperialism, 7, 61, 83, 112-13, 114-15
Centrifugal strategy, 20-2
Chaliand, Gerard, 74, 75
China (PRC), 30, 117
Chinese revolution, 21, 65, 67
Chomsky, Noam, 97
Class: creation of classes and their supersession, 64-5; and culture, 89-90; and ethnicity, 65-7; and social division of labour, 107; variables defining, 62-5; see also class analysis; petty bourgeoisie; wage earners; déclassés
Class analysis, obstacles to in African setting, 59-62
Como, Battle of, 23
Conakry, 24
Congo (Brazzaville), 30
Cuba, 9, 30, 117
Cuban revolution, 21, 65
Cubists, 13
Companhia Uniao Fabril (CUF), 15, 23, 39, 48, 49
Culture: and class, 82, 89-91; and colonialism, 86-8; definition of, 84-5; function of, 85; and identity, 83-4; and national liberation, 82-3, 88; and petty bourgeoisie, 89; Portuguese attitude toward, 82, 86; and revolutionary capacity of peasants, 85, 97-9, 90, 91; and tribalism, 83; see also National Liberation and Culture
Cunene province, 27

Damas, Leon, 61
Death Pangs of Imperialism, The, 116, 117, 121
Déclassés: divisions within, 73-4; emergence in Guiné, 73; as intellectual faction, 74; revolutionary potential of, 74-5
Development, indigenous reflex to, 5-6; see also underdevelopment; mode of production
In Defense of the Land, 46
Dien Bien Phu, 22
Djassi, Abel, 13
Dogon, artists of, 13
Dyulas, 66

Egypt, ancient, 55, 104
Elections, for general assembly, 25
Emmanuel, A., 124, 126
Engels, 110; and peasants, 69, 100, 110; 'The Peasant Wars in Germany', 73; and the state, 92
Esso, 26
European settlers, see Guiné

The Facts about Portuguese Colonialism, 13-14
Fanon, Frantz, 1, 7, 10; and 'Black Skin, White Masks', 77; and class theory, 62; and the colonial personality, 68, 89, 98; and colonial proletariat, 11; and the colonial state, 98; culture and personality, 83; and detribalisation, 68; and the Lumpenproletariat, 75; and the national bourgeoisie, 80, 124, 128; national liberation as the revolutionary force of our time, 121; and parallels with Cabral, 8-9; as radical nationalist, 10; and the theory of imperialism, 7, 112; and the theory of revolution, 8-9; and underdevelopment theory, 58; 'The Wretched of the Earth', 2, 8, 61, 62, 75, 98, 115, 123, 124, 127, 137, 138
FARP, 20, 24
France, 2, 15, 28, 30, 31, 116, 119
Feigoa, 39
FLN, 18, 62
Food and Agricultural Organisation (FAO), 36, 37
Frank, Andre Gunder, 10
FRELIMO, 20, 31, 133
Fromm, Erich, 107
Fula, 14; agricultural production, 38; burning-off practices, 39; and class, 65-6; emergence of a state amongst, 94, 102; groundnuts, 38-9, 57; semi-feudal structures, 65-6; Fulacunda, 43-6

Garvey, Marcus, 6
'German Ideology, The', 5, 100, 108
Germany, West, 24, 30, 31, 116
Ghana, 15, 26, 56
Godelier, M., 109
Gramsci, Antonio, 77, 130, 133
Groundnuts: disadvantages to grower, 43-6, 70-5; and war in Gabu, 23
Guerrilla warfare: Maoist principles of, 12; strategy and problems of, 21-2
Guevara, Ernesto (Che), 12
Guiné: colonisation by Portugal, 14-16; economic relations with Portugal, 15-16, 48; European settlers in, 69; population, 2; post-war problems, 32-5; present economic situation, 32, 34; productive forces in, 106; social conditions pre-revolution, 12-13; topography, 16
Guinea, Republic of, 14, 15, 20, 34, 39
Guro, 101

Hayden, Goron, 102
Hebrew civilisation, 54

Hegel, G.W.F., 7, 129
Hilferding, Rudolf, 4
History: and concept of aborted history, 98-9; and phases of human development, 103-4, 108
Hobson, J.A., 4, 60
Ho Chi Minh, 112

Identity and Dignity, 89
Illich, Ivan, 59, 107
Imperialism: African theory of, 7-8, 112-14; and blocked development, 118-20, 122; classic theories of, 4; and class theory, 5; The Death Pangs of Imperialism, 116, 117, 121; failings of, 111, 125, 126-8; labour aristocracy and, 119; Leninist theory of, 110-11, 125; Marxist theories of, 110-12; mode of production and, 114-15; monopoly capitalism and, 110-12, 116-17; national liberation and, 118; Is Portugal Imperialist? 116; requirements for theory of, 6-7; as revolutionary force, 107, 117-18, 125, 126; Third-World theories of, 5, 112-14
Indo-China, 1, 2, 14, 22, 25, 30
Iran, 133
Islamicised peasants, 65-6; see also Fula
Ivory Coast, 56

Jalée, P., 59

Kanza, Thomas, 83
Kautsky, Karl, 111
Kenya, 125, 126, 128
Kola nuts, 39

Lafayette, 30
Land Utilisation in Black Africa, On, 49-51
Latin America, 120, 136; models of underdevelopment, 6, 7; theories of underdevelopment, 120, 125-6
Lenin, V.I.: 'The Development of Capitalism in Russia', 57; 'Imperialism', 4, 60, 110, 111, 121, 122, 125; and narodism, 84; The State of Revolution, 92, 156; theory of imperialism, 4, 178, 180, 198; and theory of the state, 98
Leys, Colin, 76, 81, 97, 125
Liberated zones, 21-2, 23-4
Libya, 133
Lisbon, 2, 14, 15, 20, 26, 30, 31
Luanda, 28
Lumpenproletariat, 73-5; see also déclassés; Marx's characterisation of, 74
Lumumba, Patrice, 1, 7, 55, 83

Luso-French Convention, The, 14
Luxemburg, Rosa, 4, 111, 121, 122

Machel, Samora, 61, 82
Makonde, artists of, 13
Malawi, 126, 136
mangoes, 39
Manjak, 14
Mao tse-tung, 12, 121
Marcuse, Herbert, 92, 107
Marx, Karl, 107, 110, 114, 129, 135; and Bonapartist state, 92; 'Economic and Philosophical Manuscripts', 54; 'The German Ideology', 5, 100, 108; and Lumpenproletariat, 74, 75
Marxism: and anthropology, 100-3; and development, 129; and theory of imperialism, 3-4; petty bourgeoisie, definition of, 76-7; soviet Marxism, 3, 4, 11; technology and, 6-7, 107
Massacres: at Luanda, 28; Meuda, 28; Pidguitti, 28; see also Pidguitti
Mboya, Tom, 61
Mbuti, 101
Mechanisation of Agriculture in Guiné, On the, 51-4
Meillassoux, Claude, 101, 108, 126
Metheun, the treaty of, 116
Military actions, 20-5
Miliband, Ralph, The State in Contemporary Capitalism, 92
Millet, as food substitute for rice, 38-9
MING, 70, 78
Mode of production, 3; 103-4 and productive forces, 104-7, 107-9
Mondlane, Eduardo, 7, 61, 82
Morel, E.D., 13
Mozambique, 1, 2, 13, 14, 15, 26, 28, 30, 35, 116
MPLA, 20, 31, 133

Namibia, 31
Narodism, 84, 91
National Liberation and Culture, 89, 157
NATO, 1, 30, 31
Negritude, 5-6; as stimulus to nationalism, 61-2
Neo-colonialism: differences from colonialism, 120-1; emergence of petty bourgeoisie, 77, 78, 79; growth of déclassés during, 74-5; as revolutionary, 80; transformation from, 122-3
Neto, Agostinho, 82
Nigeria, 126, 128
Nixon, Richard, 30
Nkrumah, Kwame, 7, 10, 55, 60, 61, 82, 102, 113, 115

Nyerere, Julius, 61, 102

Oil palm, 40
Our People are our Mountains, 12

PAIGC PAI founded 1956, 2, 10, 12, 17; and centrifugal strategy, 20-1; concept of political party, 18; party and the army, 22; earliest demands for political independence, 17-18; earliest political programme, 17-18; and Marxism, 18; and democratic centralism, 19; and people's stores, 32, 33; and political mobilisation, 17-20; and principle of collective leadership, 19; the state in the liberated zones, 96; and UN representations, 30
PALISARIO, 17
Peasant, 67-9; Balanta peasants, 67; culture and revolution, 68; Fula peasants exploited, 67, 68; no land alienation in Guiné, 67; limitations as revolutionary class, 67-8, 69; as most exploited class in Guiné, 68
perennial crops, 39
Petty bourgeoisie, 75-81; and class suicide, 122-5; character in colonial Africa, 77; creation of in colonial conditions, 77; dilemma facing, 78; factors determining its revolutionary capacity, 78-9; Marxist definition of, 76; as revolutionary class, 78; and state power, 97; two factions of within Guiné, 77-8; varied attitude toward revolution, 77-8; various accounts of, 75-6
Picasso, Pablo, 7
Pide (a state police) 17, 19, 25
Pidguitti, massacre at, 17, 19, 26, 28, 71
Praia, 25
Pre-colonial societies, 5
Poland, 58
Portugal, 1, 2, 3, 15, 30, 32, 58, 116; backwardness of, 12; colonialism of 4, 11-14; failings as an imperialist power, 117; foreign investment and, 26-7; foreign monopolies and, 15; imperialism of, 13, 14, 117; political opposition to in Guiné, 14, 17; refusal to decolonise, 15-16; settler schemes of, 28; troops in Guiné, 2; war materials from, 30
Potlatches, 107
Productive forces, 3; as motor force of history, 108; and social formation, 101-2
Prometheus, 135

Reich, W., 107
Return to the Source, 71-2
Revolution in Guiné: military actions, 22-5; in Cape Verde, 24
Revolution in the Third World, 11
Rice coup, 33-4
Rice growing, 38-9
Rhodesia (Zimbabwe), 31, 50
Rodney, Walter, 102
Roman civilisation, 54
Rome Conference, declaration of, 31

Sal, island of, 24
Salazar, 14, 28, 82
São Tomé, 13, 16, 26
Schultz, Governor Arnaldo, 27
Senegal, 14, 15, 16, 39, 43, 49, 56
Senghor, Leopold, 61
Shivji, Issa, 76, 97
Société Commerciale d'outre, 23
Sorgum, 46
South Africa, Republic of, 2, 13, 15, 24, 26, 30, 31, 78, 126
Soviet Union, 30, 136; empire of, 136; Soviet Marxism, 3, 11, 112, 134; Soviet revolution, 134; see also Marxism
Spinola, 27
State/ discussion of in A Brief Analysis, 93-5; discussion of in The Weapon of Theory, 98-9; emergence of among Fula, 94; exotic form of, 94; and failure of African nationalism, 95-6; Marxist view of, 92-3; as repressive apparatus, 93-4; as semi-autonomous, 93
Surrealism, 13
SWAPO, 17

Tanzania, 30, 136
Technology: and development, 6, 7 and underdevelopment theory, 106, 7
Ten Years after Pidguitti, 27-8
Terray, Emmanuel, 101, 108, 126
Third Reich, the, 86
Touré, Sékou, 7, 10, 55, 61, 115
Tribalism, and political mobilisation, 29
Tribe, as economic system, 66-7

UAR, 30
Underdevelopment theory, 125-8; Latin American models of, 6-7; and technology, 106, 107
Understanding the Problem of Soil Erosion, 46-7, 55
United Nations, 9, 17, 20, 25, 30, 31, 35
United States, 1, 30, 31, 119, 133, 136

Vietnam, 2, 26, 30 (NLF), 67
Vietnamese revolution, 1, 2, 21, 65, 101, 104; US tactics during, 1, 21

Wage earners, in Guiné, 70-3; dependence upon petty bourgeoisie, 72; limitations as revolutionary class, 72; and peasant culture, 72
Wallerstein, Immanuel, 126

Warren, Bill, 81, 124, 126
Weapon of Theory, The, 98, 116, 118, 122
Weber, Max, 7, 129

Yoruba, 50

Zaire, 75, 126, 128
Zimbabwe, 31, 50

For Product Safety Concerns and Information please contact our EU representative GPSR@taylorandfrancis.com
Taylor & Francis Verlag GmbH, Kaufingerstraße 24, 80331 München, Germany

www.ingramcontent.com/pod-product-compliance
Lightning Source LLC
Chambersburg PA
CBHW052128300426
44116CB00010B/1814